C000145866

JOHN LENNON
LIFE, TIMES & ASSASSINATION

THIS BOOK IS DEDICATED TO:
Harry & Dodo, Jay & JD, Vince & Christo, Gerry, Andy, Barbara,
Simon, Guy, Selena, Maddee, David, Kathy, Paola, Cherry.

© Phil Strongman 2010
Published by The Bluecoat Press, Liverpool
Book design by Michael March, Liverpool
Printed by JF Print, Yeovil
Front cover photograph by John 'Hoppy' Hopkins

The author would also like to thank:
Roy Carr, May Pang and Colin Wilkinson.

ISBN 9781904438946

JOHN LENNON
LIFE, TIMES & ASSASSINATION

Phil Strongman

THE BLUECOAT PRESS

CONTENTS

AUTHOR'S INTRODUCTION

Like John Kennedy and Martin Luther King, also victims of assassination, John [Lennon] has become a figure larger than life, a true icon of our times.

Sir George Martin

Political rock – and around the time of The Beatles, CSN&Y, the Byrds and Pink Floyd, most rock had some sort of a political imaginatively militant dimension – has helped produce a world where everyone is forever young. It won a kind of battle. It had to fight hard to do it, and in a way the fight is over. Rock isn't against the conventional world anymore, it is the conventional world.

Paul Morley, M Magazine 2009

The 30 years since John Lennon's death have not diminished his standing, only added to it. When he was shot dead in New York, on 8 December 1980, his reputation, his cultural and financial wealth and his track record had already been established. His comeback had thrown him back into the public eye and the charts once again, but he was already acknowledged as a vibrant and much-loved influence.

What surprised many of the more mainstream commentators was the fact that the period of mourning for Lennon lasted so long and went so deep and so wide; across oceans, across generations, across races, religions and continents. According to tabloid reporters, only Princess Diana's death matched Lennon's for impact. Everyone, bar the bigots of the Far Right, felt his passing. Not just the usual suspects – the thirtysomethings who'd grown up with him, the hardcore Beatle and Lennon fans – but young Punks as well, and New Romantics, Rappers and, to their own surprise, many of the middle-aged cynics who'd been dismissing Lennon for years.

Lennon's alleged killer was Mark David Chapman. His family name came from the medieval 'Chapmans', the men who delivered material and messages to Britain's cottage industry weavers. Like Lennon's name, it is one that has some Irish connections. This particular Chapman, Mark David, was from Georgia, USA, the Deep South. He was, we were told within hours, a 'schizophrenic', a 'loner', a 'Beatles obsessive', an 'attention-seeker' and a 'manic autograph-hunter'.

Of equal importance was the 'fact', we were smoothly assured, that Chapman was a 'lone nut'. Just like all those other 'lone madmen' assassins of recent American history; Lee Harvey Oswald, James Earl Ray and Sirhan Sirhan. We were told that Chapman was a 'half-crazy' fan of John Lennon – 'Lennon's Biggest Fan!' – a stalker who would do almost anything to be famous.

As anyone who has studied the case knows, these are actually *all* myths. Chapman was *not* a big John Lennon fan; nor was he a Beatles fan; nor was he an autograph-hunter; nor was he an attention-seeker; nor was he crazy, nor yet was he a loner. Three decades on it seems increasingly likely, as we shall see later, that Chapman did not even fire the fatal shot. He was, however, still significant and would have been even if this attempt to kill Lennon had failed. Significant not just because of his actions but because of his connections; those who knew him, those who trained him, those who supported him then – and still support him now.

But myths have always surrounded the legends of stage, screen and sound and Lennon was no exception. The working class boy from the Liverpool slums, allegedly

7

born in the midst of a Nazi bombing raid, was actually just as much a member of the lower middle class. After five and a half uneven years with his bohemian showgirl mother, he was offered to his sailor father and then traumatically snatched back, before being left with his Uncle George and Aunt Mimi. From then on his life was to have structure, support and, last but not least, regular meals. But, for all George's kindness and Mimi's strict affection, John was not living with his mother, while his father had quite simply disappeared. The bitter rejection that most people do not feel until their teens or twenties came earlier to John; came earlier and cut deeper. George's death only added to this. In that sense, as the nuclear family began to implode across the west, Lennon was to become symbolic of a growing phenomenon; a child raised by people who were not his parents, a child relying on the kindness of relative strangers.

Yet this difficult start undoubtedly helped to make him the artist he was. It explains, if only in part, the dynamic drive that was to take him from obscurity – and a total lack of qualifications – to stardom and wealth beyond his wildest dreams, the life of a best-selling recording artist, singer, poet and writer, a life where he could count presidents and kings as virtual equals. He was to be connected to some of the biggest events and the most famous names of the twentieth century: Kennedy, Luther King, Nixon, Reagan.

It may seem that these are pretty big names for a guitar-playing Liverpudlian to be amongst, but many of us too often underplay the potency of music – easily done now its most unruly child, rock'n'roll, is, in the main, 'a toothless old man' (and an 'old man' moreover, whose audio wares are now virtually valueless, easily picked up for free on the world wide web).

It's easy to forget that Irish war drums were banned

for centuries, that Beethoven's music was considered far too sexy, causing young maidens to 'swoon', that Tchaikovsky was thought to have bewitched the Russian Tsarina as much as Rasputin and that even in the staid classical theatres of the 1920s, new works by Ravel and Prokofiev could provoke violent arguments and even riots. The Sixties' beat groups – like the Fifties' rock'n'rollers before them and the Seventies' punks afterwards – really did cause angry newspaper editorials, really did raise questions in parliament and really did change many of the leading lights of several generations; for both better *and* worse.

We forget too that, following John Lennon's death, there were memorial gatherings that were, in total, millions strong. Millions more joined in a ten minute worldwide silent vigil.

Popular music had power and generated big money. Less so now, but worldwide profits still number in the billions for CD recordings, downloads, ringtones, tours and live concerts.

During the key Cold War period of 1945-1991, popular music was strictly controlled. Right into my lifetime, right up until the early Eighties, popular music shows on British television lasted for less than 30 minutes a week. When *The Old Grey Whistle Test* was being broadcast it crept up to one hour. That was it. The limit. Live music – even a single guitarist – was licensed like a dog in Britain.

But recorded music is everywhere now, like the air we breathe, and like the air we depend on, it's easy to take it all for granted. Many of us, including myself, took John Lennon and The Beatles for granted – right up until that foggy day in December 1980 when every TV screen in every electrical goods store showed only one image: John Lennon. Everyone then knew that the news about Lennon was the worst it could be. Rock stars could only lead the news in those days by dying.

Millions of us suffered a little death on 8 December 1980. The Beatles had been part of our childhood, our adolescence, our youth, our lives. To almost every young man and woman Lennon's Beatles were once 'everyman', just like him next door and that lad over the road. They knew us, we knew them. A smile, a wink, a song. Except that The Beatles were just that bit more talented, that touch more amusing and though age and honesty later revealed their faults, we still loved them then, and love them still.

Lennon was the sarcastic leader who was also the idealistic dreamer; the angry poet who was also the passionate lover; the man who stripped naked for love and went to bed for world peace was also the absent husband; the one-night stand merchant was also the repentant father; the last serious Jack-the-lad was also the first male feminist.

John Lennon was also, most shockingly, the first Beatle to die, something that should have been obvious to all of us from the start.

At the time of Lennon's killing, Reagan and the men behind him were busy trying to hot up the last decade of the Cold War. I didn't, at the time, see that there could be any strong connection with what had just happened in New York. It was probably just sheer ignorance on my part but I'd also like to think it was an 'age thing' as well; you just don't see the 'connectedness' of everything when you're younger. It takes time to see the wider picture.

The bigger, clearer picture – the *vision* – was something that John Lennon had acquired by the time of his death. It was a widescreen vision that went beyond petty national boundaries, a vision that some people feared, including members of America's intelligence agencies.

Despite his musical roots in the 1950s – and his chart success and growing cultural power during the Seventies and early Eighties – John Lennon will always be tied in with the Sixties. At the start of that decade The Beatles were playing for pennies in the bars and brothels of Hamburg. By the middle of the Sixties they *were* the Sixties. The biggest musical act ever. And their leader, Lennon, didn't shrink from embracing the radical causes that flowed out of that time – anti-racism, anti-sexism and the growing battle against the horror of war, in particular the pointless slaughter of the Vietnam War.

Killing John Lennon was, Chapman later bragged, like killing the Sixties. It was a hollow boast, you cannot murder a decade any more than you can murder a century. You *can* kill an idealist, of course, but you can't, ultimately, kill his ideals. But who really was John Lennon, what were his ideals and why did he die? There have been some 45 books written about John Lennon, and that's just the number published in the years 1981 to 2003, one of them by myself. Is there anything new to say? I believe there is. Not just about his life but about his death – and his legacy.

The following then is not purely a book about music, for John Lennon was not just about music, but an attempt instead to give an up-to-date and full account of Lennon's life and times, how they shaped him, how he in turn affected them and how this very affect led directly to his shocking death. How a boy becomes a man becomes a catalyst becomes an icon – becomes a target.

CHAPTER ONE

ANOTHER TIME, ANOTHER PLACE

The lights in the screening room go down and we find ourselves in cosy, womb-like darkness. A switch is clicked behind us and a projector splutters into life; uneven at first, its jerky start soon settles into a solid purr as the images start to flicker up on the screen at twenty four frames per second – they're not very bright as the black background platforms the skinny, white countdown numbers: 10, 9, 8, 7, 6, 5, 4, 3.

And then we're there. Moving pictures, transporting the airless room into a portal on the world and all its past, present and future glories. And within seconds we are transported as well. Although we're not quite as gauche as the Parisian audiences of the 1890s, who screamed and dived for cover as film of a moving train rolled toward them, we too are soon believing what we see; ducking for cover as the hero ducks, twitching during the fights, tapping our feet to the music and feeling the anger, pain and joy just as he does.

Liverpool, England, 9 October 1940. The port city is not as uncluttered as much of it is in the twenty-first century – the Luftwaffe and the post-War planners have yet to wreak their full havoc – though the sea-front area and many of the older buildings still have the wide-ranging space and self-confidence of the Victorian era that made them. Many of these buildings were funded by the profits from African slavery – and from the lesser, but endless, exploitation of local workers. Neither subject is considered fit to be discussed in school in the 1940s, or in the newspapers, nor will they be for decades to come.

It is a very different world from today's. Trams rumble through streets where a few men still wear wooden clogs – only a few, though, this isn't Wigan Pier in the Hungry Thirties – most of the men smoke cheap cigarettes at work in the docks, or in factories, cafes and offices. Virtually everyone wears a hat outside, and even most of the kids wear school caps out of school, the boys stuck in short trousers until they leave school, the majority bowing out of education at the ripe old age of 14. Most of these kids, like their parents, will never have used a telephone or a refrigerator. It will take the 'miracles' of modern warfare, mass production and a social sea-change to introduce these other wonders into the homes of the majority.

In the cold autumn, the majority of homes that have coal or firewood are belching out smoke. Combined with the acrid smell of burnt brickwork and melting bakelite that still hangs in the air, courtesy of a bombing raid several days before, it gives Liverpool the aura of Guy Fawkes' Night come early. Britain and France have been at war with Nazi Germany for over a year. France has already fallen under German Occupation, as have Poland, Holland, Belgium, Luxembourg and Holland.

In the Oxford Street Maternity Hospital 26-year-old Julia Lennon, a cinema usherette, gives birth to John Winston Lennon. The newly-born's first name, John, had been suggested by Julia's older sister Mimi Smith. This pair have three other sisters so the arrival of a boy will lead to much celebration. The boy's middle name comes from Winston Churchill, Britain's inspirational war-time prime minister since May that year, when Labour MPs forced him on a reluctant Tory-dominated government (by December 1940 it is a national government). The child's father, Alfred 'Freddie' Lennon, is away at sea at the time of the birth, fulfilling his role as a head-waiter in the merchant navy (a once safe job that now, with British vessels being torpedoed every week, is no longer quite so cushy).

Mimi, however, visits daily. On the 10th she even ducks and scurries her way through a bombing raid to visit Julia and her child. Her interest, and the future pattern of the extended family, is already set before the child has left the maternity hospital.

Freddie's roots lay in Ireland – Liverpool was then regarded, only half-jokingly, as being 'the capital of Ireland' – and he was later to claim that his own father was a member of Ireland's famous Kentucky Minstrels (an assertion dismissed by other members of the family). He is usually described as 'forthright', a euphemism for awkwardness, for being 'bolshy', something which could only make his marriage to the musically talented, 'flighty' Julia Stanley, a bit of a rollercoaster. As part of her job she had already spent thousands of hours in cinemas, nightly absorbing vast silver screen dreams that few men, least of all Freddie Lennon, could ever have made true.

Within three years of their registry office wedding, the relationship – damaged by a war that extended Fred's absences – was already dying. Although he sent money, at first, to help his new-born son, Fred has hardly seen the child and doesn't have a prolonged conversation with him until the latter is almost six years old.

Once the payments stop, Julia abandons all pretence of being happily married and starts to see other men. She'd already left little John Lennon with his Aunt Mimi within six months of his birth. Mimi and her husband George Smith will be his effective parents for most of the next 15 years.

CHAPTER TWO

ROOTS

The Second World War had also brought change to America's security forces. The FBI, under the control of J Edgar Hoover since 1934, did monitor *some* of the activities of America's pro-Nazi German Bund, although the Bund did not suffer any serious harassment before December 1941, when Nazi Germany declared war on the US. As late as that autumn, Nazi propaganda movies were still being regularly screened in American cinemas, mainly in Yorkville, then the German quarter of New York City.

1941 was a key year in every sense – during the twelve months between 1940 and '42, almost everything changed. The European war went global in spectacular fashion as Nazi Germany invaded Soviet Russia in June. Secret memos concerning the Wannsee Conference flew back and forth in Berlin in December. Hitler himself did not bother to attend the conference, which didn't actually convene until January '42, but it was at that meeting, in a leafy Berlin suburb, that the decision was taken to implement the genocidal 'Final Solution'. "Who, today, remembers the Ottoman massacre of the Armenians?" Hitler had later asked, in order to show how easily he felt such crimes were forgotten.

In July 1941 the French Vichy regime, having already ceded half of France to the Nazi aggressors, then allowed the Third Reich's Far Eastern ally, Imperial Japan, to take over Indochina. This was the area dominated by the nation later to be known as Viet Nam, later still to be called by the one word name Vietnam. While the

Japanese forces there did not often behave with quite the same ruthlessness as they exhibited in Nanking, Korea and the Phillipines, the locals did still suffer, far more than their French 'protectors'. The only real opposition to the 'official invasion' came from Ho Chi Minh's native Communist guerrillas.

From Indochina, Imperial Japan could strike out at British Malaya, which, of course, it did, the very same day that America's Pearl Harbour was struck, 7 December 1941. The latter was a disaster for the US Navy, particularly its Naval Intelligence wing, which had no idea such a whirlwind was about to land on America's doorstep. With the US and Japan involved, the conflict that had begun in Poland in 1939 had truly become a World War in 1941.

In the USA, the CIA's predecessor, the obliquely named Office of Strategic Studies (OSS), also came into being in 1941 on the orders of President Franklyn D Roosevelt. Its founder was one Colonel William 'Big Bill' Donovan, a lawyer from the Deep South. From the start, as its own OSS War Report stated, it was envisaged that journalists would be used in order to engage in 'psychological warfare', while OSS staff operatives were told that 'psychological warfare' was a brief wide enough to include misinformation, sabotage and even 'assassination'.

Whether a liberal Democrat President like FDR had ever genuinely wanted to work with Donovan in the long term is debatable, but the latter was acceptable to US military intelligence and Roosevelt was a sick man – he would not outlive the war. He was also already in debt to the US military after the events of 1934. Back then an attempted coup d'etat by a far right element of the US Army would have succeeded – and FDR *would* have been assassinated – had not most officers at the time stayed loyal (many, no doubt, with some reluctance).

This failed coup has almost been written out of American history – some historians don't even bother to mention the coup at all, although there was a reference to it in the original *Citizen Kane* script – but it *was* serious for several reasons. Firstly, because the coup itself could have succeeded in changing US and world history. The attempt was also important because – even if one forgot the shoot-out and the death and injuries – it did still show the depth of feeling on the American Right.

Even Roosevelt's mostly moderate reforms were to be opposed by any means possible, even by violence. This was treason of the highest order, an armed attack on the President (an attack, moreover, that was supported by some of the very men who had pledged to defend him, their head of state). This was a lesson with deadly implications, a lesson that few of Roosevelt's Democratic successors seem to have taken on board.

One lesson that his opponents did soon learn was that FDR's constituency – unions, blacks, Latinos, Jews, Catholics, small farmers, women and middle class liberals – was unstoppable at the ballot box. The Republicans might have had the Rockefellers, Howard Hughes and William Randolph 'Citizen Kane' Hearst – and all the billions such men could raise – but it wasn't enough to defeat the masses.

FDR won the 1932, 1936, 1940 and 1944 elections – by which point the Right gave up trying to defeat him and instead concentrated on changing the law. Their aim was to prevent such a popular personality ever again holding sway and they eventually succeeded – an amendment was passed that prevented any future President from holding office for more than two terms.

The newly created OSS was to handle America's overseas enemies, just as the FBI dealt with the domestic variety. Because these enemies would sometimes overlap

– a US citizen travelling abroad to sell state secrets, say, or a German spy working within the US. The two agencies had to liaise from point one. This cooperation was something that had been emphasised by British spymaster, Bill Cavendish-Bendinck, a former soldier who'd been irritated by the constant in-fighting amongst London's various intelligence services.

Cavendish-Bendinck was, initially, something of an influence on the fledgling OSS. After Pearl Harbour the British and Americans were allies in all theatres of the conflict – not because the US had declared war on Nazi Germany, the Bund and the right-wing of Republican Party were still strong enough to prevent Roosevelt doing this, but purely because Hitler had turned the tables and declared war on the US – part of the Fuhrer's vain attempt to get Imperial Japan to declare war on Russia where his armed forces were already starting to struggle.

Even at the height of the war though, there were those on the right within the US intelligence services who'd have preferred an armistice to outright victory over the people they considered natural allies – the Fascists of Imperial Japan and Nazi Germany.

There are certain incidents that look remarkably suspicious today, in an age when double-cross and doublethink are widely known about – if not widely accepted. In mid-June 1942, just after the Battle of Midway had seen the US Navy defeat the sea-borne forces of Imperial Japan for the first time, the *Chicago Tribune* newspaper ran a front page story detailing how the triumph had been made possible by the Navy's 'Magic' code-breaking system. The latter, one of America's most important wartime secrets, had been put at serious risk by a story that could have cost millions of Allied lives.

Luckily Tojo's high command did not believe the newspaper story, but it was not mere coincidence that the

Chicago Tribune was actually owned by Robert McCormick, a onetime colonel who had friends in Washington DC (the isolationist McCormick was also violently opposed to both FDR and the whole anti-Fascist war effort).

In May 1945 Nazi Germany surrendered, as the OSS, occasionally helped by the Vatican and British Military Intelligence, began to secretly smuggle hundreds of Nazi war criminals down the 'rat-runs', the secret routes that led to the USA and South America aka Operation Paperclip. Although unspoken anti-semitism no doubt played a part in these actions, the main two reasons were loot and anti-Communism (several US generals had reached Western Germany with the words' 'On to Moscow!').

Martin Bormann, Hitler's deputy and the keeper of the Nazi's Swiss bank account codes, was saved by the loot factor. Although he was supposed to have died in Berlin in May 1945 as Nazi Germany collapsed, the actual body belonged to an unfortunate lookalike, for Bormann himself had been whisked off to Britain in a joint OSS/MI action (the action's code name, according to former Royal Navy spy John Ainsworth-Davis, was OPJB).

Through Bormann the Allies got most of the Nazi cash out of Switzerland and he was then allowed to flee to Paraguay and a life of luxury. He died there some 14 years later, in a red soil area, which accounts for the *terra rossa* earth found around Bormann's skull after its official, miraculous 'discovery' in Berlin in 1973, in an area that had been thoroughly searched several times at the end of the war, an area which – like the rest of that part of Germany – is completely bereft of red soil.

The Bormann episode, not fully revealed until 1996, is telling in several ways – it showed the immorality of the Western intelligence services, who were prepared to work with, and then grant a life of ease to, a war criminal responsible for many thousands of deaths. It also demonstrated the lengths those services were prepared to go to cover-up their activities – dozens had died in the secret operation, including the unwitting Bormann lookalike who'd already undergone imprisonment and extensive plastic surgery before his untimely death.

The evacuation of another top Nazi – Klaus Barbie, the French-based 'Butcher of Lyons' – was also conducted in 1945, Barbie being prized for his extensive knowledge of France's resistance fighters, many of whom were Socialists or Communists.

The Russians were not informed of Barbie's evacuation, of course, for the Cold War had already begun.

As the war ended, John Lennon began to attend Liverpool's Dovedale Primary School, a couple of miles away from the Strawberry Fields Children's Home with its sprawling gardens. That children's home may have briefly housed his half-sister – his biological mother Julia having given birth to a baby girl in 1944. The father was not Freddie and she quickly offered the child up for adoption. Nineteen forty-five, however, saw her more seriously involved with a local man, John Dykins. They were to have two children together but, by then, the forthright Aunt Mimi had taken John to live with her and her kindly husband George, a dairy manager.

John's first year with Mimi and George was happy enough – the war, and the fading threat of bombing, was finally over and he was beginning to settle down well in the lower middle class enclave of Mendips, 21 Menlove Avenue, in the comparatively prosperous suburb of Woolton. Visits by Julia, or by John to the Dykins, seemed to cause him no great confusion, beyond asking Aunt Mimi why he couldn't call her 'mummy' too.

But massive ructions shook the boy's world during the following summer holiday. Lennon's father Fred returned to the Liverpool area with the idea of emigrating 'down under', to the new land of New Zealand, and he now wanted to take with him the son he hardly knew. By then though, mother Julia had decided she wanted the little boy back herself.

In a cheap Blackpool hotel the tearful child watched as the increasingly vicious arguments raged back and forth amidst the peeling wallpaper and cracked windows. And then, agony of agonies, the little boy was asked by Freddie to chose between his absent father and his previously uninterested mother.

Lennon chose his father. Then minutes later, sobbing in the street, he changed his mind and tried to chase after his departing mother. A disappointed Freddie did the decent thing and withdrew quietly. John then stayed with his mother, but only for a few days. Before the week was out Julia Lennon had returned to her new partner, after going to Aunt Mimi's to drop off an emotionally shattered John Lennon. He was not yet six years old.

In Vietnam, then still French Indochina, the returning Gallic authorities decided that maintaining law and order – i.e. combating the spread of Socialist Ho Chi Minh's growing popularity in the north – would best be served by a huge new infusion of armed militia. Indochinese natives were at first shocked and then visibly angered when the French expedited this strategy by freeing and then re-arming some of the Imperial Japanese troops who had oppressed the locals for over four years.

Ho Chi Minh and his men were no angels – they had brutally repressed Vietnam's own Trotskyites – but they had fought the Japanese and also opposed their re-arming. Indochina's first post-war election gave a majority to Ho Chi Minh. The ruling French ignored the result and a war of independence began.

Looking back over all this almost seven decades later,

the chain of personal and international events seems both strangely interwoven *and* as inevitable as death and taxes – desertion and secrecy, lookalikes and assassinations, public morality and secret crime, West and East, hot war and Cold War; Britain, Germany, America, Japan, Vietnam.

The changes within the above nations were to later impact heavily on that small child then living near the banks of the Mersey. It's as if John Lennon's destiny – his first musical residences, his biggest romance, his travels, his political protests, his life and death – had already been mapped out for him before he'd begun his first year in junior school, before he'd hardly spoken his first words. As he told his father on Blackpool sands, when he grew up he wanted to go on the stage, or become Prime Minister. Politics or entertainment? Although neither he nor his father could have guessed it at the time, John was eventually, indirectly, to choose both.

CHAPTER THREE

ART FOR ART'S SAKE

Presidents and kings come and go
but the CIA goes on forever.

Anonymous

Paralytic sycophants, effete betrayers of humanity,
carrion-eating servile imitators, arch-cowards and
collaborators, gang of women-murderers, degenerate
rabble, parasitic traditionalists, playboy soldiers,
conceited dandies.

Approved terms of abuse for East German
Communist Party speakers to use when referring
to Great Britain in 1953.

The headmaster of Lennon's first school described the young boy as being 'sharp' – intelligent but also spiky. His defiance of teachers, although only occasional, became legendary and amongst his playground friends he was always the one who ended up in charge. Order and harmony hadn't often come from above; he would have to impose his own when he deemed it necessary.

At home in Menlove Avenue he would create his own magazines, newspapers and posters. And the visual arts some became his first love as he doodled and drew for hours. His work had quality too and one of his pictures was exhibited in the Dovedale school hall (it was a drawing of a bearded Jesus Christ, friends later remarking that the picture strangely resembled the way Lennon was to look circa 1968).

After he'd passed the 11-plus exam he found himself at Quarry Bank secondary school, arriving in September 1952. Quarry Bank was an upmarket state school where the teachers wore gowns and even mortar board hats. Its mild pomposity inevitably became a Lennon target once he'd become a fan of the ground-breaking *Goon Show*. The Goons were, essentially, Spike Milligan aided and abetted by Harry Seacombe, Peter Sellers and Michael Bentine. All four were young war veterans, Bentine had been present at the liberation of the Nazi death camp at Bergen Belsen, and all of them had a healthy disregard for both the authorities and convention.

Their Home Programme radio show was a half hour blast of surreal, often hilarious, comedy that somehow smuggled funny voices, early electronic sound effects, bizarre scripts and even 'dirty jokes' – or, at least their punchlines – past the BBC's censors. Their weekly broadcasts ran from 1951 to 1960, with repeats on the BBC's Light Service – despite hiccups like Bentine's departure, Milligan's nervous break-down and Sellers' growing workload as an increasingly successful film actor. Lennon rarely missed a show, the four 'Goonsters' appealing greatly to his own unreal brand of humour.

The Central Intelligence Agency was created in 1947 – the same year as the House of Un-American Activities Committee first began its hearings, the start of the anti-red witch-hunts that Senator Joe McCarthy later took to frightening heights of hysteria.

The CIA was the child of the OSS and its even more secretive OFC branch. From the start, the CIA saw its role in the widest possible terms. It wasn't just the obvious targets – overseas enemies, spies and troublemakers – that were to be covered. Foreign *and* domestic Anarchists, Communists, Socialists and even their alleged 'fellow travellers' – liberals and civil liberty lobbyists – were to be watched and harassed every step of the way, and in every single sphere of life.

The fact that much of this intruded on FBI territory didn't worry the new organisation's directorate overly – collaboration with Hoover's boys was usually pretty good and when it came down to any kind of confrontation, the CIA had the ultimate card to play. The latter was a crude set of photos of Hoover and his assistant Colson engaged in homosexual activity, copies of which were owned by the ruthless James J Angleton, ex-OSS officer and CIA counter-intelligence chief. There is, of course, a certain grim irony in this – Hoover himself gets caught out, the blackmailer blackmailed – but the end result was neither good for the US nor for democracy.

On those few occasions that Hoover tried to confront the CIA over their growing excesses, his position was weakened from the start by the black and white photos that Angleton possessed. Later on, such a situation was to lead to several horrifying conclusions.

The CIA never seriously tried to have Hoover removed from office for the very same reason – why lose a man you can easily threaten, to have him replaced with a stranger you might have no 'dirt' on?

With the coast clear, and assured of FBI help, the CIA began to infiltrate every post-war industry, even those connected with the Arts. Amongst the more conservative elements of the art world, for instance, there was great concern at the way major figures like Picasso had so publicly embraced Socialism (something that was arguably expressed in pre-war works like *Guernica* and post-war efforts such as *Charnel House*).

Determined that the Cold War art agenda was not going to be influenced in any way, shape, or form by the left, the CIA created a series of fronts to promote artists whose work – whatever its true long term merit – and general attitudes were deemed either mainstream or apolitical. A useful distraction!

The Congress For Cultural Freedom, Britain's *Encounter* magazine and the American Newspaper Guild, were merely the tip of a very large iceberg of liberal media endeavours that secretly received tens of thousands of CIA dollars (something that the US press did eventually reveal, but not until the spring of 1966 – almost 20 years after the Arts and Media infiltration programme had begun).

The British film *Animal Farm*, an animated version of George Orwell's ant-Stalinist book of the same name, received seed funding from a CIA front in 1954 and was produced the same year. Although Stalin had actually died the year before, the film, like the original parable, was generally taken to be anti-Communist and the last scene of the cartoon was given a different ending from the book – in the new cinematic version the animals start to rise up against their 'red' rulers just before the end titles roll.

Meanwhile the price of paintings by abstract expressionists Jackson Pollock and Mark Rothko soared at an incredible rate during the Fifties, even though the former's work was often mere drips and splashes while the latter dealt principally with mesmerisingly large blocks of blended colours. Although part of that can be put down to inflation – and a larger part to 'art inflation' – much of the huge price rise for works considered mildly daring at the time simply cannot be accounted for – unless the CIA's efforts are taken into account.

While Pollock was mostly too busy drinking to care that much – he was dead drunk by 1955, dead by '56 – Rothko was a man very much at odds with the brash ethos of modern America and he saw his own contemplative canvasses in a vaguely left-field light – a notion that lasted until 1959, when he was offered the commission to produce a large piece of work for an upscale restaurant in Manhattan's Wall Street business district. Here was the perfect opportunity for subversion, for cooking up an artistic snook right under the very noses of the new cheque-book Czars; a chance to make the undeserving rich choke on their caviar. But it was not to be. After merely ordering a single meal in the restaurant, and even before, it's said, the first course had arrived, Rothko saw the impossibility of it all. It was blatantly obvious to anyone of any intelligence – nothing in his oblique style could possibly cause comment, let alone offence, in such an atmosphere of deal-making, gossip and conspicuous consumption. He wasn't going to break any boundaries in Wall Street, only provide chewing gum for the eyes, a backdrop for power brunches and discordant, drunken celebrations in the evening (a disgusted Rothko swiftly refused the commission, thus losing several thousand dollars).

Andy Warhol is another US artist who allegedly received a boost, again unwittingly, from the same tainted source. And it is true that *after* 1965, when he stopped silk-screening his more disturbing images of Americana – car crashes, police attacks on civil rights marchers, Jackie Kennedy in mourning – demand for his work went through the roof. His block-coloured celeb pictures continue to rise in value even today, a self-fulfilling principle in art once someone, or something, has started the ball rolling.

Photographer and Warhol associate, Nat Finkelstein, was a man of radical disposition who was a first-hand witness to how rapidly Warhol and his gang went from being cultural subversives to the art establishment's court jesters. Finkelstein himself stayed on the edge, photographing not just Warhol, Edie Sedgwick, Lou Reed *et al* but also the growing number of Civil Rights marches and anti-Vietnam War demonstrations ("I was fully involved, recording the information before me; the brutality, the glee of the oppressors, the courage of the kids"). He fell out with his biggest outlet, *Life* magazine, after they refused to run pictures of policemen attacking marchers, and by the end of the Sixties Finkelstein was helping organise demos and was himself followed by the FBI. When he started to associate with the Black Panthers, the Feds' harassment of Finkelstein went up a notch. Strangers would appear in the street and spend hours fixing their cars directly outside his home.

With floods of secret CIA cash behind them, America's pop and op artists thus became the world's most important artists – a lead they held through the Fifties and much of the Sixties. A first for the United States in the arts. Thus, brightly coloured consumerism was to be celebrated, not attacked, and even though some of the above works were done with irony, and sometimes even brilliance, the end result was the same; the founding of a strong new tradition that increasingly demanded that 'art' could be literally anything – from a blank canvas, to a shiny cartoon, to an unmade bed – as long as it was without practicality, meaning, or politics (and preferably without any of the above three).

John Lennon was aware of pop art and like many of his contemporaries he had a sneaking regard for some of it. In a dreary post-war Britain of drizzle and rationing – still paying back its Lend Lease loans to a US determined to ensure the complete death of the Empire – it was perhaps inevitable. Everything was in a drab monochrome in the UK of the Fifties, from the two TV stations, to the newspapers, to the children's comics and even most of the newspaper cartoons. Even Britain's Easter egg chocolate was second-rate, then being 'chocolate-flavoured vegetable fat'; it seemed the once glorious Imperial future was now a distinctly mundane present.

There was, of course, some safety and jobs-for-life in Britain, as well as a 'glorious' past, but even this past was celebrated in films that were 90 per cent black and white, both literally and artistically. In such an environment, anything in full colour, let alone an exciting new art genre, would have had appeal. Yet Lennon, showing surprising maturity, soon tired of the high gloss, high colour future. As increasingly bright images, posters and films began to filter in, he developed a marked preference for the classic *film noir* look, something that was originally pioneered by Germany's UFA Studios before being taken up briefly by war-time Hollywood and then Britain. It was a black and white, day and night view of imagery, a world of highlights and shadows that Lennon became interested in. It was to appear on the striking covers of several Beatles' albums, courtesy of Lennon.

Film noir is, in essence, stylish tragedy, and tragedy was to hit Lennon hard in his mid-teens, not once but twice. When he was 14, kindly Uncle George, Lennon's substitute father figure, died of a haemorrhage. Stunned, John took to his bedroom, brooding for days. His school work, erratic since leaving Dovedale, plummeted in both quality and quantity. Lennon was to leave the all-boys' school at the age of 16, without having passed a single O Level or A Level exam. In his last two years in school Lennon, together with his disruptive pal Pete Shotton, were regarded by Quarry Bank's staff as the academy's biggest disciplinary problem; something that got Lennon caned on several occasions. He was, the staff consensus went, lively and clever but also awkward – and increasingly capable of cruelty.

As if sensing her boy now needed him, his mother Julia began to visit John on an almost daily basis. She had mastered the banjo by now, just as her son – fired by the

DIY music craze skiffle – had picked up the guitar and started his own skiffle band, The Quarry Men. Occasionally, mother and son would even 'jam' together.

But on the evening of 15 July 1958, just seconds after visiting John and Mimi, the 44-year-old Julia Lennon was run over and killed. The driver, an off-duty policeman, was felt to be at fault and was even prosecuted in court, but he was swiftly acquitted, adding insult to young Lennon's injury. Whenever he was asked in future about his mother's demise he would almost always say the same thing, "She was killed by a drunk-driving cop". As with the death of step-father George, Lennon had giggled hysterically for a moment then brooded darkly for days.

By then, Lennon's Quarry Men had been in existence for over a year. Their skiffle style – acoustic guitars, banjo, tea-chest bass – had been inspired by the UK's leading exponent of the form, Lonnie Donnegan, whose version of 'Rock Island Line' had crashed into the British charts in January 1956, some four months before Elvis Presley had made the English hit parade.

The Quarry Men were initially named The Blackjacks – they wore black jeans with green piping – and John was the undisputed leader on guitar and vocals. Rod Davis picked the banjo, Eric Griffiths the guitar and Shotton played the washboard (the latter eventually replaced by young drummer Colin Hanton). Lennon abruptly changed the group's monicker to The Quarry Men and added two occasional recruits, 'tea-chest bassists' who took turns to play gigs: Nigel Whalley from the Bluecoat Grammar School and Ivan Vaughan from the Liverpool Institute. Another lad, Bill Smith, played bass for a time, before Len Garry took on the task, with Whalley concentrating on finding the band gigs (it helped that Lennon was, at first, prepared to play for nothing).

After a one-off gig at the Cavern – then a jazz joint

whose audience booed when Lennon dared deviate away from 'pure' skiffle and into the rock'n'roll that many then regarded as 'yobbish' – the band secured a gig at the St Peter's garden fete in Woolton. It took place on 6 July 1957 and would probably have been just another outdoor gig, especially for a group whose sole ambitious member was Lennon, if it hadn't been for the crowd. For in there, only a few feet away from a mildly shocked Aunt Mimi, was one Paul McCartney, a teenage friend of Ivan Vaughan's.

McCartney was then only 15, almost two years younger than Lennon, but he was a pretty good guitarist who also knew all the chords *and* the various words to many of the new rock'n'roll classics. After Vaughan had invited him back-stage, McCartney tuned and played Lennon's guitar and scribbled down some Eddie Cochran lyrics. Lennon was impressed with the youngster, as McCartney was impressed by the fact that the older boy had actually got a live group together; a group, moreover, that actually rocked a bit. A couple of months later McCartney finished with the Boy Scouts and joined the Quarry Men. A few months after that his fellow Liverpool Institute schoolmate George Harrison – a talented guitarist – also joined the line-up.

Lennon began his first term at Liverpool College of Art in September 1957, some weeks before his 17th birthday. The fledgling musician was now a full-on teddy boy, complete with quiff, and would not have got into college at all had it not been for the quality of his art work and the enthusiasm he'd displayed at the interview.

His enthusiasm for art and the LCA was short-lived, however. Lennon's sketches came in later and later, fewer and fewer. Painting was alright but music, that was the real thing, his real love, and it was now rock'n'roll more than skiffle that inspired him. Films like the early Elvis vehicles and *The Girl Can't Help It*, fed the fantasy of widescreen stardom, the movies affecting him as they had his mother before him. Lennon even recruited his biggest art college pal – the talented but shy Stuart Sutcliffe – into his dream of rock'n'roll success.

And dream it certainly seemed. By the autumn of 1957 Britain had produced only one rock'n'roll star and he, Tommy Steele, had quickly shifted into the more lucrative ballads market, mainly to prolong his career. Steele was to release only two more uptempo numbers on single after 1957. The ascendance of the second big English rock act, Cliff Richard and his Drifters – later called The Shadows after name problems with the US originals – was over a year away, in late 1958. No British act of any musical genre had ever had an American Number 1, or even sold that well in continental Europe. Music was not a major breadwinner for a post-War economy that even had to ration its sweets until Lennon was a teenager.

Britain exported family cars, fast but unreliable motorcycles, radios, steel, coal, the occasional film and a bankrupt sense of mild superiority – mainly to the former Empire: the Commonwealth of Canada, Australia, New Zealand, Hong Kong, Singapore, Nigeria, Uganda, Jamaica, South Africa, Kenya and Malaya. In fact, the South-East Asian state of Malaya was the site of another British export relevant to this book – the 'hearts and minds' policy. As with most other Asian colonies, the post-war period in Malaya saw a growing resentment of both government and big business systems that were managed by representatives of the European 'mother countries', the imperial states who had failed to protect their subjects from the Imperial Japanese invasion.

This anger blended with support for Communist guerrillas – the latter had often been the only effective opposition to Japanese troops – support which mushroomed after the war. The initial belief among many of the colonists was that life could go on as it had before 1941. In the neo-racist parlance of the ex-pats, the locals "simply weren't up to the job" of running the place and it was too early to even think about letting them try. A little patience on all sides might have brought forth peaceful resolutions, but patience, post-'45, was in short supply.

When Chairman Mao's guerrillas finally completed their take-over of China in 1948, the trickle of support for neighbouring revolutions became a river and then a flood. In October 1951, Malaya's British High Commissioner Sir Henry Gurney was killed in a Communist ambush. Armed attacks on British forces had been rising in the area for months – along with terrorist attacks on economic targets such as rubber plantations – and Gurney's killing signified the real start of the 'Malayan Emergency'.

Thousands of young British conscripts were sent to deprive the red guerrillas of local support (in the UK National Service was still going strong and the majority of teenagers were to serve two years in the armed forces right up until the year 1961). The official British response to the Malayan insurgency was not, however, purely military, instead the stick was to be balanced with the carrot. It was the birth of the so-called 'Heart and Minds' programme.

In the jungles and along the rivers – areas of most support to the insurgents – the communities were isolated and, in many cases, depopulated. Unlike the French forces in Algeria, the British rarely resorted to massacre. The natives were, instead, to have their hearts won over with free medical treatment for children, extensive literacy courses, the digging of fresh water wells etc. If they 'had' to be moved it was usually done with some kind of notice.

The problem was, however, that the atmosphere of oppression remained – troops of a distant European country, foreign soldiers of a foreign race, were evicting thousands of locals from their ancestral homes, all in a desperate attempt to defeat native rebels who could slip from territory to territory overnight.

The Malayan Emergency continued through most of the Fifties. By the end of the decade, the British seemed to have won – the terrorists were on the run, local and national government had kept going and the local resentment of London seemed slight. As the Malayan Federation moved towards limited independence, it looked as if the Mother Country might even manage to keep its export market for finished goods.

One observer of all this was British writer Anthony Burgess, then working within the UK Civil Service out in Malaya. The future author of *A Clockwork Orange* met several times with US intelligence officials – men fascinated by the seemingly successful 'hearts and minds' scheme. And men who had schemes of their own.

It was at this time that CIA agents first began work on MKULTRA aka MHULTRA aka MK-ULTRA a 'mind control' scheme born of the ARTICHOKE and BLUEBIRD projects. Although it was supposed to be purely to help with interrogations, the programme rapidly became one that the CIA hoped would yield either assassins – to eliminate foreign trouble-makers – or 'patsies', the fall guys on whom such killings could be blamed.

It was believed that, with sufficient work, neither assassin nor 'patsy' would have any idea of what crimes they had committed or why (the subject of Burgess' 1962 book *A Clockwork Orange* was actually aversion-therapy, the manipulation of the brain – years later author Roger Lewis tried to access the CIA's Anthony Burgess file; he was told that whether such a file existed or not, it was not available for viewing for reasons of 'national security').

The CIA does not have a gloriously honourable record when it comes to mind control. After starting the

MKULTRA plan, allegedly at Fort Bliss, the Agency soon shifted its operations into several different US cities and using several different techniques: manipulation of the brain's Alpha waves, sodium pentathol, the so-called 'truth drug', 'deep hypnosis', auto suggestion and hallucinogenic drugs.

Huge doses of Lysergic Acid, LSD, were dished out. These hallucinogenic drugs were not given to volunteers, who might have been prepared, or at least willing, but to low level and unwitting CIA workers and 'outside Agency' civilians. Sometimes these doses were given to casual passers-by, lured into hotel rooms by false invitations, or by hired prostitutes. At other times they were injected – often with big doses of mescaline – into those attending hospitals for minor psychiatric ailments.

In 1953 alone, at least two American civilians – Frank Olson and Harold Blauer – died in these experiments. The former was a scientist working for the CIA who leapt through a ninth floor hotel window to his death. Blauer was a depressed tennis pro' who died foaming at the mouth after his hospital deliberately gave him a massive mescaline shot on CIA orders. The dead men's families were not, of course, told the real reason for the deaths of their husbands and fathers. The fact that, in a similar situation, the Russian and East German secret services would almost certainly have behaved in a similarly ruthless fashion is not, ultimately, a good excuse. No matter how much the West might exploit certain classes, its entire twentieth century *raison d'etre* had become the protection of the rights of the individual.

The CIA was busy on other fronts too during the mid-Fifties. The democratically elected but left-wing Arbenz government of Guatemala was overthrown in 1954 in a bloody CIA-backed coup d'etat. It was a coup that was to leave the small Central American state in the hands of generals for the next 40 years, during which time they and their death squads killed 100,000 Indians, as well as thousands of opposition activists. Nearly all of these victims were unarmed civilians and amongst their number were tens of thousands of senior citizens, women and children.

The same year saw the first major inter-power conference on Indochina. There the French colonial forces had been fought to a standstill, despite some Agency backing, by local guerrillas made up of both nationalists and Ho Chi Minh's Communists.

At 1954's Geneva Conference, America's representative John Foster Dulles had been spoiling for a fight, for a chance to extend the first Vietnamese war. But skilful manoeuvring by Britain's foreign secretary Anthony Eden and China's Zhou Enlai led instead to a French agreement to withdraw. The treaty also gave Cambodia and Laos the chance to establish themselves as independent nations, while the 'Buddhist Socialist North Vietnam' and the 'Catholic Capitalist South Vietnam' were to remain separate countries temporarily, until nationwide elections could be held.

But the CIA's own secret polls quickly revealed the inevitability of Ho Chi Minh's second electoral victory at the ballot box and the US President of the time, Eisenhower, was later to privately admit that some 80 per cent of the Indochinese would have undoubtedly voted for Minh again – if given the chance. But they weren't allowed that option, as the US moved heaven and earth to make sure the nationwide elections were postponed indefinitely.

As in Guatemala, as in Vietnam, when democracy offered the wrong result – i.e. left-of-centre government – or even just the possibility of the wrong result, it was to be ignored. It was a position of discreet hypocrisy that obtained throughout most of the twentieth century. These machinations were – *are* – public knowledge in much of the Third World but not in Middle America, where many citizens still, even today, do not understand the Southern Hemisphere's bitter resentment of the superpower that so often armed and supported their oppressors.

The US answer in divided Viet Nam was eventually to cancel the elections while donating arms and guns to the South. This did not end the tensions in the police state south which, while dominated by a Catholic minority of a million, was in essence also a Buddhist country with a Buddhist majority of almost 13 million (the word 'Buddhist' here covers the Caodaism faith plus various Taoist and Confucian off-shoots).

In 1960 Communist guerrillas known as the Viet Cong started the National liberation Front. From the start the NLF were clever enough to court the favour of the Southern peasantry. Popular priests were usually left alone while unpopular ones were beaten; brutal landlords and police chiefs shot, their gunmen driven out and the food surpluses of the bigger farms were stolen and redistributed. All the US-backed South Vietnamese authorities could do to counter this was to threaten torture and/or summary execution to anyone who was caught helping the Vietcong. Such a response was crude, but it was not, in the end, effective.

And by then, several thousand miles away, John Lennon's Quarry Men were no longer The Quarry Men. A name change had been on the cards for some time, with Lennon anxious to lose the name that had not brought success – or cut his ties with his old school. One of their last gigs under the old Quarry name had been playing at the opening of the Casbah coffee club, where the much-loved owner Mona Best ruled the roost, and where her son Pete occasionally played drums. By the end of 1959 Lennon's men were known as Johnny & The Moondogs – and this was the name under which they failed the audition to join the talent stable of 'star-maker' Carroll Leavis.

After dozens of local gigs, they became 'The Silver Beetles', an idea of Stuart Sutcliffe's, in honour of Buddy Holly's backing band The Crickets. The newly re-named Silver Beetles failed yet another audition in May 1960, this time to become the touring band for the moody-looking star known as Billy Fury. But that day was to produce some good news, the lesser-known but 'up-and-coming' pop singer Johnny Gentle thought the Silver boys were good enough to be his backing band on a forthcoming Scottish tour.

These first regular gigs to pay good hard cash encouraged Lennon, and within two months the group had taken on the more straightforward monicker The Beatles (allegedly from a line in *The Wild Ones* movie, the seminal leather'n'motorcycles epic starring Marlon Brando and Lee Marvin, a film that was banned in the UK for over 20 years, lest its lawless spirit further inflame Britain's own bike-riding rockers. It was also a play on the words 'beat' and 'beatnik' – the latter being the name for the black-clad existential youths whom the Press, not without some justification, regarded as gothic middle-class Teds).

In July Lennon left the Liverpool College of Art for the last time, just days before facing probable expulsion (it has been said that only his friendship with the brilliant Sutcliffe had prevented this happening before). Although John had gained a 'classy' and devoted girlfriend from the LCA experience – the bottle blonde Cynthia Powell – he had once again left an educational institution without a single qualification. He was nearly 20 years old and beginning to realise that he had to get serious about his music if he and his pals were to stand any chance of 'making it' in the fast-changing world of pop.

With increasing persistence he began to harass Allen Williams, the Welsh manager of the Jacaranda Club – a place, close to the LCA, where groups would hang out, with Williams sometimes booking them gigs. Lennon was convinced that Williams could help launch the Beatles or, at the very least, get them on to another paying tour, and, in a way, he was to be proved right. For Williams received a telegram that summer from the Royal Caribbean Steel Band, regulars at the 'Jac', saying that they'd discovered that there were great opportunities for beat groups where they were currently playing – Hamburg, the major northern port of a Germany divided in half since the end of World War Two.

After a quick trip to Hamburg's sleazy all-night Reeperbahn district, Williams booked The Beatles into Bruno Koschimider's Kaiserkeller Club for an extended residency starting in late August 1960. The band, Williams was told, could make good money. "We'll be making a hundred pound a week each," Lennon had excitedly told friends (£100 then is perhaps £2,000 in today's money). This, of course, turned out not to be the case. But for The Beatles – Lennon, McCartney, Harrison, Sutcliffe and new drummer Pete Best – Hamburg was still to be a baptism of fire.

CHAPTER FOUR

LOVE ME DO

I just wanted them to be my friends, that's why I managed
The Who, that's why I managed any group.

Pete Meadon

As a busy port, Liverpool had its own tough spots, its own violence – future *Merseybeat* editor Bill Harry once saw bouncers throwing girls off-stage head first – as well as a few low key brothels (the tram-connected Lime Street area was once notorious). There were several late night bars and strip-clubs too in the late 1950s. The Beatles had even supported one 'strip tease artiste' for a couple of Merseyside gigs. But nothing had prepared them for Hamburg. It was a city still scarred by the mass bombing raids of the war, raids in which fire-storms had killed thousands of civilians. The hastily rebuilt port areas were soon funnelling through millions of tons of cargo – and thousands of sailors, servicemen and tourists – as America's Marshall Plan reconstructed West Germany and its nearest western neighbours.

Cash was king and for seamen who'd crossed the Baltic or the Atlantic there were no holds barred for those with money to blow. Strip-clubs, sex clubs, brothels, night clubs and bars ran all night – the latter almost always with live music till at least 2 or 3am. In the streets, and some of the bars, there were shouts, screams and fights, sometimes knife fights, till dawn. Sirens were punctuated with the occasional gunshot. It was the same city where pimps, prostitutes, transvestites and even a few trans-sexuals continually partied and where, just a couple of years later, a pre-Slade Noddy Holder was to be accosted by men who would pay serious deutschmarks to watch others defecate on glass tables.

For the teenage Beatles – John was the oldest at just 19, Harrison was a mere 16 – it was a big, big shock. The 'hotel chambers' they'd been promised turned out to be shocking too; three filthy rooms with battered camp beds, a few thin blankets and dirty shared toilets. Bruno didn't care, the British beat boys were here now and Koschimider, a former Panzer tank officer, was going to work them hard. After a false start at the tiny Indra Club, Lennon's boys were transferred to the Kaiserkeller itself, a venue where fellow scousers Derry & The Seniors had already established a reputation.

For the next four months The Beatles were to play between five and seven 45-minute sets from between eight in the evening until around two in the morning. A weeks' worth of gigs in a single night. This was to be done six nights a week, sometimes seven. And if Bruno thought the band weren't doing enough, he'd bellow encouragement, or threats, up at the stage. 'Not all the club owners here are ex-Nazis, they just act like it,' as one piece of short-lived graffiti proclaimed.

For someone doing gentle ballads, or short piano-recitals, it might have been physically easy. But for five inexperienced Liverpudlian youngsters performing high-energy rock'n'roll it soon became utterly exhausting. Only the 'prellies' – Preludin tablets – got them through it. These slimming pills, when combined with alcohol, affected the body like 'speed', amphetamines, quickly producing long-lasting bouts of energy and sometimes aggression. Such tablets were also capable of inducing short sharp spells of depression and even mild psychosis.

As Lennon baited older members of the crowd – "What

did you do in the war? Bloody Krauts!" the band became tighter and tighter, their act, partly stodgy before, becoming diamond-hard. Most of the audience were just passing through and were too busy, or too drunk, to do much more than whistle or jeer. Occasionally, as with Liverpool, there would be fights that involved the band. Although as likely to run as the next man when faced with serious odds, one-to-one Lennon seemed to enjoy a good scrap – as he had since his primary school – especially when fuelled with drink, when he would get incredibly angry, and reckless.

Not that the entire Kaiserkeller crowd always consisted of drunken sailors. Some local 'beatniks' did attend there though and one couple, young illustrator Klaus Voormann and his stunning girlfriend Astrid Kirchherr, became Beatles fans from the off, the latter instantly realising that Lennon was the leader. When Kirchherr became Sutcliffe's girlfriend, Voormann was naturally disappointed, yet he remained enough of a Beatles' fan to persuade his pal, photographer Jurgen Vollmer, to start attending the Kaiserkeller nights.

The Hamburg kids had never heard rock played so wild – nor had they ever seen the band's pointed 'winkle-picker' shoes or short jackets before. And nor had they dealt with such musicians previously – aware, intelligent, stylish, questioning. But the arty young Germans also had a few ideas of their own to offer. And the Beatles were clever enough to accept their input, something that was already, unwittingly, adding an international aspect to the band. Although there had always been a steady trickle of imported records to Liverpool – as befits a major port in the age before containerisation – and although Lennon and McCartney were fast becoming aware of the new Gordy-Motown labels, the 'exis', Hamburg existential beatniks, gave them a truly original and international edge.

Unlike Elvis Presley, Gene Vincent *et al*, The Beatles – despite the *Mersey*-beat label that was soon to be stuck on them – were not totally in tune with just one time or place as they artistically grew up. They were not just a product of Liverpool, or the American Deep South, because, whilst retaining much of their home town's attitude and sardonic wit, the simple fact is that in Hamburg, The Beatles began to move beyond provincialism, began to move into an entirely new cultural world; a world that they themselves were helping create.

The black-clad Astrid was the first to persuade Stuart to try a new haircut – grease-free and brushed forward – as well as collarless jackets. Lennon jeered at first, something he often did with the laid back Sutcliffe – perhaps to hide his true affection for him – then adopted the new look. Before this change was complete, Kirchherr was to take some classic photos of the early 'rock'n'roll Beatles – and before the decade was out, Voorman would fulfil his dream of designing album sleeves for the same band.

Without knowing it, Brian Epstein had been looking for The Beatles for years. Not that he knew their name, of course, or even that they'd turn out to be a rock'n'roll group, but he was looking for *something*. Anyone who was classically cultured or Jewish or comparatively wealthy could often feel a little out of place in Liverpool back then. Epstein was all three. He was also homosexual in an age when such a lifestyle was completely illegal. At best it meant constant vigilance and trusting the 'kindness of strangers'. At worst, it meant a lifetime of blackmail, harassment, public shame and occasional court appearances (which could, and sometimes did, lead to short, sharp prison sentences for hundreds of people). The sensitivity that gave Epstein certain insights also left him with a hefty dose of guilt over his sexual preferences,

preferences that were usually indulged only with help from his family's cash.

Serving record store customers, even when most had a certain respect for him, was not really his idea of fun. But the family music shop was the one place where he could see, and talk to, young people. Those in their teens or early twenties, those who were a few years – and several lifetimes – younger than him, those who seemed so much freer and happier than he ever did.

And then, in late October 1961, the *something* he'd been looking for casually walked into the NEMS music emporium. 'Something' was a teenage boy asking for a German record by *Tony Sheridan and The Beatles* (the German label actually called them The Beat Brothers on the first pressings). Epstein thought he had heard of the band but couldn't think where, since the store didn't normally stock German imports. He, or one his acquaintances, may have seen the name in Bill Harry's *Merseybeat* magazine which had launched that summer, complete with Lennon's humourous history of The Beatles. And then the boy told him that the band weren't actually German, they were local, an underground 'beat combo' who were playing regularly at Liverpool's Cavern night-club.

After returning from Hamburg the previous December, virtually penniless and with Harrison temporarily in custody for working without a visa under-age, Lennon returned to Mendips and Aunt Mimi. Not only had he not made a fortune – though he'd sent some money back to Cynthia – he had also lost his best friend in the band; Stuart Sutcliffe had stayed behind in Hamburg to paint canvases – and to live with Astrid Kirchherr. He had, more or less, left the group. McCartney, embarrassed by Sutcliffe's mediocre bass-playing was relieved and shifted to bass himself. For John the problem was more than musical. Stuart, as he'd told Astrid a number of times when on the 'prellies', was his soul-mate, someone he loved.

That spring the battered but unbowed Beatles got themselves a residency at The Cavern, a venue that was no longer dedicated exclusively to jazz. Word began to spread and soon there were respectable crowds to see the band. Summer saw their one, brief, recording session from Hamburg, backing Tony Sheridan, finally get released, but it was only issued in Germany.

The next month saw the booming Liverpool music scene get its own magazine, Bill Harry's *Merseybeat*. Interest in The Beatles was such that Lennon was asked to contribute a story on the band. His amusing 'Short Diversion on The Dubious Origins of Beatles' more than filled the brief. Over the next couple of years he would contribute many short stories, jokes and word-play poems to Harry's publication.

In October Lennon and McCartney had hustled up enough money to take a holiday in Paris with Jurgen Vollmer. The only 'happening' people they saw in the French capital – a mere handful – seemed to have the new scruffy brushed-forward haircut that the Beatles were pioneering, only the Parisian trendies didn't yet wear their hair quite as long as the band or their German friend. To have the male forehead covered by hair was vaguely subversive in 1961, after two world wars and a major economic depression which encouraged both conformity, uniformity, and a 'short back and sides' haircut for men.

Wherever they went in the French capital a few heads would turn. It confirmed to John and Paul – now a serious song-writing team – that the group's new look was indeed the way to go. After two weeks they returned to Liverpool. Demand for the band was such that lunchtime sessions were now taking place several times a week at The Cavern, attended by growing numbers of both students and teenage schoolgirls, eager to see the new 'beat sensation'.

On 9 November 1961, Epstein determined to check out this new 'Mersey beat' group for himself. In the basement heat of the Cavern, with their 'wild' hair and black leather, The Beatles – both toughened and seasoned by their endless Hamburg nights – seemed irresistible to Epstein. He loved their clever semi-educated roughness, the fact that they were handsome, spontaneous, talented and dangerous. And *free*. Everything he'd wanted to be at their age, everything he wanted to be *now*. Whether they could ever be polished enough to reach the very top was another thing entirely. But to Epstein that no longer mattered, he was already hooked. He instantly saw that Lennon was the leader and spent most of the next few days winning him over. Within a month he'd become The Beatles' first serious manager, promising to use his position as one of Liverpool's leading record retailers to arrange auditions with major labels.

On 9 December they played their first live event in the South of England. Only 18 punters bothered to turn up at Aldershot's Princess Hall. If the Beatles faith was shaken in Epstein's organisational abilities, they were rapidly proved wrong after he pulled a few strings and arranged a New Year's Day audition at Decca Records – then one of the biggest labels in the UK and the home of million-selling stars such as Tommy Steele, The Tornados and Terry Dene.

The Beatles attended the Decca audition in a different musical world to the one Lennon had fallen in love with some five years before. Rock'n'roll had now been totally eclipsed by lightweight pop, by a string of smooth young crooners. Some actually had a bit of talent – Ricky Nelson and Paul Anka, for example, as well as Britain's Billy Fury, one of the few who wrote some of his own material – but most were interchangeable; glossy, pretty and manufactured. The boy-bands of their day.

Of the original rockers, Elvis had never fully recovered his musical drive after being drafted into the US Army; Chuck Berry had been jailed for violating the Mann Act; Buddy Holly and Eddie Cochran had died in travelling accidents; while Gene Vincent fled to Britain and then France after problems with both promoters and unions. In Britain, Johnny Kidd had broken through some two years before with the seminal rocker 'Shakin' All Over'. But he was the only one, the exception that proved the rule. And Kidd, despite getting some radio play, seemed to be confined to the rocker ghetto. He never cracked the America chart and 'Shakin' was to be his only major pre-Beatles hit. Even Steele and Cliff Richard, who'd sparked riots at one point, now sounded like the new pop dream boys.

The Beatles already had quite a few Lennon-McCartney songs, but Epstein wanted them to mostly play covers at the audition, preferably ballads. And on New Year's Day 1962, that's exactly what they did, at Decca's studios in West Hampstead, London. Lennon, Harrison and McCartney, resplendent with their longer ungreased hair and drummer Pete Best still with his trademark Teddy Boy quiff.

Pop covers, balanced with some McCartney-dominated ballads, did not go down well. Decca's chief A&R Dick Rowe rejected the band with the words that have now become almost legendary, "Guitar bands are on the way out", although that didn't stop him signing up another guitar band, Dagenham's Brian Poole and The Tremeloes, later that same day. At least two other major labels were to say 'no' to the Beatles over the next few weeks.

The boys' disappointment was alleviated, at least a little, by their first radio session for BBC Manchester in March. 'Dream Baby, Memphis Tennessee' (sung by Lennon) and the early Motowner 'Please Mister Postman' were recorded and duly broadcast the next day. The radio plays clinched it for Epstein – during the last week of March the band finally agreed to his suggestion that they wear suits on stage for *most* gigs.

Lennon saw the matching suits as the first and, in some ways, the biggest compromise of the Beatle years. It now sounds an excessive comment but its hard to exaggerate the importance of clothes to young people in Britain during the years between the mid-Forties and the late Eighties.

Clothes could get you – or lose you – a good job, a steady girlfriend, police attention or a new set of friends. Clothes were an indication of class, attitude, imagination, sexual orientation and even politics. The Beatle suits were chic and collarless, and some were as black as the leather they'd just dumped, but they were still *suits*, the uniform of every bank clerk and junior civil servant. Suits, even sharp ones, just didn't cut it as far as young musicians then were concerned.

But to make it to, in Lennon's words, "the toppermost of the poppermost", you had to do what was necessary. You had to be a tough bastard. And the Fab Four, he once boasted, were the biggest bastards going.

In April the band returned to Hamburg, to a Star-Club residency and the news that young Stuart Sutcliffe, Lennon's soul-mate, had just died – killed by a brain haemorrhage, probably the result of a beating dished out by thugs after a gig in Liverpool – which didn't stop various writers from later claiming that it was Lennon's violence that was chiefly responsible for his best friend's death. Lennon reacted exactly the same way he had when his mother and step-father had died. After laughing hysterically for a few moments he faked indifference, though it was also a kind of tough love that he used on others, forcing Sutcliffe's girlfriend Astrid to live, to go out and to go on – she later said he helped to save her from an endless, deep depression.

A few weeks later Epstein sent a telegram from England with good news. EMI had agreed to audition the band. EMI was then the biggest label outside of America, and its US subsidiary Capitol even managed to sell millions Stateside as well, with big name artists such as Frank Sinatra.

Epstein didn't tell his boys that the EMI producer-A&R in question, George Martin, worked for Parlophone, one of the smaller EMI labels. It was also a label more usually associated with novelty or comedy records by the likes of Peter Sellers, Bernard Cribbins or Charlie Drake. By now, though, Epstein was hip enough not to say anything that would cut into the band's confidence, though he did add 'Please Rehearse New Material' to the foot of the telegram.

Paul's ballads and the usual rock standards hadn't worked at the Decca audition and the band were fast running out of time. Bill Harry had started the *Merseybeat* magazine for a good reason, namely because there were already dozens of beat groups playing live in the Liverpool area (by the end of 1961 there were over 90, by mid-1963 the number was said to be an amazing 300). Many of these groups had hundreds of fans, including Kingsize Taylor and the Dominoes, Derry & The Seniors, Cass & The Casanovas, The Big Three, The Clayton Squares, Rory Storm & The Hurricanes and Gerry & The Pacemakers. Newcomers such as Billy J Kramer & The Dakotas and Ian & The Zodiacs were also making waves. At any time any one of them could, theoretically, be signed up to a major label to steal The Beatles' thunder and claim the Mersey sound as their own, thus relegating the others to being, at best, followers, at worst also-rans. Or, perhaps, a new musical trend from America, or London, might just make merseybeat itself seem old-fashioned and redundant before it had even really broken. The EMI Parlophone audition had to be the Beatles' best – they might not get another one.

At EMI's Abbey Road Studios on 6 June 1962 the band were told to play four numbers. They did a Coasters' cover, plus 'Love Me Do' and two other originals. McCartney handled most of the lead vocals with John singing 'Ask Me Why'. Despite having reservations about Pete Best's drumming, George Martin expressed serious interest in the band. The actual decision to sign them was taken a few days later after, allegedly, a desperate Epstein had phoned EMI and told them in no uncertain terms that his NEMS shops would no longer stock EMI product if his group got rejected.

With EMI's permission Martin signed them up, and within days the major label's influence began to get results. On 11 June the BBC Light Programme – then Britain's only national radio station – did their first session with The Beatles for the Beeb's *Here We Go* show.

July 1962 saw the very first Lennon lyric to appear on record as Darren Young, aka Johnny Gentle, had his 'I've Just Fallen For Someone' issued as a single, complete with an uncredited middle 8 by The Beatles' founder. The next month things were anything but gentle as Pete Best was finally fired. The drummer had been with them for two years but Martin's critical comments had added to a growing rift that already existed between Best and the rest of the Beatles (principally, it's said, over Best's refusal to lose his somewhat dated teddy boy quiff – if true it must make it the world's most expensive haircut, since it was to eventually cost its owner at least £250 million). After Best left, to be replaced by the Hurricanes' Ringo Starr, an old pal from Hamburg, some of his more dedicated Cavern fans physically attacked both Ringo and Harrison, with Lennon saving the latter from a severe beating on at least one occasion.

August was a hectic month at the Cavern for John Lennon, even aside from the Harrison fight. Before one gig his girlfriend Cynthia Powell told him that she was pregnant and they were secretly married on the 23rd – without Aunt Mimi's approval, or presence – the day before Granada TV had sent a film crew to cover the Cavern Club and its strange array of new beat bands. The Beatles were filmed topping the bill as they performed 'Kansas City' and a Big Three favourite, the up-tempo jealous guy anthem 'Some Other Guy'.

A quarter of a century later, Granada presenter, Tony Wilson heard a rare audio tape of the Beatles performing their entire set of that night and described it as sounding as explosive as the Manchester performances of the Sex Pistols, the punk founders whose television debut was to be on Wilson's *So It Goes* show.

On the first day of October 1962, with the release of their first 45 'Love Me Do' just four days away, The Beatles finally signed a proper management contract with Brian Epstein's NEMS Enterprises Limited. It looks a curiously dated and one-sided document now. As McCartney and Harrison were under 21, their respective fathers, James McCartney and Harold Harrison, had to sign for them, while NEMS management solemnly promised to do its best to promote:

A group of musicians to be known as The Beatles, in the following branches of the entertainment industry: (a) Vaudeville and revue (b) Motion pictures (c) Balls and dances whether of a public or private nature (d) Radio and television broadcasting (e) Concerts, private parties, cabarets (f) Phonographic and tape recording (g) Sponsorship projects.

The contract was to run for five years, but under Clause One's proviso, either party could terminate with just three months notice, as long as that notice was delivered by registered post. Epstein, despite the EMI deal, was giving himself an out, though on 22 January 1963 Epstein persuaded the band to cancel this op-out proviso.

In purely monetary terms it was not the 'Mister Ten Per Cent' contract of showbiz legend. Epstein was to get 15 per cent of The Beatles' earnings, if those earnings should total less than £400 per week. This management cut rose to 20 per cent if the group's received monies exceeded £400 per week, but were less than £800. If the group's earnings broke the £800 per-week mark (perhaps £16,000 in current values) then NEMS/Epstein were to get a massive 25 per cent. From late 1963 onwards, Epstein was thus to be the best paid 'Beatle' of all. Sadly, though, the inexperienced NEMS MD wasn't so good at extracting percentages from EMI. From the start Epstein was said to have been convinced that EMI boss Sir Joseph Lockwood, as an English gentleman, couldn't possibly sanction a deal that was unfair to any artist. With a good recording royalty then being between 7 and 10 per cent, Epstein accepted a deal that, in real terms, got the group a lot less than three – much later it was renegotiated upwards to prevent embarrassment for either Epstein or EMI.

The same week they signed the contract, The Beatles travelled South to meet the music press. Some of those present were shocked by the fact that the band turned up with 'uncut hair' and wearing leather and jeans. Their appearance prompted questions about whether the group would wear such clothes if ever Epstein got them on nationwide television. NEMS press agent Andrew Loog Oldham, future Rolling Stones manager, and his assistant Tony Calder, both sat in the wings, Oldham taking careful note of the intense interest the Beatles' 'scruffy looks' had generated.

Two weeks after signing with NEMS, the now besuited

Beatles appeared live on Granada TV to promote their original 'Love Me Do' debut. Although their fan base had leapt from hundreds to thousands overnight, the national press had still not noticed the screaming girls who mobbed the band whenever they were north of Watford – perhaps partly because the US-Soviet confrontation known as the Cuba Crisis, had selfishly grabbed the headlines by taking the world to the brink of World War Three, and complete nuclear annihilation.

After three days of the Cuba Crisis people started cracking sick jokes in the morning, "Well, we're still here then!" After five days people stopped laughing. Across the world millions held their breath as millions more frantically prayed. American and NATO forces were, like those of Russia's Warsaw Pact, placed on red alert as fleets of jets and bombers stood ready on the ground, while others circled in the air champing at the bit for the Go-Code – the last order.

In a crumbling garret, Robert 'Bob Dylan' Zimmerman began to furiously scribble the song 'A Hard Rain's A-Gonna Fall'. It was made up of single lines from all the various unfinished songs that he no longer believed he'd live long enough to complete.

CHAPTER FIVE

1963

Will the people in the cheaper seats clap your hands?
And the rest of you, just rattle your jewellery.

John Lennon, November 1963

Like 1941 before it, and 1968 after, 1963 was a key year in many many ways. Artistically, in the film world, several people attempted to push the medium on to a higher level. Rough cuts of the first three hours of the extravaganza *Cleopatra*, in today's money a 200 million dollar movie, are said to be amongst the most dramatic of any costume drama ever shot. But rather than indulge director Joseph L Mankiewicz for a few weeks longer, the studio seized the footage already shot and cobbled together the 'finished' epic. Even then, half-finished on some levels, the Liz Taylor and Richard Burton epic still garnered four Oscars.

Hollywood did, of course, make a contribution to the Cold War debate – how could it not when the 13 days of the Cuba Crisis had taken the world to the brink of oblivion? Tinseltown gave us films such as *On The Beach*, which showed the aftermath of a limited nuclear war and in which the planet's remaining humans gather in Australia and wait for the terminal clouds of radiocactive poison to reach them. In the final reel, as suicide pills are handed out, Salvation Army banners tell us 'There Is Still Time'.

Stanley Kubrick's chilling black comedy *Dr Strangelove* or *How I Learned To Stop Worrying And Love The Bomb*, had another take on the subject, foreseeing a nuclear disaster deliberately being provoked by a USAF officer. Its release was delayed, it wasn't issued until 1964, and its portrayal of the US military led to anguished articles in American newspapers and magazines. Another film completed in '63, but not released until the following year, was *Seven Days In May*, the story of a conspiracy by US generals to bring down a liberal Democrat President after the latter begins negotiations with the Russians to rid the world of nuclear weapons. After seeing a sneak preview of the film President Kennedy told its director, John Frankenheimer, "That [a US Army coup] is exactly what would happen to me if I ever tried such a deal."

Meanwhile, in England, in May 1963, Joseph Losey, a Hollywood director who'd fled the McCarthy witchhunts, finally got to see his film *The Damned* hit British screens. It was his version of H.I. Lawrence's cult sci-fi novel *The Children of Light* and it had been shot and edited by him way back in 1961. Amongst the film's rising stars were Shirley Ann Field, Viveca Lindfors and a young Oliver Reed. But Hammer Films, the producers, were used to more mainstream 'horror' and they were, quite simply, outraged by the movie's anti-nukes' sensibility. After viewing it again they agreed to postpone its release until late 1962.

By turns touching, thought-provoking and sinister, *The Damned* concerns liberal 'nice guy' Simon, an American tourist played by the middle-aged MacDonald Carey, who picks up a girl and eventually helps her get away from her restrictive brother King and his gang of leather-clad bike thugs, who mug Simon while singing along with the film's 'Black Leather' theme song.

The movie ends in spectacular fashion. The lovers and King stumble on a secret under-cliff 'prison' of radioactive children who have never seen the sunlight, children who have been kept secret so they can be used by the state after a nuclear war. The unlikely trio free the young inmates and are then hunted down before King is killed. The two lovers escape by boat, shadowed by an Army helicopter and unaware that they are already dying of radioactive sickness. The children themselves are rounded up and swiftly re-imprisoned, ready once again to reluctantly serve the post-nuclear war state 'when the time comes'.

The Damned ends with the sound of the children, now finally aware of the outside beauty they're missing, crying hopelessly, *"Help us! Please somebody help us!"* as the camera pans over the distant holidaymakers on Weymouth's glitzy beach. The cries are obviously meant to be the cries of humanity, *our* cries, *our* screams for help in a world gone MAD (Mutually Assured Destruction, the deterrent theory of nuclear weaponry).

They're also the cries of anyone – or everyone – with a damaged childhood, the 'Rosebud symbol' of the atomic age (the 'Rosebud symbol' comes from Orson Welles' pioneering *Citizen Kane* film of 1941, with its reporter's quest for the meaning of a media tycoon's dying words. We finally discover, though the reporter does not, that Rosebud refers to Kane's snow sledge and the aborted childhood it represents. Lennon's own childhood was similarly deconstructed, though he perhaps turned his driving ambition into something more worthy than Kane's megalomania).

Then the October '62 horror of the Cuba Crisis – and the nuclear war it very nearly led to – made Hammer postpone *The Damned's* release for another seven months. Finally the following May, after sneak rave previews of Losey's follow-up *The Servant* had already started Oscar rumours, *The Damned* was publicly screened in London, buried in a double bill and with some 13 minutes hacked out of it. Its US release, as *These After The Damned*, was postponed for another two years and even then it was only allowed out as part of a similar low budget double bill.

Despite such treatment, the UK's leading indie film critic of the time, Raymond Durgnant, predicted that *The Damned* might yet be seen as "one of the most important films of the Sixties" while its screening at the first Trieste Science Fiction Film Festival led to a standing ovation before it won the festival's main award.

Although often poetic exciting and passionate, all of the above films are visions of the crackling present, their subliminal soundtracks the buzzing rattle of the Geiger-counter, and all of them – despite their brilliance – *are* ultimately horror films, genuine horror, the nightmares of the non-future the Cold War had given us.

On the British music scene, in early 1963 maverick producer Joe Meek was expecting six figure royalties from his, and Britain's, first ever American Number 1 hit – the strange, space age instrumental 'Telstar' by The Tornados. Unfortunately the money never arrived for one of the world's very first independent producers. Instead Meek – who also designed and built his own EQs and sound compressors – was slapped with a costly writ that froze his monies for over four years. By the time the case was settled in Meek's favour, the gay wildman of British pop production was dead. The deep-in-debt sound wizard had blown his own head off with a shotgun a few minutes after he'd killed the landlady of his tiny Holloway Road recording studio. There was a lesson here too, of sorts. You could be as independent as you liked, but when it came to big deals and big monies, then it was still the big lawyers and the big distributors – like the big film studios – who called the shots. The Beatles would change that, at least for a time, but it was a change that came too late for Joe Meek and many others.

John, Paul, George and Ringo had started 1963 with their only single hit to date – 'Love Me Do' (top position Number 17, just for a week) dropping slowly out of the charts despite their furious efforts to promote it during a five-date mini-tour of Scotland.

The Scottish gigs had earned them just under £200 – by the end of the year they were getting over £4,000 for the same number of concerts (£80,000 today). The excellent rocker 'Please Please Me', was their first Number 1, though the chart used by the BBC judged it to be no higher than Number 2. It was an all-out piece of pumping, melodic magic that was initially refused US airplay. Many Stateside radio producers objected to it on two grounds: One; it was too crudely played and recorded and, Two; it was lyrically about nothing more than oral sex, something which was never totally true and it was not, in any case, an explicit song in any sense. No one in British or European radio had seriously considered the possibility that listeners would interpret the words that way. Lennon had first played it to George Martin at their second ever session together but back then it had been a slower, Roy Orbison type slice of melodrama, a slow ballad. Now it was Britain's first real rock'n'roll hit for years.

The group themselves had also racked up three other Number 1 hits by year's end. The first was 'From Me To You', which charted, while 'Please Please Me' was still on the hit parade. As if to add to the celebrations that April, John's young wife Cynthia gave birth to Julian Lennon – full name John Charles Julian Lennon – at Liverpool's Sefton General Hospital.

But like his father before him, Lennon was absent for the birth, rehearsing with the rest of the 'Fab Four' in London. Lennon's fame, and Epstein's outdated showbiz need to keep the marriage to Cynthia secret, lest it damage record sales, meant it was another 48 hours before John was finally smuggled in to see his first born son. Even then he had to depart early, for a one-hour Beatles' gig at Birkenhead's Majestic Ballroom.

The next Beatles' chart-topper that year was 'She Loves You', a third person narrative that raced out of the traps and contained the 'yeah, yeah, yeah' chorus that was to enter the language, and newspaper headlines, of the world. This was the age when, both in schools and polite British circles, words such as 'yeah' and 'okay' were still considered rude, yobbish and vaguely subversive.

The last Beatles' Number 1 of the year was 'I Want To Hold Your Hand' with its abrupt build-up of an intro, accented choruses, manic hand-clapping and superb cut-dead ending. It was one of the last songs they bothered to record in a foreign language version; these were usually, after Hamburg, in German. By casually demolishing this showbiz tradition, The Beatles unwittingly boosted English round the world – millions of youngsters learned it, at least in part, so as to better understand the Fab Four's songs – and, since they sang in casual language they also helped introduce a new verbal informality that spread into native tongues. In some of the Scandinavian countries, for instance, forms of address between strangers switched abruptly from the impersonal to the personal 'du' during the Sixties. Across the globe the last vestiges of Victoriana were finally being swept away.

All of these 1963 hits were classics, and all of them were pure Beatles, although, unlike later songs, these are so much *of* the band that they have rarely been covered, despite their continuing popularity. The first and last of these – 'Please Please Me' and 'I Want To Hold Your Hand' – were principally written by John Lennon. Although the Beatles songs' by McCartney or Lennon – or both – were all credited to 'Lennon-McCartney' after the first few singles (when the order had been reversed), something that was adhered to for the next eight years, many songs are known to have been almost wholly written by one or the other. McCartney had first started writing back in 1957, probably as he'd read about Buddy Holly and Chuck Berry composing much of their own material, and Lennon had soon joined in. The torrent of songs that they actually wrote together, 'eyeball-to-eyeball' as Lennon once put it, was to quickly slow to a trickle after their first two years on Parlophone. From then on, as the creative rivalry between them grew, the contributions they gave to each other's songs usually consisted of nothing more than a bridge, or an alternative word, or a recording suggestion.

By the time 'I Want To Hold Your Hand' was released, over half a million orders for it had been received and the word 'Beatlemania' had entered the language, as the English South, and the rest of the UK, finally surrendered to the Fab Four. Now mobs of young teens, mainly girls, pursued them on almost every street corner and every grand entrance and exit required decoys, fast cars and hundreds of police officers. In their TV appearances Lennon dominated the stage, standing with legs slightly apart, head back and well in command, looking down his long regal nose when he wasn't singing intensely. The others performed well enough onstage – and the 'Ooh-Oohs' when John shared a mic with Paul, sent the girls wild – but any student of psychology would only have to study the scene for a few seconds to see that Lennon was top dog here. He wasn't arrogant about it anymore, merely self-confident. He'd started the group, he'd pretty much led it and, though the input from McCartney – and Harrison and Kirchherr – had been critical, it was still *his* group. He was, he rightly felt, slightly more important than the others.

At November's Royal Command Performance at the Prince of Wales theatre, The Beatles, though way down the bill, completely stole the show. McCartney's yearning rendition of 'Till There Was You', from the hit musical *The*

Music Man, showed the oldies that the boys could manage a decent, respectable song properly, while Lennon's knock-out attack on the Isley Brother's 'Twist & Shout' brought the house down. For the last number Lennon gave the following introduction to the assembled lords, ladies and gentlemen (and the millions watching on television), "For this number, we'd like to ask your help. Will the people in the cheaper seats clap your hands? And the rest of you, just rattle your jewellery."

It was the perfect remark for the occasion, cheeky enough to appeal to the young and the 'young at heart', without being really offensive. Offence had already been taken though. Several days before the Royal Show the *Daily Telegraph* newspaper had compared The Beatles to Hitler, and their gigs to Nuremberg rallies that filled young people's heads with 'hysteria'.

Lennon himself, as with the other Beatles, had seen the growing tumult at every concert as being, in part, a sociological phenomenon. The band were just being used, he said, "as an excuse for people to go wild." It was fun, at first, but the constant screaming soon began to annoy them – Lennon often ended songs with a bellowed obscenity that no one could hear amid the mayhem, just as no one, at many gigs, could hear the music clearly.

And Lennon had originally been going to use a four letter word during the Royal Variety Show as well, which would have been British TV's very first example of heavy swearing. But he allowed a nervous Epstein to talk him out of it. It was almost certainly for the best, creatively speaking; the outrage that followed the Sex Pistols TV swear-in 13 years later effectively ended their live career, and the subsequent pressure probably helped break up the original line-up too, since tunesmith Glen Matlock was swiftly fired – allegedly, in part, for being a Beatles' fan, according to Pistols' manager Malcolm McLaren – to be replaced by the late Sid Vicious. Only two more original Pistols songs were recorded and released before the band imploded.

Such a media storm might just have done similar damage to The Beatles (comparisons with the Pistols are not wildly out of place here – not, at least, in media terms – as they also caused a great outcry, making the front pages time after time, and just like the Beatles, the new 'John, Paul, Steve and Glen' had started out playing wild gigs in strip clubs, bars and dank jazz basements).

Lennon's verbal restraint at the Royal Variety Show was rewarded with a dozen rave reviews in the national newspapers – the band were already beyond music press only coverage – and The Beatles were lauded as wits as well as talented musicians and composers. They were seen as real talents 'who didn't need off-colour jokes or obscenities'. If only the hacks had known about Lennon's planned remark, or his notoriously sick sense of humour – most of his school, college and *Merseybeat* jokes had mocked rabbis or the physically handicapped – perhaps something that might initially be expected from a sarcastic 'abandoned' child of above average intelligence. But when Lennon witnessed genuine anti-Semitism – as when fellow Quarry Bank pupil Michael Isaacson was verbally abused in school – he was appalled and refused to join in the attacks. Isaacson has always said that he and John "got on okay". Lennon wasn't racist. The only sick thing about him was his sense of humour, though even that would probably be considered almost mainstream by twenty-first century standards.

As well as handling the media, Lennon was also learning a little about recording studio technique along the way and, like Hendrix after him, he is supposed to have attended some mastering sessions; mastering being, in essence, the final 'mix' as a silver cutting disc is prepared from which the moulds for thousands of vinyl copies are to be pressed.

At these sessions frequencies could be boosted or reduced, special effects pulled down or pushed up and vocals stressed or half-buried and compression added to give the recording some mid-level punch, usually necessary to cut through the chewing-gum, rusty juke-box radio fog of the intended target audience of the time.

Later John was to complain about the crude stereo mixes that were done in his absence in the early days – "I dunno what they were thinking of!" – mixes that had most vocals on one side, most instruments on the other. These were used on the rare stereo releases since most radios, record decks, juke-boxes and radios were then mono, the format for which the biggest pressings were reserved and on which Lennon had worked hardest. The stereo versions were minor sellers during 1962-64 – which now makes many of them as highly collectible as India's 78rpm Beatles singles – but it was those stereo tapes that got used on most re-releases and compilations.

Two Beatles albums had reached Number 1 in the UK during '63 – *Please Please Me* and *With The Beatles*, long-players that were to spend a staggering total of two and half years on the British album charts. They both also contained 14 tracks on each and this in an age when 11 or 12 was the norm. The 14-track album was an act of generosity to the fans, an act that only happened because Lennon had insisted on it.

A Parisian residency had been booked for 1964 and tentative plans were made for some kind of American tour after assurances from EMI's US subsidiary Capitol that the 'I Want To Hold Your Hand' single and *Meet The Beatles* album – the US version of *With The Beatles* – would finally receive serious promotion. Capitol had actually turned down the first few Beatles singles which had then only appeared Stateside on smaller labels such as Vee Jay and Swan, and it had taken the latter five months, and The Beatles' US TV debut, to get 'She Loves You' into the charts.

Gerry & The Pacemakers, the young Rolling Stones and Billy J Kramer & The Dakotas all scored hits in 1963 with Lennon-McCartney songs and in December *The Times* and *Sunday Times* called Lennon and McCartney the most 'outstanding' English composer of the year; the finest young talents since the heyday of Beethoven.

But in the world outside England there were several other incidents in 1963 that were to have great importance both for John Lennon and the world.

On 16 September, as Lennon travelled to Paris with wife Cynthia for a well-earned holiday, British Malaya became Malaysia. Local celebrations on gaining independence rapidly escalated into attacks on the symbols of former British rule. The violence culminated in an angry mob of over 100,000 rioters sacking the British Embassy. Once it had been effectively looted it was burnt to the ground. Despite all the rhetoric and gestures, both real and fictional, the British were to lose most of their influence in Malaya. Their exports to the Asian state were to fall dramatically too.

No one in British military intelligence really wanted to talk about it – and nor, of course, did the American spooks already planning to apply some of the same failed philosophies in Vietnam – but the fact was now obvious to anyone with the eyes to see it; for all its short term successes, over the long haul the 'hearts and minds' programme had simply *not* worked.

In October America's President, John F Kennedy, issued National Security Action memo NSAM 263 on Vietnam which, after a three line intro, opened with the lines:

The President approved the military recommendations contained in Section I B (1-3) of the report but directed that no formal announcement be made of the implementation of plans to withdraw 1,000 US military personnel by the end of 1963.

Although the wording might seen ambiguous, it does indicate, especially when taken together with memo NSAM 111, that JFK was about to start pulling out of the Vietnam morass. Kennedy's own remarks to the Press in September, about the war ultimately being the responsibility of the Vietnamese people, echo this theme:

It is their [the South Vietnamese's] war. We can help them, we can send them equipment, we can send our men out there as advisers, but in the final analysis it is their people and their government who have to win or lose this struggle.

In his next three public speeches Kennedy repeated his resolve "never" to send a US draftee to solve problems that only the Vietnamese could solve. On 2 October he asked Secretary of Defence, Robert McNamara, to tell waiting pressmen that a thousand US advisers were to be brought back from South-East Asia before 25 December 1963 and that he expected the last American military to leave there before "the end of 1965, and that means all the helicopter pilots too."

But McNamara was still, at that point, convinced that the Vietnam War could easily be won and he twisted JFK's words, announcing only that "the major part of the US military task" could be completed by the end of '65. Kennedy, however, was determined to make himself clear and he returned to the same subject again, in a public speech at the end of October '63: "Our object is to bring home *every* American technician, helicopter pilot and military adviser by the end of 1965." A fortnight later he even announced that the first thousand men were starting to pack and would be US-bound by Christmas.

Presidential NSA memo NSAM 273 then reversed *all* of this. While the rest of the ten point document is similar to NSAM 263 – though the line *'plausibility of denial'* has been added to point 7 concerning attacks on North Vietnam – the key opening paragraph about withdrawal is missing in its entirety. The withdrawal policy has been effectively put into reverse.

The reason for this reversal is quite simple. NSAM 273, the later memo, is dated 26 November 1963 and was issued by a different President. America's new leader was a brutal career politician from the Deep South, 'LBJ', one Lyndon Baines Johnson, a man convinced that the 'hearts and minds' programme, backed with sufficient military force, would soon lead to a spectacular US victory in Vietnam.

The reason LBJ was now President was also simple – four days before, on 22 November 1963, John F Kennedy, the 35th President of the United States of America, had been assassinated, shot to death in broad daylight in Dallas, Texas.

CHAPTER SIX

HAPPINESS IS A WARM GUN

So what if he [Kennedy] screwed a few women? Every President since has screwed the entire world.

Shirley MacLaine

The facts are that President Kennedy was withdrawing from Vietnam at the time of his murder.

John Newman, author of 'JFK & VIETNAM', writing in the *New York Times* March 29 1992.

[JFK] would have opted against a large-scale American war in Vietnam.

Frederik Logevall, author of the award-winning *Choosing War: The Lost Chance For Peace & The Escalation of War In Vietnam* (2001).

Kennedy had come to power after defeating Republican Vice President Nixon in the 1960 election, thus ending eight long years of Republican rule. The latter had been the favourite to win, having been a high-profile supporter of the McCarthy witchhunts, as well as being Vice President between 1952 and January 1961 when JFK was inaugurated.

Having been bounced by the CIA into approving the Bay of Pigs attack on Castro's Cuba – an invasion carried out by 1,300 Cuban exiles and US mercenaries on 17 April – JFK was horrified when the locals failed to rise up in support of the incursion, an uprising the CIA had assured him would happen.

Despite coming under considerable pressure from the

Agency and the US military, JFK then refused to order a massive US air strike – such a move, with the attendant deaths of thousands of civilians, was the only action that could possibly have made the invasion a 'success'.

As well as angering the USA's intelligence community and military top brass, JFK's refusal to blitz Havana also annoyed the American Mafia. The organised crime syndicates had run most of the bars, brothels and casinos in pre-Castro Cuba and military action seemed the only way they'd regain their tax-free cash-cows.

In the aftermath of the Bay of Pigs fiasco Kennedy swore he'd smash the CIA and scatter them "into a thousand pieces". Within weeks CIA boss Allen W Dulles was dismissed. JFK caused further outrage amongst US security forces during the October '62 Cuba Crisis – when the Cuban installation of Soviet nuclear missiles, presumably to deter another Bay of Pigs attack – and also to balance the US missiles that had recently arrived in American air-bases in Turkey – led to a US Naval blockade and a 'Mexican stand-off'.

For almost two weeks it seemed the US and Soviet Union would go to (nuclear) war, possibly ending all human life on planet earth. Bobby 'RFK' Kennedy, the Attorney General who was JFK's brother, eventually persuaded Russian leader Khrushchev to remove the missiles, partly in exchange for a discreet US pullback in Turkey – though not before General Curits E. LeMay, the USAF's Chief of Staff, had tried to start the apocalypse by firing a missile at the Soviet Union. Curits E. LeMay was the same man whose pilots had fire-bombed Tokyo and other Japanese cities in early 1945, killing over 220,000 civilians and terrifying a young Yoko Ono.

LeMay's missile, with a dud warhead, flew over a thousand miles towards the Russians – tracked all the way by frantic Red Army radar operators – before it ditched harmlessly in the sea. At the same time, CIA big-wig Bill Harvey was also trying to provoke a US-Soviet war by continuing to send anti-Castro commando teams on raids along the Cuban coast. RFK discovered this and in a justifiable fury demanded that Bill Harvey be sacked. Although he was temporarily removed from his post, the CIA did not, in the end, sack Bill Harvey but instead sent him to Europe.

If this all seems extreme to the point of madness well, yes, in many ways it was, but it has to be remembered that the USA at the time of the Cuba Crisis had over 5,000 nuclear war heads that could reach the Soviet Union and fellow Warsaw Pact countries. The Soviets had barely 35 such weapons that could hit the US mainland from Russia.

If the Soviets could be pushed into a nuclear war they would, effectively, be wiped out by America's superior atomic firepower. Of course, the Americans' European and Asian allies would suffer vast losses too and even the continental USA would have said goodbye to anything from a few hundred thousand to 20 million civilians. The world too would have undergone a huge climate change (no one had ever tried exploding hundreds of huge nuclear weapons on the same day before).

But to right-wing extremists, such as LeMay and many of the CIA and US Army high-ups, it was a price well worth paying in order to rid the planet of the scourge of 'godless Communism'. Besides, if the military caught the Russians on the hop there was a slight chance that US losses would be comparatively small.

Bombing raids ordered by LeMay had already killed almost 300,000 civilians during 1945 alone. Calculating such losses weren't a big novelty for him. The insane character Colonel Jack D Ripper, in the film *Dr. Strangelove*, was said to have been based on Curtis E LeMay.

Thanks to RFK's efforts though, the Cuba Crisis failed

to produce World War Three but it was a close run thing. Krushchev came under pressure from the Red Army to take a tougher stand, while even JFK's saner Chiefs of Staff had pressed him to launch air, sea and land attacks on Cuba, but we now know that the Soviet missile operators on Cuba were under strict instructions to use their tactical nuclear weapons if there was a US invasion.

At the time, though, the US Right was convinced that the peace that followed was yet another Kennedy betrayal of the nation – 'Cuba was still Red at the end, wasn't it?' said some while an hysterical LeMay called the peace 'The biggest defeat in our history!' – and JFK's next moves only seemed to confirm their worst fears. In order to reduce tension and lessen the danger of another catastrophic misunderstanding, Kennedy and Khrushchev agreed to establish a phone 'hotline' between the White House and Moscow's Kremlin.

By the time the hotline was operational, at the end of August '63, the US had also signed – along with Britain and the USSR – the nuclear Test Ban Treaty, an agreement that would eventually stop all open-air explosions, except those that the French military still occasionally mount. To the US top brass the Test Ban Treaty was, in effect, 'stopping their fun', slowing down a nuclear arms race that they felt they could win.

It later became clear that, as part of the Cuba Missile Crisis deal, JFK had also agreed that the US would not attempt another armed invasion of the island, a decision which outraged the CIA and the Joint Chiefs of Staff – and the Mafia.

In the CIA and Army, insult was added to injury when Kennedy declared that the Vietnam War was "South Vietnam's to win" and began to draw up plans to withdraw US troops. His Vice President, Lyndon B Johnson, disagreed with this but then, as JFK had told his secretary the same month, Johnson was not actually going to be Kennedy's running mate in the next, 1964, election.

With his moves to repeal the 27.5 per cent oil depletion tax loophole, JFK had dared to upset the big oil companies too, particularly those run by Dallas oil billionaire H.L. Hunt. A Rightist fanatic who had his own intelligence network, Hunt had also spent millions of dollars in the Fifties backing Congressman Lyndon B Johnson, VP Richard Nixon, fellow Republican Gerald Ford as well as Senator Joe McCarthy.

Before leaving office Republican President Eisenhower had spoken of his worries concerning the growing power of "the military-industrial complex". Now, a thousand days later, the prime movers within that complex – the CIA, the US Chiefs of Staff, the arms manufacturers, the steel and oil industries – all wanted Kennedy out of office. Permanently.

His brother's anti-Mafia crusade seemed to the Mob to be against the spirit of an 'agreement' that they later privately claimed they'd brokered with the Kennedys' father during the 1960 election. It's an interesting claim, though why the Kennedys, with 400 million dollars of their own, would want Mafia money is another question entirely, although it is thought by some experts that some alleged pro-JFK vote-rigging in Chicago had been arranged by a Mob who expected JFK's father, with his history of bootlegging, to pressure his son into honouring the so-called 'debt'. If paternal pressure was exerted on JFK it had no obvious effect. This, combined with the 'loss' of Cuba, was enough to bring the overlapping groups of organised crime and right-wing Cuban exiles into the frame – the latter hand-in-glove with their CIA sponsors. Hoover's FBI had been hostile to JFK from the start – and the fact that JFK was not prepared to postpone Hoover's forthcoming retirement date only added to the old man's fury.

71

The anti-Kennedy forces now included the FBI, the CIA, the Mob, the Cuban exiles, Big Business, and many key leaders of the Army, Navy and Airforce, as well as Vice President 'LBJ' Johnson. LBJ was scheduled to soon face corruption charges over the Estes and Bobby Baker financial scandals, charges from which JFK was not prepared to save him. All wanted Kennedy out of The White House and all were aware that, in the public's eyes, he was as popular as ever, a 'shoo-in' for the 1964 poll and his brother Bobby 'RFK' Kennedy was surely a racing cert for '68 and '72. The 'unstoppable' FDR ghost, who the Right thought they had firmly buried beneath the Cold War hysteria of the Fifties, had returned to haunt them, his torch now borne by the Kennedys.

President Kennedy was shot and mortally wounded at 12.30 Eastern Standard Time on 22nd November 1963. He never regained consciousness and was dead within minutes. He was hit on Elm Street in the Texan city of Dallas, just past the Dal-Tex Building and Texas Book Depository, and to the left of the grassy knoll which has railway yards behind and beyond it. The Governor of Texas, John Bowden Connally Jr., was seriously wounded in the attack and a passer-by, one James Tague, received a minor face burn from a bullet. The windscreen had a bullet hole and other bullets were picked off the ground in the minutes following the killing.

Witnesses spoke of three to eight shots and others said there had been 'bursts' of automatic gunfire. Tom Wicker of the *New York Times*, present that day, wrote of JFK being hit by "a bullet in the throat, this wound had the appearance of a bullet's entry."

Twenty-eight other witnesses saw gun-smoke or heard gun-shots coming from the grassy knoll and several followed at least two Dallas police officers in rushing up the knoll, but all were prevented from reaching the top for a few crucial moments as the man delaying them had Secret Service ID. This ID later turned out to be fake, as there were no SS men on duty on the knoll. Within minutes a Dallas policeman, Officer Tippit, lay dying of gunshot wounds a few blocks away.

Officially, this entire onslaught was supposed to have been carried out by just one man, Lee Harvey Oswald. Oswald had, apparently, wreaked all this havoc with a single shot rifle: a bolt action gun that was almost 20 years old.

No one on Elm Street at the time seriously believed this. No one believed all that carnage had been carried out by one man with an antique rifle. Everyone spoke of how "*they* had shot the President". Governor Connally is reported to have said, moments after being hit, "My God, they are going to kill us all!"

Conspiracy theories are often not treated seriously these days, perhaps understandably after a few ludicrous extremes. Yet the fact is that people of influence *were* murdered, *were* assassinated. And in assassination after assassination, the accepted, official version of events is not just inadequate – it is, time and again, wholly and blatantly wrong. These discrepancies are now so obvious that only the naive, or those with a vested interest, could actually continue to believe them to be wholly innocent. There are few genuine conspiracies, there are even fewer genuine coincidences.

All of the following had some impact, directly and indirectly, on John Lennon's life – and death. In fact, the existence of the penultimate conspiracy herein, the Watergate Scandal, cannot be denied by even the most blinkered of commentators. Five men, working for President Nixon's re-election campaign, *did* burgle the Democrat Party HQ at the Watergate Centre in Washington

DC. They did so in order to illegally photograph documents, copy files and plant bugs – and they *were* caught red-handed and arrested on the spot by local police. It took well over two years, but Watergate and the subsequent cover-up did eventually force Nixon to resign in shame, sparking half a decade of revelations that were to shock America.

What did *not* emerge at the time were some other unsavoury connections between Watergate and the, then recent, past. The leader of the Watergate break-in team was Bernard Barker, a CIA 'asset' and former associate of mobster Santos Trafficante. Barker's two main assistants in planning the Watergate burglary were Frank Sturgis and E Howard Hunt.

During the dying months of 1960, Barker, Hunt and Sturgis had helped General Cabell and Richard Nixon plan the Bay of Pigs attack on Cuba. More disturbing still, Barker himself has been identified by, amongst others, police officer Seymour Weitzman as being the so-called 'Secret Service agent' who prevented Dallas police officers and others from inspecting the top of the grassy knoll in the seconds after the JFK shooting.

Hunt himself, like Frank Sturgis and David Ferrie, has long been an JFK assassination suspect and Hunt and Sturgis are believed by some to be two of the fake tramps arrested in a railway car, and then photographed behind the grassy knoll within minutes of the '63 assassination.

One key aspect of the Watergate cover-up was the Watergate Tapes – White House recordings of Nixon in conversation with his confederates during 1969-74. There were various unexplained edits and deletions on the tapes, though even the words that were left behind showed that Nixon and Hunt and the other Nixon associates still had, for some strange reason, an incredibly intense interest in the Bay of Pigs fiasco, over eleven years after it had happened. Many assassination experts now believe 'the Bay of Pigs' was Nixon code for the JFK assassination, its cover-up and the CIA's involvement in both.

According to E Howard Hunt's biographer Tad Szulc, Hunt had also been the CIA station chief in Mexico City during September 1963, when a lookalike had first attempted to create the impression of a new link between Lee Harvey Oswald and the Soviet Union. The Cuban Embassy refused the spy a visa and the Russians – who were now well suspicious of Oswald, or anyone calling themselves Oswald – promptly did the same.

Much of the above was first mentioned in A.J. Weberman and Michael Canfield's 1975 book *Coup d'Etat in America; The CIA & The Assassination of John F. Kennedy,* the authors backing their allegation with a CIA memo from an aide to CIA high-up Richard Helms' aide, stating that Hunt *was* in Dallas that day, a memo that showed great concern over the possibility that Hunt's presence there might one day become public knowledge. On publication Hunt immediately tried to sue Weberman and Canfield but when the case finally came to court, his case was quickly thrown out.

In 1985 Marita Lorenz, a former CIA and FBI agent, testified on oath that CIA operative Frank Sturgis – her one-time common law husband – had been one of the men who had assassinated JFK. She also said that Hunt and Jack Ruby had visited Sturgis in his Dallas motel room on 21 November 1963, the eve of the assassination, Hunt giving them thousands of dollars in used notes.

According to Lorenz, Sturgis later confessed to his part in the JFK killing. Sturgis himself denied this, though he did later admit that he *was* indeed questioned by the FBI over the JFK assassination.

Jack Ruby was a known FBI informer and mobster who went on to kill the official assassination suspect, Lee

Harvey Oswald, on 24 November 1963, before Oswald could be tried in court. Despite having his own apartment and plenty of ready cash from the Carousel Club, Ruby sometimes stayed at the Dallas YMCA rooms, as did Oswald (the latter on 3 October 1963 and again from 15-19 October). Although no newspaper said so at the time, several were aware that Jack Ruby was also a former employee of ex-Vice President Richard Milhouse Nixon.

CHAPTER SEVEN

THE FIRST LONE NUT

... we are all puppets ...

Sirhan Sirhan

One the day of Lee Harvey Oswald's arrest, three wallets belonging to him were found by the Dallas police, two of these wallets contained full ID. One was found on Oswald, one was found in his apartment and another wallet was discovered on 10th Street, just a few feet away from where Dallas Police Officer Tippit had been killed. This strange surplus of wallets seems to confirm the theory that it was an Oswald doppelganger who attempted to get Russian and Cuban visas in Mexico, almost certainly the same lookalike who'd gone around Dallas very loudly, and very publicly, making anti-American and pro-Soviet comments in the weeks leading up to JFK's assassination.

Several showgirls from Jack Ruby's Dallas night-club, the Carousel, later stated that Ruby and Oswald had been 'bedmates' and that assassination suspect David Ferrie had visited the club regularly as well. Oswald had also been in the New Orleans' Civic Air Patrol with Ferrie – a photo has now been unearthed of Oswald and Ferrie together at a CAP gathering in 1955 – before joining the US Marines. While in the Marines Oswald suffered several mysterious but minor gunshot wounds. One fellow marine said Oswald was faking and he disappeared from barracks for weeks at a time. These disappearances, uniquely, did not lead to charges or disciplinary hearings.

When US Marine Oswald was in Japan he was quartered at Atsugi, near Tokyo, a base for America's then secret U2 spy plane – and a base that was also home to an equally secret stash of American H-bombs, officially forbidden on the soil of Japan, the nation that had suffered the world's only atomic attacks. Oswald was also described by some of his acquaintances, including former marine colleagues, as being a narcissistic homosexual who was susceptible to hypnosis, "... someone you could brainwash".

Oswald had left the marines abruptly in 1959 before 'defecting' to the Soviet Union in a rather curious manner. Despite officially having virtually no money, he'd taken a ship to Britain, flown on to the Finnish capital Helsinki, where he stayed in an upmarket hotel, and then entered the Soviet Union using a one week tourist visa and the most expensive means of transport possible. A trip which would have cost him, in today's terms, around $10,000. Who was paying for all this?

Once in Helsinki he attempted to defect to the Soviet Union but delays led him to apparently attempt suicide in order to persuade the Russians he was in earnest; an act of seeming self-harm that his new Soviet doctor, Lydia Mikhailina, did not believe was genuine – or serious. Seven months after Oswald's defection the Russians surprised everyone by capturing a USAF spy plane, Gary Powers' U2 jet, which was shot down over Soviet territory.

Although the 1 May 1960 spy plane incident seemed to be an embarrassing set-back for America – flying at 90,000 feet the U2 had been thought to be untouchable – it was paradoxically greeted with joy, in private, by both the US military chiefs of staff and the CIA top brass. Both groups had felt that US President 'Ike' Eisenhower was getting too friendly with the Soviet's moderate post-Stalin leader Khruskhev and the U2 set-back caused immense damage to relations between the two men. It happened just before an important summit meeting.

A few months after the U2 episode, Oswald, who had never been fully trusted or accepted by his Soviet handlers, 'defected back' to the USA. Incredibly there remains no record of any attempt at a debriefing by either the CIA or FBI (not even when Oswald's interest in cameras led him to a job with the Jaggars Chiles Stovall Company, a firm doing top secret photographic work for the US government). Oswald did, however, later get in touch with Dallas FBI agent James P Hosty Jr., but Oswald's last pre-assassination note to Hosty was destroyed in late November 1963 on the orders of local FBI office chief J Gordon Shanklin.

One of the other main problems with the official 'Oswald was a commie' theory was Oswald's pro-Castro 'Fair Play For Cuba' leaflets. Many of them initially had a New Orleans address stamped on the back, and an address – 544 Camp Street – that was linked to both US Naval Intelligence and anti-Castro gunmen, as well as assassination suspects Guy Banister, David Ferrie and Clay Shaw. Shaw was taken to court in 1967 by New Orleans District Attorney Jim Garrison, a case that was the basis for Oliver Stone's 1992 film *JFK*. Banister died of an alleged heart attack within ten days of the last Warren Commission hearing into the JFK assassination, while Ferrie, who told friends he would never commit suicide, was found dead with not one, but two, suicide notes before he could testify before Garrison. Shaw himself was eventually acquitted, partly because most other American States refused Garrison's request that they extradite witnesses to New Orleans.

Anyone who has seriously studied the Oswald evidence rapidly comes to several contradictory conclusions about the man. Recent revelations, however, have made it easier to establish some sort of coherent whole.

Oswald started to work with the CIA after joining the marines in 1959. He had been groomed for the role by gay right-wing mentors like CAP volunteer David Ferrie, a devotee of the Rev. George A Hyde of the Orthodox Catholic Church. The Agency were already 'running' a passable Oswald lookalike when the 'original' was still in his mid-teens. This accounts for the innumerable discrepancies between the short shy Harvey Oswald schoolboy from Yorkville in New York and the pushier, taller southern boy Lee Oswald from New Orleans – it also explains how, when Oswald was in Russia, Lee Oswald could still be seen attempting to buy trucks and guns in New Orleans, and how Oswald could be seen in the USA at the same time as another Oswald was making waves in Mexico City – an Oswald who, according to young Mexican radicals, was obviously *not* the leftist he claimed to be.

Using such young people was not so new in the spook world – Britain's Royal Navy spy Christopher Creighton, aka John Ainsworth Davis, claimed to have been groomed and recruited when he was barely 16 years old and the Soviets had a phrase that summed up their young 'sleeper' schemes – 'wine cask fill' – which literally meant new wine in old bottles. An identity might be built on a fading faked photo from the British Raj or pre-war Paris and then combined with a forged ID. Before long a teenage graduate of the Minsk spy school would be starting a new life in Europe, Asia or America, trained to put up an endless front, trained to observe and wait for years if necessary.

Oswald was a similarly youthful recruit to America's spy system, and again similarly, he too was used abroad. Oswald was also a confused homosexual in an age when such a lifestyle was regarded as being both shameful and illegal. He voluntarily underwent deep hypnosis as he got further into the US foreign intelligence services: US

Naval Intelligence and liaisons with the CIA. The alter ego that emerged after such hypnotic sessions was no longer gay but heterosexual, sometimes aggressively so – a ladies man, a 'programmed' ladies man.

Whilst in the US Marines, during his fake injury recovery periods, Oswald is learning Russian. He also learns a few of the U-2 spy secrets. These he is to give to the Russians in order to widen the gap between the US and Soviet leadership.

After the US U-2 project has been betrayed, Oswald has another secret mission in Russia (after he's been photographed a few times by those few US tourists who are in the Soviet Union at the time, tourists who just happen to be in exactly the same parts of Russia that he is). That mission is to try and lure the daughter of a KGB high-up, a man connected to the Minsk spy school, to the West – with her father soon to follow, hopefully. A defector 'fishing trip'.

Marina Pruskakova is intrigued by Oswald's move, as are the KGB who are soon briefing Marina. They allow her to marry Oswald and even let the couple leave for America (there are no real secrets beyond the U-2 spy plane that Oswald has ever been privy to, so no more he can give the Soviets).

Back in the USA, the CIA, in conjunction with the FBI, arrange for Oswald to infiltrate and subvert the pro-Castro Fair Play For Cuba movement. The ultimate aim is to destroy it, of course. Oswald gives out pro-Cuban leaflets – quickly scrubbing out the Camp Street address after he notices it – and engages in fake fights and media debates which he knows he will lose, because his primed opponents know they can always drop the 'he's a defector to Russia' bombshell.

Whenever Oswald got into real trouble, he amazed local police by summoning the FBI, who would always get him released within minutes (hardly the service they'd render a real 'red'). He also made friends, secretly, with Dallas Police Officer Tippit and got reacquainted with Jack Ruby who also seemed to know Tippit.

At the same time, the other, taller, tougher 'Oswald' was creating quite a stir with his outrageous anti-American remarks – he also ordered guns via mail order, something quite unnecessary then in Dallas, since any kind of gun could have been bought over the counter for cash by anyone over 18, but mail order slips do leave a nice circumstantial trail to the quieter Harvey Oswald.

As the day of JFK's assassination moved closer, those who are in on it within the CIA heirachy coordinate their own Agency-mob 'shooter team', as well as back-ups from Cuba and the Middle East. Hoover got various warnings – including the 17 November 1963 FBI memo giving notice that a 'MILITANT REVOLUTIONARY GROUP MAY ATTEMPT TO ASSASSINATE PRESIDENT KENNEDY ON HIS PROPOSED TRIP TO DALLAS, TEXAS, 11-22-63' – and he ignored them completely. The shooters who were important enough to be interested were told that, with Kennedy dead, Cuba could be won back and North Vietnam liberated from Communism. If that damaged East-West relationships, so much the better. If it even provoked all-out war with the Soviets then so be it – better now than later when the Soviets would be stronger and possess more nuclear weapons.

A few weeks before the assassination the quiet but arrogant Harvey Oswald was told that his next assignment was to help expose shortcomings within the US Secret Service. When Kennedy visited Dallas a shot was to be fired close to the President. The subsequent shake-up would improve the Secret Service's presidential protection squad.

On 22 November, the unwitting Harvey Oswald went to work, making no attempt at disguise or subterfuge, and allowed three men, including one dark-skinned Cuban, into the Texas Book Depository. Other gunmen lurked in the Dal-Tex building, on the grassy knoll, in the Elm Street storm drains.

As the clocks struck 12.30, President Kennedy's Lincoln 'Lancer' turned into Elm Street and slowly started to straighten up – a perfect target. A single shot shattered the silence. It was followed two seconds later by a series of shots from a Mauser rifle and two new automatic rifles – proto-type M-16s – fitted with silencers. They peppered the presidential Lincoln and the area around it – a bullet flew down the triple underpass as another sent concrete chips of sidewalk up into the air. Others hit human targets.

All the while the shooters' radio coordinator on the ground barked "Shoot! Shoot! Shoot!" into his mini-radio mic as an umbrella flapped up and down beside him. Then, amazingly, 'Lancer', against all the rules of presidential driving, slowed to a virtual halt. An even easier target.

Of the 15 plus Secret Servicemen in the JFK motorcade, only three made *any* move to help the President. The shots continued to slam in from left and right as the SS men behind the car twitched hopelessly.

One TV reporter described the shots as being three "bursts" of automatic gunfire and dozens of other witnesses recall hearing four or more shots. Even many of those who only hear three shots testify that they were *not* evenly spaced (later to be a key issue).

Governor Connally was seriously wounded, the Lincoln's windscreen was holed, passer-by James Tague got away with a cut cheek, and then, after almost eight seconds of mayhem, Kennedy finally had the back of his head blown away. The fatal shot comes from the front, on the right, piercing Kennedy's right temple, shattering the back of his skull and splashing his wife with brain, blood and bone.

With Kennedy's head open and parts of his brain in his wife's lap, the blood-splattered wife Jackie is torn between two awful choices; the agony of holding her dying husband, or trying to survive herself by climbing out of a car that's still being hit by bullets.

After almost seven seconds of slowing down, and with Kennedy now seriously hit, 'Lancer' finally started to accelerate away, as an SS man leapt uselessly on the back bonnet. Did the SS man help Mrs Kennedy stay in the car or was it her that prevented him from falling off as the Lincoln gathered speed? It doesn't matter, the gunshots had at last stopped with the police sirens drowning out the screams. And the 35thPresident of the United States of America was fatally wounded, minutes away from death.

Angry passers-by joined motorcycle cops in running to where over 25 people have seen gun-smoke or heard gun-shots – up on the grassy knoll. Bernard Barker used his fake Secret Service ID to turn most of them away.

Seconds later the news filtered down to Oswald, still on one of the Book Depository's lower floors. He had half expected the first shot; this was surely the Secret Service security test his handlers had warned him about – but as the other explosive sounds continued to penetrate the quiet of the book warehouse he knew something had gone awfully, fatally wrong.

Within seconds he knows that Kennedy has been shot, that Kennedy is seriously wounded. "No, no," says someone with a good view of the last, fatal head shot, "President Kennedy is dying!"

By 12.33pm the news is on the wires but those hoping to get confirmation direct from Washington DC are disappointed. No one can get through, the entire DC phone network has been sabotaged.

Halfway across the country, one of the Latino maids looking after JFK's children is said to have remembered the bloody military coup d'etats of her own country and starts to dress the youngsters for a quick getaway.

Eight miles above the mid-Pacific, en route to Vietnam, Kennedy's cabinet see a ticker-tape message announcing that JFK has been 'seriously wounded' in Dallas. They try and use code to contact Washington DC but the presidential code-book is missing. The US government's leaders are completely stranded, unable to contact Washington and with their current peace mission to Vietnam now rendered meaningless.

Oswald at last realises what the hypnosis sessions, and his in-built sense of superiority have kept from him. He – the 'pro-Castro commie', the red who came back from Russia – is the fall guy, the patsy, the kid in the frame. There was no Secret Service readiness test.

He tries to remember the emergency plan, the back-up in case anything ever went wrong – Tippit, the .38 handgun, the one-two car horn beep, the Dallas police shirt, the out-of-town airfield.

Oswald goes to leave the Book Depository – two cops stop him but quickly let him go. He even isn't sweating, they quite rightly reason, so how can he possibly have run all the way down from the 6th floor from where the shots are supposed to have come.

Oswald gets back to his new apartment in time for his landlady to witness Tippit's cop car pulling up outside – it beeps its horn twice then moves slowly forward. Oswald goes to his bedroom, grabs the .38 and the police shirt that he hopes will get him out of town. The shirt is probably unnecessary, he only brings it in case Tippit has forgotten his spare police shirt – all part of the back-up plan.

Oswald hurries down 10th Street to see a horrifying sight – Tippit is with another man. The latter points at

Harvey Oswald, urges Tippit on. Tippit is part of it too – Tippit is supposed to kill him!

Fighting back a wave of nausea, Oswald spins on his heel and starts to run-walk off down a side street. He glances back as the CIA op with Tippit runs out of patience and actually turns and shoots the police officer. He kills Tippit on the spot (later the spare police shirt, the same size as Oswald's other shirts, will be found in the back of Tippit's squad car – no official explanation is ever offered).

Oswald sees the operative drop something on the ground near Tippit but by now he's running too hard to think. The Texas Theatre and Ruby. That's his last and only hope.

It's not until Oswald is within sight of the Texas Theatre cinema that he recalls the obvious – the CIA operative with the gun looked a little like himself. He's to be framed for Tippit's killing too.

Although this is Dallas, where half the cops are Ku Klux Klan supporters who hate Kennedy, the embarrassment of 'losing' the President is now compounded by the very real police anger that surrounds the killing of Officer Tippit. No one's fatally shot a Dallas cop for over a dozen years – *that's part of the plan too, it's so obvious now, Oswald's not going to be taken alive, surely he's going to be shot 'while trying to escape'.*

Oswald charges into the Texas Theatre and prays that this contact, this last sole contact, will be true. But within moments the electric whine of the DPD tells another, more bitter tale – there's no one trying to contact him. He's to die alone, but as the nano-seconds turn into seconds into moments into minutes – or what seem like minutes – Harvey Oswald realises that they're waiting. The cops and the FBI and the Agency and the Secret Service. All Just waiting. Where's Jack Ruby?

The obvious thing to do is just run out of the back fire exit – but that's too obvious, that's why they're waiting, that's *where* they're waiting, the others. Oswald knows there'll be half a dozen gunmen round the back – he'd be dead within seconds, without witnesses. Killed while trying to escape.

He has to make them do it here. Make them blow him away in front of all these teenagers and housewives, right here in the movie theatre before hundreds of witnesses.

Suddenly the house lights start coming up and several cops, guns drawn, begin to wander cautiously down the aisles. But there's just a glimpse of daylight through the tired drapes behind one of the cops. By the entrance. A flicker of hope. Oswald might just be able to make a run for it back into the street and grab a car and run. *But where to?*

A cop eyeballs him, turns away but keeps moving in roughly the same direction, closer, closer. Another flicker of daylight hope through the drapes, drapes like a funeral parlour. Oswald grips the .38 in his sweating hand as the nervous couple each side of him start to scramble away. Harvey Oswald leaps up, knows he can't get past the nearest cop without shooting. He aims and fires but the only sound is a hollow click.

Click! The .38 is useless. *They've been in his apartment, they've sawn the hammer off the handgun's firing mechanism. The trap is complete.*

Struggling with the cop, two more closing in – none of them firing. Stricken faces of the kids in the tip-up seats, backing off.

Struggling with the police officers, Oswald takes two more punches as the cinema audience start to squeeze out of the fire exits at the side – kids playing truant, housewives holding the wrong man's hand. The wanted man sees he has to make a fuss or he might still die where he stands. A shotgun butt smashes into his back. Oswald suddenly screams out loud, "I must protest this police brutality! *Police Brutality!*"

A couple of the crowd slow down, turn and look back. Then dozens start to stare. Oswald is not killed. The useless gun is taken from his hand and he's turned around and cuffed.

It's still almost midday, not even two. An hour and a half ago Oswald was still a semi-retired spy, serving the USA to the best of his ability. *Now what?* The hypnosis words come back into his head – *calmness, Lee, calmness, there is nothing to be afraid of, your father's gone, there's nothing to be afraid of, there's just calmness, calmness, calmness.*

Within seconds Oswald's face has a faint half-smile – he seems lost in a self-induced world. As they push his head down to get him into the police car's back seat, Oswald glances up and back at the Texas Theatre. Through the glass double doors he sees the drapes being pushed asunder. He looks back around him – six, seven, eight police cars. *Calmness. The name of the lawyer to ask for is Abt. John Abt. John Abt.*

His eyes count the police cars again. *Two four six eight.* There's safety in repetition. Calmness, calmness, *calmness*, the internal tranquillity is balanced with fear and sadness. He doesn't know why. *His life's been a lie since he was 14.* The Northerner playing a Southerner, the second generation German American with the Polish accent. The 'happily married' man who can only make love when he's programmed – and that with a woman who he still half suspects is a KGB junior. A woman now with child – a true Cold War family, with dad under arrest.

And he still doesn't know why, a bit-part patsy in his own life story. It is impossible to tell what he is thinking of – the U-2 betrayal? The FBI meets? The YMCA circuit? The gay sessions? The Cuban fakery?

In the back of the police car Oswald finally realizes how fully he will be exposed, he looks up for a moment and says – ruefully, sadly – "now everyone will know who I am ..."

As the Texas Theatre curtains flap open, several people see Ruby step out into the foyer, his teeth already chewing his bottom lip as he watches Harvey Oswald's own little motorcade scream away.

We didn't get him, Ruby thinks, over and over, *we just didn't get him. What the hell went wrong?* Muttering obscenities, Ruby gets in a big car, 1958 vintage, as his driver puts it in gear.

Oswald's brother Robert, when visiting him at Dallas Police Station the day after he'd allegedly shot JFK, stared into his sibling's eyes looking for any hint of sorrow or conscience. There was calmness to the point of zero, 'nothing'. Several Dallas law enforcement officials were later to speak of Oswald's mysterious post-JFK calm in custody, a calmness that – to them at least – suggested deep hypnosis or some kind of 'programming'.

Within hours of the JFK assassination word of Oswald's 'Communist' links had begun to leak out. Phase One, in CIA parlance, begins. The story of the 'red sniper'. If any low level cop or FBI agent starts to seriously investigate Oswald's background, and discovers the fake nature of his so-called Marxism, then the Agency will shift its press and police contacts towards Phase Two.

Phase Two is the 'lone nut' theory. This is even less believable than the 'red sniper' theory *but* it is backed up with the threat of real fear. The inquisitive will be told that if an investigation goes any further then the serious depths of Oswald's Communist roots will be revealed – not just a red sniper but a Soviet one – any serious investigation of the case will result, allegedly, in a nuclear war with Russia. Phase Two will be supported by a commission of inquiry of 'impeccable integrity'.

If and when Phase One and Two fall apart, then Phase Three of the cover-up stands ready, years later, to give out a few clues that will lead everyone to blame those who were merely the help, the hired help, the gun help. Blame it *all* on the Mafia, the mob.

Of course, all these cover-up levels, these phases, depended on one thing – that there would be no public trial; that Oswald would not be allowed to speak in a courtroom; that Oswald would be killed while being arrested; 'shot while trying to escape'. But that hadn't happened.

After 24 hours of almost non-stop interrogation – for which, incredibly, no tapes are used and no shorthand or longhand notes are taken – the Dallas Police prepare to transfer Oswald to the county jail. As his wallet, and of his two full ID sets, has been found near Officer Tippit's body, Oswald is already being charged with that murder. He is to be transferred through the basement where the world's press, now in a feeding frenzy, wait for him.

In the basement one cop lets Ruby in through a side door as another shelters him from the impatient cameras of the press. Although no one knows it yet, Ruby has already been accidentally photographed near Elm Street, just a stone's throw from both the grassy knoll and at the Texas Book Depository, and then again at Parkland Hospital as JFK was dying and then *again* at a police press conference. It is Ruby who hastily dives in when a police spokesman links Oswald with the right wing Free Cuba movement, "It's Fair Play for Cuba!" Ruby shouts, worried lest anyone should get the wrong – or rather the right – idea. Ruby's claim on oath – that he was an apolitical person who decided to kill Oswald purely to save Jackie Kennedy the trouble of going to court – simply does not bear water.

Oswald's last recorded words, delivered over his

shoulder as he is led away from the last brief Q&A session, are almost a scream; "I'm just a patsy!"

Now dressed in sober black jersey and white shirt, Oswald comes out of the lift, a little wired but, in the circumstances, actually quite calm, calmer than anyone else in the room.

It's 11.21am and Oswald is brought forward slowly – too slowly, but that's inevitable since the 1963 Ford Galaxie that's supposed to be whisking him away is backing up towards him at far too leisurely a pace.

As he wonders if the car's slothfulness is deliberate, Oswald approaches the crescent of pressmen. A familiar face – Jack Ruby's – appears from behind the sheltering police officer. Oswald goes to give a half-smile but before the expression even reaches his face it goes into reverse. Ruby is rapidly raising a handgun. As a shocked Oswald cringes, Ruby fires a single shot into his abdomen.

Ruby is instantly dragged to the ground and arrested.

"What did you do that for, Jack?" asks one cop, more irritated than annoyed. Everyone at the station knows Jack Ruby, virtually all the cops there have had drinks in his strip club.

An unidentified police officer leans on the stricken Oswald's abdomen and starts giving him artificial respiration, the worst possible treatment for an abdominal gunshot wound.

An ambulance is on the scene with suspicious speed. Barely 90 seconds after Ruby pulled the trigger, the medical team begin to drive down into the basement. Before 11.30 – less than nine minutes after the shooting – they have Oswald in Parkland where, in under two hours, he is declared dead.

Vice President Johnson has already been sworn in as the new US President, Jackie Kennedy by his side, her pink Chanel suit now caked with blood. Johnson's elevation to the presidency means he can now avoid the Estes and Bobby Baker financial scandals that could have put him in jail. No wonder photos taken that fateful day show him grinning and winking. His first two major actions are straightforward. He cancels Kennedy's memo NSAM 263 pulling US troops out of Vietnam and instead sends more (within five years he will pour over a million US troops into the Vietnamese quagmire).

And then LBJ tells a smiling Hoover that he won't be forced to resign his FBI directorship the next year.

As questions continue to be asked over the JFK assassination, Johnson sets up the Warren Commission to investigate. Its panel includes right-wing Republican Gerald Ford and former CIA director Allen W Dulles, the man who JFK had fired over the Bay of Pigs fiasco. By the time they first meet, the leftist Fair Play For Cuba committee is history, having been forced out of business by its faint but controversial link with 'volunteer' Lee Harvey Oswald.

In late 1964 the Warren Commission announced their verdict: Lee Harvey Oswald was JFK's sole assassin, committing the killing from the sixth floor of the Texas Book Depository. Using one ageing second-rate rifle and firing three evenly spaced bullets, Oswald had hit Kennedy's neck before wounding Governor Connally and then finally killing JFK with a headshot.

This miracle of solo marksmanship was accomplished against a moving target, in under 4.6 seconds, and from a distance of over 260 feet – and all done with a 20-year-old weapon that was in such a dangerously poor condition FBI riflemen refused to test fire it until a complete barrel re-bore had been performed.

The ammo round that wounded Connally has since become known as the 'magic bullet' since, in order to hit JFK in the back, exit upwardly through his neck and then go on through to wound Connally, the bullet must have changed directions several times, both before and after hitting the governor. To compound the 'magic', the bullet in question is found in virtually mint condition. Its discovery is similarly unreal, being conveniently found on Connally's previously clean hospital stretcher.

The Warren Commission ignored the possibility that the 'magic bullet' was in such good condition purely because it hadn't hit anyone. That would mean there were more than three shots fired and any more than three shots meant there must have been a second gunman, and therefore a conspiracy.

The Warren Commission ignored the slight wound suffered by passer-by James Tague, which again would mean there were more than three shots fired.

The Warren Commission ignored the photos of FBI and Secret Servicemen picking up bullets from the roadside, which again would mean there were more than three shots fired.

The Warren Commission ignored the bullet hole in the presidential Lincoln's windscreen, which again would mean there were more than three shots fired.

The Warren Commission ignored the several witnesses who heard bursts of gunfire, suggesting at least one automatic weapon, which would again mean there were more than three shots fired.

The Warren Commission ignored the witnesses who heard four or more gunshots, which would again mean there were more than three shots fired.

The Warren Commission ignored the 28 witnesses who heard gunshots, or saw gunsmoke, coming from the grassy knoll, which would again mean there were more than three shots fired – some from the front and not from the rear where Oswald was.

The Warren Commission accepted the FBI and CIA

statements – since proved false – that they had had no contact with Oswald in the months leading up to the assassination.

The Warren Commission ignored the numerous witnesses who had seen Oswald with Ruby before the assassination.

The Warren Commission ignored the fact that Oswald's 'work' for the Fair Play for Cuba Committee had been patently designed to discredit the FPCC. Oswald's actions were actually anti-leftist, something else to which the Commission chose to turn a blind eye.

The Warren Commission ignored what is, undoubtedly, the most important evidence of all – the testimony of the 12 doctors and nurses, both operating and observing, who tried to save Kennedy. All of them stated unequivocally that at least one of the shots that hit JFK had come from the front. This rules out Oswald as the lone assassin firing from behind. This medical testimony on its own is proof of an assassination plot, of conspiracy. The Commission's refusal to take it into account in any way at all adds the final note of sick farce to what was already one of the judicial scandals of the century.

The resulting Warren Report blames Oswald and Oswald alone and it is now, rightly, seen as a complete 'whitewash' by virtually all serious assassination researchers. Public scepticism has grown apace too – currently over 90 per cent of the American public disbelieve the commission's official findings.

Some have claimed, both at the time and since – including Robert Goldberg, author of *Enemies Within* – that one of the roles of the Warren Commission was to dispel rumours of a foreign Moscow-driven conspiracy to assassinate the President. It was something that Johnson, when President, self-consciously played along with in a phone call to Warren Report commissioner Senator

Richard Russell. "We've gotta take this out of the arena where they're testifying that Krushchev and Castro did this and did that and ... kicking us into a war that'd kill 40 million Americans in an hour."

Yet LBJ himself had been the *first* major American politician – and the most senior, as the new President – who had claimed, within hours of the assassination, that 'international Communism' was to blame for JFK's death.

For anyone who still believes in official government denials, 'lone nuts', 'commie agents' and 'magic bullets' that defy medical evidence, there is one other simple statistic. Between the winters of 1963 and 1967, fifteen JFK assassination witnesses, who had been interviewed by the Warren Commission, the Dallas Police, or the FBI, died prematurely. The causes of death were a bizarre blend of gunshots, hit-and-run car crashes, highway accidents, unexpected suicides, undiagnosed heart trouble, cut throats and karate chops.

When the *Sunday Times* got an actuary to compute the life expectancy of the dead witnesses, he concluded that the odds, on 22 November 1963, against all 15 of them being dead before February 1967 were a staggering One Hundred Thousand Trillion to One. Or, to put it numerically, in excess of 100,000,000,000,000,000 to 1.

But by the time the actuary had completed his careful calculations they were already out of date – because four more assassination witnesses had died in suspicious circumstances.

US Army intelligence destroyed their file on Lee Harvey Oswald in 1973. This was done, they claimed, purely for routine, 'space-saving' reasons. As with RFK, Martin Luther King, Malcolm X and John Lennon, the CIA files on JFK remain incomplete and, for the most part, unseen.

CHAPTER EIGHT

INVASION!

*The Beatles were always supposing they were
Smokey Robinson.*

John Lennon 1980

And the truth will set you free.

Biblical quote officially engraved outside CIA HQ

On 9 February 1964, The Beatles, then Number 1 on both sides of the Atlantic, made their first live appearance on American television. The *Ed Sullivan Show* was watched by a staggering 73 million viewers that night and crime levels dipped to their lowest level in years as everyone from bank managers to schoolgirls to car thieves decided to check out the latest musical sensation.

Though the media culture vultures mostly sneered – the *New York Times* critic found the boys 'incoherent, schematic', within days, The Beatles were holding the top five chart spots in the US, a feat never before, or since, matched.

There are a hundred reasons why The Beatles got so big so fast in the US – talent not being the least of them – but timing was a big part of it. A stunned America was still mourning the death of JFK less than three months before, and The Beatles were, for young people at least, the perfect way to lift the gloom. They were young, hip, energetic, witty and also foreign, whilst still speaking English that was different but understandable. They offered something a bit more raw than the usual pop pap.

They had a certain honesty and even their detractors admitted they also had humour;

Reporter: Will you sing something for us now?

John Lennon: We need cash first.

Reporter: How would you account for your success?

JL: We've got a good press agent.

2nd Reporter: When do you rehearse?

JL: We don't.

Paul McCartney: Yeah, of course we do.

JL: Paul does, we don't.

3rd Reporter: But surely you don't need all this police protection? Surely you can handle it all yourselves?

JL: Maybe you can, you're a lot fatter than we are.

Everyone from radical poet Allen Ginsberg to teenage cheerleaders to an 11-year-old Nile Rodgers fell for the Fab Four magic. "Yeah, I dug The Beatles. The thing is, Afro hair just don't shake like that," said Rodgers, the co-founder of Chic and later a producer for David Bowie, "so when I wanted to do that shaking moptop thing I'd put my running shorts on my head, grab my tennis racket guitar and then start shaking my ass off!"

The Fab Four were now a worldwide sensation, with Epstein making hundreds of thousands of dollars – and losing millions more – on merchandising, as Beatles toys, Beatles wigs, Beatles lunch boxes, Beatles posters, jeans, boots, jackets, t-shirts, handbags, stickers, sweets, chewing gum cards and cakes swamped America.

According to legend, Epstein nearly cost the band even more than that. Within hours of arriving in the US, jet-lagged and hung-over, he'd done something he wouldn't have ever dared do back in Britain – he'd picked up a boy in his late teens, straight off the street, in broad daylight. Having whisked his 'rough trade' back to his hotel, Epstein was about to consummate the 'relationship' when a faint motorised whirring could be heard. A photographer, trying to stalk the Beatles from a fire escape, had instead grabbed a shot of Epstein doing something that was illegal in 38 states – including New York. There were many industry people hoping the Fab Four would fail, and Epstein's outrage, if it had ever become public, might just have led to that happening.

Luckily for him, after he'd scrambled to the phone, Capitol allegedly had staffers on the case within seconds. Minutes later the photographer was manhandled on the door-step of his own apartment and had his film stolen – a large amount of cash was slapped in his hand as compensation for his 'time and trouble'. He was then told to just forget all he'd seen that day – to forget it or risk being sued. Apparently he has forgotten it because, even up to this very day, the photographer – if he ever existed – has maintained a dignified silence.

Between the first and second Beatles visits to America came *A Hard Day's Night*, movie debut with a Lennon theme song and much frantic direction from Dick Lester. The story was the Beatles under siege, going through the new lifestyle of pop stardom – 'a getaway car, then a room then another car' – was basic enough but the fresh performances and the driving soundtrack gave it something more. Only the last reel, an adequately filmed piece of concert miming, slowed things down, and even then the fast-cutting end titles finished things on something of a high.

During the filming Lennon got to know, and like, actor Victor Spinetti, a friendship that would prove lasting. *A Hard Day's Night* was, however, still shot in black and white. Although The Beatles had sold millions they were still regarded by United Artists Films as being a bit of a risk, not worth wasting colour film on. *Any of these pop bands could completely fade away at any minute, couldn't they? It's all just a short-lived fad, isn't it?*

The Beatles first 'proper' American tour came in

August 1964, covering two dozen cities coast to coast, during 34 hectic days. It was a triumphant series of concerts despite their receiving bomb threats in Las Vegas – possibly over Lennon's public refusal to play segregated Southern gigs. "The audience would be segregated and black people have to sit at the back," said Lennon. "We've never played segregated gigs and we're not gonna start now." His comments were relevant internationally too, for '64 was also the year that the CIA policy of shopping the 'dangerous Communist terrorist' Nelson Mandela to the South African police paid off. He was caught and sentenced to life imprisonment on Robbin Island.

In Kansas The Beatles had played for $150,000, some three million dollars today, a record fee of almost five thousand dollars a minute. By the following Easter, The Beatles accounted for over 85 per cent of *all* American singles sales of the previous year.

After returning to the UK, Lennon casually helped save the career of comedian and writer Peter Cook. Dudley Moore's comic partner had returned from New York after losing thousands on a Broadway show that flopped. With no offers on the table – and the satirical show *That Was The Week That Was* off the air because of the forthcoming UK election – Cook found himself near bankruptcy. When Moore, a talented piano player in his own right, got offered a one-off BBC TV show, he was told that Cook could only appear as part of an all-star line-up. If such a thing could be found quickly.

Lennon heard the news, instantly volunteered to appear and did two sketches for a show that got rave reviews. The 'one-off' quickly morphed into the long-running *Not Only But Also* series, swiftly making household names of Cook and Moore.

In Britain the left-wing Labour Party won the general election, ending 13 years of Tory rule and making Harold

Wilson prime minister. On the same day, 16 October, Red China exploded its first H-Bomb. In Russia, the Communist Party decided that with the Americans killing off their liberal leader, JFK, the Soviet Union no longer needed to tolerate its own reformer and Khrushchev was forced into a dacha and early retirement.

Glasnost was postponed for over 20 years as the more militaristic Brezhnev became the effective leader of the USSR. He increased the mass production of Inter Continental Ballistic Missiles at the behest of the Red Army. News of this, when combined with reports about China's H-bomb test and Britain's 'left turn', gave the world balance of power a subtle shift. A nuclear war no longer seemed so winnable or so desirable for most of America's hawks, a reasonable notion that managed to last for a decade and a half. Now, aside from the routine harassment of Cuba, all the hawks' imperial aggression was to be aimed at Vietnam.

The hawks' own political leader, privately, was LBJ. Publicly they favoured Republican presidential candidate Barry Goldwater, who had gone into the November 1964 US election with the slogan 'Goldwater: In Your Heart You Know He's Right!'

Goldwater had once threatened to use 'small scale' tactical H-bombs in Vietnam and President Johnson's Democrat supporters swiftly responded with the most devastating TV advertisement in electoral history – 'Daisy Girl' – wherein a small child picks the petals off a daisy in a kind of countdown. In the last few seconds of the advert the child is shockingly bleached out while the picture becomes an atomic explosion, as Goldwater's boast is twisted against him; 'In Your Heart You Know He Might!' Young Democrats later came up with an even crueller parody; 'Goldwater: In Your Guts You Know He's Nuts!'

Not surprisingly, Johnson won the election with the biggest landslide ever seen in US history. The Democrats also took both Houses of Congress and the majority of governorships. Guilt over Kennedy's death was no doubt a factor in Johnson's triumph – all of which was bitterly ironic in the light of LBJ's reversal of Kennedy's Vietnam withdrawal policy.

The second Beatles feature film, 1965's *Help!*, was a colour extravaganza that started in the Bahamas – for tax reasons – and involved endless set changes and jet-setting, and every type of music from Lennon's bitter-sweet rocker of a title tune to Beethoven's 9th Symphony. The Lennon theme song was one that, like the 'A Hard Day's Night' single, was taken as being lyrically something of a humourous number. Why would wildly successful John Lennon ever want or need help?

Yet Lennon did want help, for he *was* worried about his weight, his song-writing, his direction, his marriage. Cooped up in his big new house in the Southern stockbroker town of Weybridge, Lennon felt torn between London's bright lights, the new experiences he felt he should still be seeking out, and guilt over the beautiful wife and young boy child he'd already neglected far too much.

For The Beatles, 1965 ended with the December release of *Rubber Soul*, an LP that leapt in at Number 1 – their sixth album in a row to reach that exalted slot – garnering praise from various quarters en route. In London it was the first Beatles album since their first to grudgingly win secret praise from the nation's top mods, whilst in America sales exceeded a staggering six million copies, despite the US version not containing 'Drive My Car'; a soulish, uptempo number about stars and their power.

The Beatles were now more than a mere beat group and everything about *Rubber Soul* reflected this, from a cover that didn't even bother to mention their name, to songs that included several Lennon gems such as 'Girl', a bittersweet anthem to the ultimate cool girl bitch, which came complete with a Greek bouzouki solo and John's sharply drawn breath on the choruses, and 'Norwegian Wood' ('This Bird Has Flown') Lennon's acoustic take on Bob Dylan. A fair enough source for him to use since Dylan had now gone electric and was fairly obviously soaking up quite a bit of influence from the beat bands in general, and the Fab Four in particular. Dylan had introduced the band to cannabis the year before – the first illegal drug – bar the speedy 'prellies' – that The Beatles had ever come across. Both Lennon and McCartney were fast becoming heavy regular smokers. Despite the drug's effect, which was usually tranquilising, the pair argued more during the album's recording than at any previous Abbey Road sessions. As even the studio staff noticed, the duo, who had been increasingly writing apart since 1963, were headed in different directions.

Perhaps *Rubber Soul's* most haunting track though was 'Nowhere Man', Lennon's ode to, about, and for the common man and the power for good the everyman unwittingly had – and didn't use. Many at the time, and since, have felt that John was also aiming the song squarely at himself.

CHAPTER NINE

UNDER FIRE

*What's the point of all this fame if I can't do
something useful with it?*

John Lennon

Burn The Beatles!

Memphis banner 1966

As The Beatles arrived in the Phillipines on 3 July 1966, the *New York Times* ran a Lennon quote about how show business was 'an extension of the Jewish religion'. Despite some muttering, in a less politically correct age this comment was accepted without serious criticism. But three weeks later, after riots at both Japanese and Filipino gigs, *Datebook*, a US magazine aimed at high school teens, finally ran the Maureen Cleeve *Evening Standard* interview which she'd conducted with John Lennon some four months previously. Lennon was now John Lennon MBE, an honoured Member of the British Empire, which made the interview seem even more shocking to US eyes. Lennon had secretly wanted to reject accepting the MBE from Britain's new Labour prime minister Harold Wilson, but Epstein had insisted. John had quietly retaliated by smuggling some joints into Buckingham Palace where he and the band used the toilets to smoke them, undoubtedly the first cannaboids to be consumed in 'Buck House' since Victoria's reign.

Datebook ran the Cleeve interview as a front page

story with, of course, Lennon's sensational remarks on religion to the fore: "Christianity will go, it will vanish and shrink. I needn't argue with that; I'm right and I will be proved right. We are more popular than Jesus now; I don't know which'll go first, rock'n'roll or Christianity. Jesus was alright, but his disciples were thick and ordinary. It's them twisting it that ruins it for me."

In 58 casually spoken words, Lennon had sparked a controversy that would plague him and The Beatles for the rest of their careers Stateside. For Lennon, the same words would haunt him for the rest of his life. They would even, some later claimed, play a role in his death, for what looked like Lennon being his usual pushy opinionated self in Britain, played like outrageous blasphemous arrogance in the US, especially the Deep South, where Christian churches often tended to be run by, and for, fundamentalists.

In Alabama there were 'Beatle-burning' rallies organised by local radio and TV stations, at which thousands of the groups' records, posters and magazines were publicly torched. Dozens of other similar events spread across the South, and 30 radio stations banished the Beatles from the airwaves. As the Vatican complained about 'beatniks' dealing in 'profanity', worries grew about security for the forthcoming tour of the US. The fact that the group's next single, released just a few days later, was the McCartney-dominated 'Eleanor Rigby' – with its lines about a lonely priest failing to 'save' anyone – only made matters worse.

No one said so publicly at the time, but Lennon's remarks were also a chance for US pundits to vent their growing resentment of the 'British invasion' and the 'scruffy' foreigners who'd spearheaded it since early 1964. Music and film were, *are*, multi-billion dollar industries in America; major cash cows that local professionals will defend vigorously, often with help from the State (the type of protectionism the US government usually condemns when it defends Third World farmers or European vineyards). In 1965, for instance, the US Labor Department had responded to this new cultural 'invasion' by making moves to ban British bands from playing Stateside. For years afterwards only the very biggest English groups could easily tour the USA.

America's private sector is, of course, even more zealous and was so even back then. When big money is threatened it can often react aggressively, sometimes even with violence. At the height of their teenybopper fame, one of the Jackson Five began to 'go steady' with a particular girl, something that could have threatened all the boys' 'young, free and single' image if it had become public knowledge. When the Jacksons' father asked a record executive what could be done about the girl, he was allegedly told that a fatal 'accident' could quickly be arranged. Jackson Senior angrily rejected the idea and subsequently nothing happened to the girl in question. But such an episode does show how much more seriously such things are taken in the US.

The Beatles' US record label, Capitol, took Lennon's Jesus remarks pretty seriously themselves in August '66. They had no choice, as talk of bans and boycotts spread across the country. On the 6th Brian Epstein had told the New York press that "John Lennon's views have been misrepresented, displayed out of context."

It wasn't enough. Two days later, as all Beatles' records were banned from South African airwaves – a ban that, in Lennon's case, held until his death 14 years later – the US radio blacklist mushroomed to 35 major stations.

As the US tour grew ever closer, Lennon himself still stood by most of his words and he told Epstein he'd rather the gigs be cancelled than have to fully withdraw the remarks. After much persuasion it was decided that Lennon would make some sort of clarification-cum-apology at a pre-tour press conference in Chicago on 11 August. By this point Lennon was willing to offer some sort of apology but the seriousness of the event was only just beginning to dawn on him. Beforehand, press officer Tony Barrow told him to expect outright hostility as Epstein finally expressed his fear that the tour, without a sincere apology, could end with both Lennon and the entire band being assassinated. Both Barrows and Epstein were still astonished to see, for the first and last time, tears in Lennon's eyes. Almost weeping at the thought of endangering the others, John told them he'd do 'anything' to make matters right.

The following Astor Towers Hotel press conference was tense from the start. As the band arrived the journalists at the front were told to 'kneel for The Beatles', an accidental 'blasphemy' of the organisers that was uttered purely to allow photographers at the back to get a chance to glimpse the group.

After saying that he might have got away with saying "television is more popular than Jesus," Lennon stumblingly added, "I used the word 'Beatles' as a remote thing, not as what I think. Not as Beatles, as those other Beatles, like other people see us. I just said 'they' are having more influence on kids and things than anything else, including Jesus. I'm not saying we're better or greater, or comparing us with Jesus Christ as a person or God as a thing or whatever it is. I just said what I said and it was wrong. Or it was taken wrong."

"But," a DJ demanded, "are you actually prepared to apologise?" Lennon tried to clarify things further. "I'm not anti-God, anti-Christ or anti-religion. I believe in God but not as an old man in the sky." He then added words that were almost Buddhist in their simplicity and meaning, "I believe what people call God is something in all of us."

The press circus ended with Lennon being as blatant, and as irritated, as circumstance allowed: "I'm sorry I said it really, I never meant it to be a lousy anti-religious thing. I apologise if that will make you happy. I still don't know quite what I've done. I've tried to tell you what I did do but if you want me to apologise, if that will make you happy, then okay, I'm sorry."

It was enough, *just*, to satisfy most of the media – and most of the American public. The Vatican accepted Lennon's apology but America's Southern Baptist Convention did not – and the burnings of Beatles' records, and Lennon's *Spaniard in the Works* and *In His Own Write* books, continued. The Beatles tour went ahead, although the Louisville, Kentucky concert was cancelled and, at the Washington DC gig, Ku Klux Klan members staged a noisy demonstration outside.

Worse was to come when the tour finally reached a Deep South venue, the Mid-South Coliseum in Memphis, on 19 August. The band started well enough, despite record-burning sessions from WAAX radio, anonymous death threats and a promise from the local KKK chapter that there would be a reception the Beatles "would never forget". But halfway through, a gunshot rang out amidst the girlish screams and The Beatles looked anxiously around – at John first, and then at each other – to see which of them had been shot. It turned out to be just a fire-cracker, thrown either by an idiot 'fan' or by one of the anti-Beatles protesters. A year and a half later, however, the gunshots were to be real as civil rights leader the Reverend Martin Luther King was shot to death in the city.

Three days after the Memphis gig, an undeterred Lennon stunned his Capitol 'handlers' by attacking US involvement in the Vietnam War at a New York press conference. "We think of it every day. We don't like it. We think it's wrong." John's comments were timely, the year had started with the US military resuming its bombing campaign against North Vietnam and June had seen a particularly heavy strike against the northern capital Hanoi, which had left hundreds of civilians dead and thousands injured. There were grumblings about Lennon's remarks but the US press as a whole surprisingly failed to display serious outrage.

But it was almost certainly at this point, in August 1966, that the FBI and CIA files on John Lennon were started. For a major, internationally famous, entertainer to speak out against the Vietnam War and for that act, at that time, not to have sparked official, if covert, action, is almost inconceivable. Before Lennon, a whole series of entertainers had had CIA and FBI files opened on them, almost always for criticising either US foreign policy or the nation's civil rights record. Among them were Charlie Chaplin, Paul Robeson, Eartha Kitt and Jean Seberg.

Any man who threatened the political purity of America's youth was a man who, however vaguely, threatened America's future as a reactionary world power. Such a man was Lennon, the frontman of the biggest pop band ever.

We cannot know definitively, of course, the exact date the files were opened, as neither Lennon's CIA or FBI file have ever been released in their entirety. The CIA, in particular, has a system that allows agents to start so-called '201 files' on the slightest pretext, files that rarely ever emerge for public, or even congressional, scrutiny. Only four pages of Lennon's CIA file have ever been released, and these have only come to light because they were forwarded to, or in some cases sent from, the FBI. The FBI's own Lennon files are also impossible to access in full. Despite the existence of America's Freedom of Information Act, it still took Professor Jon Wiener almost a decade of court action to get access to nearly 300 pages of John Lennon's FBI file. To this day, many released sections, as well as several whole documents, remain unseen on grounds of 'national security'.

The day after the NYC press conference, The Beatles were at Shea Stadium where the crowd was huge but down on the previous year's total, from 56,000 to a 'mere' 45,000. After more death threats, The Beatles played their last ever 'proper' gig a few days later, behind six-foot high iron cages at San Francisco's Candlestick Park, a venue some 4,000 miles from their English home-town.

Not one of the first big rock festivals – at Monterey, Woodstock, Altamount and the Isle of Wight – were to feature The Beatles, the band who'd made them all possible. John Lennon's Beatles, the most popular group in the world, could no longer play live anywhere – especially in the USA. It had, quite simply, become too dangerous.

That same month of August 1966 saw the release of the band's most accomplished LP so far, *Revolver*, a set still widely seen as one of the finest ever made. Its stark yet intricate cover, a black and white gem from Hamburg pal Klaus Voormann, blended photos, drawings and mask-like facial sketches. The 'masks' were of the faces of the Beatles, of course, but the eyes of the sketches were 'real' photos. It was as if Voormann, and presumably the band, were trying to point that there were real human beings underneath the growing legend.

While there was the usual token Harrison composition, in this case the powerfully acerbic 'Taxman', there were also some fun tracks like McCartney's soul-pumping 'Got To Get You Into My Life' – recorded with help from Eddie Thornton and Peter Coe of Georgie Fame's Blue Flames – and the kiddy anthem 'Yellow Submarine', the latter with a dazzling array of nautical sound effects and John adding a deliberately comic repeat of Ringo's verses. But there was also some serious and mature ammunition in *Revolver's* chambers; McCartney's bitter, string-laced 'Eleanor Rigby' for one, plus those cuts mostly written by Lennon; the subtly disturbing 'I'm Only Sleeping', the druggy 'She Said, She Said', the defiantly independent 'And Your Bird Can Sing' and the controversial drug-referencing Doctor Robert. Plus, of course, the rhythmic yet dreamy loop-drive of the Indian-influenced 'Tomorrow Never Knows', with its huge drums, its drones, its dazzling backwards' tracks and its swirling George Martin atmospherics. It was an epic; one of the world's first great psychedelic tracks. It was also a track that betrays more than a trace of its subject matter; 'acid', the hallucinatory Lysergic Acid drug. Its composer was starting to take increasing amounts of dangerously strong acid by then. 'Letting go' and 'ego-destruction' were lyrical themes of the record and of Sixties' acid guru Timothy Leary – and it's a testimony to both Lennon and the band as artists that something of such originality, and such musical value, as 'Tomorrow Never Knows' could emerge from such risky over-indulgence.

In the same year that the Beach Boys had issued *Pet Sounds*, The Who *My Generation* and Dylan *Blonde On Blonde*, The Beatles had shown that their abilities were as relevant, and as strong, as ever. Despite much new rivalry in the pop world – and despite the angry bigger-than-Jesus backlash in America – *Revolver* still sold an astonishing 5 million copies Stateside plus almost a million more back home in England. The group were still the world leaders in their field.

On 9 November 1966 John Lennon had visited the Indica art gallery in London's West End, there to attend the opening night of a nine-day show by Yoko Ono, *Unfinished*

Paintings and Objects. The avant garde Japanese artist had previously been based in New York, where she'd made a few waves with her outrageous life shows. Audiences at one performance, for instance, were encouraged to use scissors to cut away her clothes as she sat mute onstage. She would sometimes end up virtually naked.

Despite this, there was also a naivety and innocence about much of Ono's work – the apples she sold as 'art', her peace obsession – increasingly relevant as Vietnam raged – plus her quiet outrage upon discovering that items such as grapefruits were essentially man-made (the fruit actually being a modern, but pre-GM hybrid of oranges and lemons). She was now living in London with her daughter Kyoko and her somewhat chauvinistic American husband, Anthony Cox, a jazzer-cum-smalltime film producer who was also active on the underground art scene, usually in tandem with Yoko.

Lennon was amused but also intrigued by her, and by the simple positivity of her 'Yes' artwork (the word was taped at the top of a tall ladder). Ono, not being a follower of pop music, was not sure who he was, though she had, of course, heard of the Beatles – like virtually every urban citizen in the world by late 1966. They talked together for a few minutes, Lennon smiling when Ono asked him to pay five shillings so he could be allowed to hammer in a nail. "Well, can't I pay an imaginary five shillings and hammer in an imaginary nail?" he shot back. They shared a smile then parted, both of them discreetly impressed by the demeanour of the other, though that wasn't to stop Lennon describing Yoko as just being "that crazy artist" whenever anyone asked about her.

By now Lennon's drug use had shifted completely from its previous, fairly moderate, blend of cannabis and alcohol into huge daily doses of LSD. He and his wife

Cynthia had first tried the new 'wonder drug' unwittingly, when it had been slipped into their coffee when they visited a trendy dentist with Harrison and his teenage wife Pattie, a model who had appeared in *A Hard Day's Night*. Lennon liked acid, at first, and started taking it regularly as he began to seek out "better and stronger tabs". His new wealth meant that this was no big problem. The problem was that his wife didn't like the drug and she, quite naturally, feared for young Julian's stability as the child began to wander down in the mornings to find his quietly wasted father too tired to talk. Occasionally he'd still be talking to a drug dealer or a gaggle of stoned musicians. There were no huge scenes then, no vomiting or violence, but it was still all faintly disturbing for Cynthia, as it would be for any mother.

At the start of 1967 the Beatles issued their strongest, strangest single yet; Lennon's stunningly original 'Strawberry Fields Forever' augmented by McCartney's melodically jaunty 'Penny Lane'. Lennon's song, named after the neighbouring children's home of his youth, was a surreal, moody concoction of subtle and ambiguous lyrics, sung through a rotating Leslie speaker that matched the shifting, grandiose backing track. It is no exaggeration to say that it was a soundtrack to a whole new way of life; a jerky yet transcendental drift – a drift between the 'eternal now' and the inner joys, trials and tribulations of remembered childhood; a recording that, over 40 years after its release, KLF's Bill Drummond still describes as one of the greatest singles ever made. 'Penny Lane' couldn't quite match this, and didn't, but it did offer a slightly more acceptable take on a similar subject. It was also, in a way, a musical counterpoint to the growing Regency fashion, a nostalgia for the clothing and graphics that had been in vogue over a century before.

Although it still sold millions worldwide, the 'Penny

Lane'/'Strawberry Fields' release received mixed reviews, as it became the first Beatles single in over four years to fail to reach the UK Number 1 slot, stalling at Number 2 for a couple of weeks before sliding away. After years of jumping in at the top position, the new 45's comparative failure was a minor shock and just a few months before it would have been taken by Lennon as a warning shot across the bows. Now he simply no longer cared.

On 25 June 1967 The Beatles performed Lennon's latest effort 'All You Need Is Love' live to a worldwide television audience of over 400 million, the world's first truly global satellite link-up. Simplistic and sentimental, it still remains one of Lennon's finest songs, perhaps the first by any major pop artist that extols a poignantly universal love. The four letter word 'love' no longer necessarily meant mum and dad, or romantic hand-holding, or a fast roll in the back of a car. In Lennon's composition it was the eternal, all-embracing everything; as much about brotherhood as Beethoven's 9th Symphony; this is why we live and die and this is what we live and die for.

The track's unreal, semi-structured finale – complete with live orchestra and hand-clapping friends – represents one of popular music's most sublime moments. The dropping in of lines from 'She Loves You' and 'Yesterday' draws us in with past reminders and yet adds emotional and cultural perspective – *Can you see how far we've come in the three and a half years since we wrote these earlier, mere pop songs ... ?*

The Beatles' following album was the ground-breaking *Sergeant Pepper's Lonely Hearts' Club Band*. The first, and in some ways still the best, pop concept album. Technically it was years ahead of its time, with producer George Martin using two synced-up four-track recorders to create mixes that are difficult to eclipse even now.

Lyrically it saw the band both as third person characters – years before Alice Cooper and David Bowie used such devices – and as future has-beens. Although much of *'Pepper'* came from McCartney, it was Lennon who composed its most dazzling track 'A Day In The Life' (he wrote all of it bar its 'alarm clock middle eight').

'A Day In The Life' starts with the bluesy tale of a millionaire's suicide, ends in orchestral cacophony and uses the drug catchphrase 'turn you on', though it was McCartney – the nice, handsome Beatle – who would, within the year, be the first in the group to admit to taking LSD, a move which some critics viewed as being an example of total, if misguided, honesty. Others saw it as being something of a PR manoeuvre, a naive 'street cred' attempt to wrestle leadership of the band from Lennon.

The year 1967 also saw the premiere of Dick Lester's blistering black comedy of British Army manners, *How I Won The War*, a superb yet surreal anti-war film that starred Michael Crawford and Lennon, the latter cast as the moaning right wing Private Gripweed. In the last reel Gripweed is fatally shot, as the Brit's North African cricket-pitch team rolls victoriously into Nazi Germany. Lennon's part ends with him mortally wounded, telling the camera that he and the audience had both known all along that this was "always going to happen", that he was always going to die like this, being shot and killed.

Lennon was actually in mourning himself, like the other Beatles, during the film's October release – in mourning over the abrupt 'drug suicide' two months before of Brian Epstein. The death of the Beatles' manager, described officially as 'accidental', was an event that even those who knew 'Eppy' well found 'puzzling'. He was a loner who was occasionally 'moody' – Lennon and the others would often send him gifts at such times – but his death was still a considerable surprise; he'd been in the studio with the band just four days before and hadn't seemed particularly anxious then. Most of his friends did not regard his mood as being suicidal. Yet if his death was accidental, it was even stranger – Epstein had taken 'downers' and 'speed' many times before and the pathologist at the inquest stated that he had been taking Carbitral, the drug that killed him, for some time.

There is one other point about Epstein and his demise; despite his public reputation as the respectable millionaire who 'cleaned up' the rough and ready Beatles – the raw rock 'n' roll group who'd played the bordellos of Hamburg – he was also a world famous liberal with radical notions, a potentially powerful figure, in cultural circles at least. And his death came almost exactly a month after he'd shocked many within the establishment by adding his name to an advertisement in *The Times*. The advert in question called for the legalisation of cannabis, the immediate release for those jailed for possession and for research into the drug's medical properties.

CHAPTER TEN

1968

Hey! Hey! LBJ! How many kids you killed today?

Student Demonstration chant 1968

Nineteen sixty-eight started off badly for President Johnson and rapidly got worse. On 19 January Japanese 'Vietniks' – anti-war students – stormed Tokyo's Foreign Ministry in protest against the visit of the *USS Enterprise*. Four days later, the US Navy vessel *Pueblo* strayed too near the territorial waters of North Korea, an erratic Stalinist state that was still at war, technically at least, with one of America's biggest Asian allies, South Korea. North Korea had signed a cease-fire but not a full peace treaty when the Korean War had ended back in 1953. North Korean sailors rapidly boarded and captured the *USS Pueblo* before it had barely had time to send a distress signal.

If LBJ was expecting a respite the next week, he was in for an unpleasant surprise. On the night of 30-31 January, the Vietnamese 'Tet' New Year – the Vietcong NLF launched a massive wave of attacks deep inside South Vietnam. All the lies that the US Army, the CIA and the Defence Intelligence Agency were still peddling were blown apart. The Vietcong was obviously not a weak, fading guerrilla force with falling morale, not when their attacks reached the heart of Saigon, the South Vietnamese capital, as well as in three dozen smaller towns.

America was stunned by pictures of dead US troops lying in their own blood within the very walls of the US Embassy, itself the scene of a fierce gun battle. The fact that regular North Vietnamese soldiers had actually taken the ancient city of Hue after savage fighting, shocked both Johnson and the Chiefs of Staff. Hue was eventually re-taken, after half the town had been flattened and thousands of civilians killed, but the short victorious war that Johnson had promised America was turning into a nightmare before his bloodshot eyes.

By 1 February 1968 over 1,400 American troops had been killed or wounded. Still deep in denial, the US government officially proclaimed the Tet Offensive a failure (though that didn't explain why over 10,000 more GIs were suddenly rushed to South Vietnam on emergency flights). Within two weeks, the USAF was forced to bomb Saigon's own suburbs as VC insurgents struck again. Despite the setbacks, LBJ pronounced himself confident of winning the forthcoming election.

For almost a year, though, anti-war intellectual Allard Lowenstein had been single-handedly running an LBJ Must Go! campaign. Because he gave lectures to the NSA, he was labelled a CIA dupe by some far left student radicals. It didn't, however, deter him from insisting that someone from the Democratic Party must run against their own deeply compromised President.

It seemed like lunacy. No one from the same party had defeated an incumbent President in decades, but Lowenstein eventually flushed out an anti-war Democrat candidate in the shape of the clever but dour Eugene McCarthy (no relation of the red-baiting Joe McCarthy). All the polls put McCarthy over 50 points behind LBJ, but as the impact of the Tet Offensive sank in, and as the trickle of US body bags returning home became a river, the tide began to turn against Lyndon Baines Johnson (now more often known by his old college nickname of Lyndon 'Bullshit' Johnson).

On 7 March Bobby 'RFK' Kennedy gave the Senate a

scorching speech demanding to know if the USA really had the right to kill tens of thousands of people purely in the cause of a "... commitment to the South Vietnamese people? Are we like the God of the Old Testament that we decide in Washington DC what cities, what towns, what hamlets are to be destroyed in Vietnam?" A week later he announced that he would run for President and a few days later Eugene McCarthy made history by defeating LBJ in the Wisconsin primary.

Since the mid-Sixties, the US Army's top brass, hand in glove with the CIA, had been pursuing a 'scorched earth' policy of burning thousands of South Vietnamese villages in order to deny the Vietcong any possible support or cover. The fact that this tactic killed hundreds of innocents, and made hundreds of thousands people homeless, was overlooked. This was all somehow supposed to work alongside the hearts and minds policy. Certain pro-government hamlets were saturated with candy, clothes, vaccinations, haircuts and medicine, while many of those evicted from smouldering villages were offered useless gifts and tiny patches of land far from their former homes.

In mid-March '68 soldiers of Charlie Company, 1st Battalion, 20th US infantry entered the My Lai 4 hamlet. No shots were fired at the US troops and virtually all the local men in the immediate area were ageing farmers in their seventies. But the American soldiers still murdered over 450 unarmed men, women and children in a daylight, four-hour orgy of rape and killing. Babies were bayoneted and shot before their stunned mothers were themselves sexually assaulted then shot. Laughing US troops kicked and punched children – the dead, the dying and the wounded – into mass graves before spraying them with bullets again. Here was the CIA's scorched earth policy taken to its ultimate, obscene conclusion. A shockingly horrific slaughter.

More shocking still, at least two reporters and one photographer had recorded the all-day massacre and one passing helicopter pilot, American Chief Warrant Officer Hugh C Thompson, was so enraged that he brought his craft down and managed to rescue ten children from the baying GIs, but Thompson only accomplished this after a furious row with Charlie Company's on-the-spot Commanding Officer, William L Calley Jr.

The US press ran stories about the attack later that same week. But these articles were run *without* pictures – and the stories all claimed that the My Lai event had been a successful 'fire fight' with Vietcong guerrillas; US troops had apparently shown great bravery while killing over 120 'armed' Vietcong insurgents. There was no mention of the hundreds of murdered women and children, only more words about the fictional VC onslaught.

No photos of the actual My Lai 4 massacre were to be printed for over a year and a half before the full story finally came out in 1970. There were other, less 'celebrated' mass killings of Vietnamese civilians by American forces at this time – noticeably at My Akn and at Southang, where 16 women and children were killed in a matter of seconds. Only two US marines were jailed for the latter slaughter – one for just five years – though their patrol leader Randy Herrod managed to get a complete acquittal after fellow marine Oliver North appeared as a character witness. No US troops were to spend years in jail over the bigger My Lai massacre since only Calley was charged and he was released after a few months' house arrest.

At the end of March '68, Johnson decided he had 'suffered' enough. He announced the suspension of US bombing against North Vietnamese forces north of the 20th parallel and concluded his speech with the words: "I shall not seek, and will not accept, the nomination of my party for another term as President."

The war in Vietnam had claimed the scalp of a second President. But, under the media spotlight, Eugene McCarthy had himself soon been revealed as being a candidate with little charm and even less charisma. Still, at least he or RFK would make some serious attempt to end the slaughter in South East Asia.

But the Democratic Party's still ascendant right wing would not accept Eugene McCarthy, or RFK, and VP Hubert Humphrey was swiftly drafted in on the 'peace with honour' ticket (i.e. the continuation of the Vietnam War with frontline US troops).

Humphrey had most of the Democratic Party machinery behind him and it soon looked more and more like the only candidate with a chance of defeating Humphrey was RFK – who had the Kennedy glamour and the support of most liberals, blacks, Latinos and blue-collar workers.

On 4 April, the inspirational black civil rights leader Martin Luther King was shot dead in Memphis, Tennessee. He had gone to the Deep South city to support the garbage worker's strike – a multi-racial dispute. King had embraced the anti-Vietnam war cause months beforehand and had fought off attempts by Hoover's FBI to silence him. During the last speech of his life he'd spoken with eerie foresight of the promised land on earth and how he "might not get there with you".

Within hours of the speech he was killed and riots erupted across the ghetto districts of America's cities. A thorough investigation of King's assassination was promised but that seemed to be undercut when officials stated, even before an arrest had been made, that there was "definitely no conspiracy".

In the end, alleged racist James Earl Ray was arrested for the crime after flying to England. The very fact that he'd flown the Atlantic seemed to prove his guilt to many

Americans and his abrupt plea of guilty appeared to confirm this. Yet a strange little FBI memo to Hoover's 'friend' Clyde Tolson inadvertently hinted at something not being quite right:

... Now that Ray has been convicted and is serving a 99-year sentence, I would like to suggest that the Director allow us to choose a friendly capable author, or the Reader's Digest, and proceed with a book on the case.

Why did the author have to be 'friendly'? The FBI isn't a pen pal organisation or a dating agency. Why friendly? What would an unfriendly one discover?

In the end George McMillan was presumably thought friendly enough and his *Making of An Assassin* book sold thousands after being given a rave review by Jeremiah O'Leary, who was later revealed to be one of 40 journalists who were actually on the CIA payroll. These 'agent-journalists' and their successors continue to work even now.

Even with other 'friendly' books, the actual case against James Earl Ray was not as watertight as it had at first seemed. As Ray changed his mind and began to belatedly proclaim his innocence, people began to ask about the Ray lookalike, complete with similar clothes and the same white Mustang car – right down to matching fender dents – seen in Memphis in the days leading up to King's assassination.

As with Lee Harvey Oswald, another man plagued by lookalikes, Ray even had an alias, Eric S Galt – and again here, there seemed to be two Eric Galts – one a shy, retiring character, the other a loud-mouthed racist drawing attention to himself.

In the seconds after the killing, one white Mustang went one way, bearing the killer, and a second exact replica appeared minutes later and went the other way. A fake police radio broadcast directed cars to chase the former car but not the latter – almost certainly allowing the real killer to escape. No attempt seems to have been made by the Memphis police or the FBI to try and track down those behind the fake and the illegal police broadcast, or to track down the owner of the second white Mustang with its curious matching dents and registration number.

And then there was the case of Marrell McCullough, the undercover Memphis policemen seen crouching over King's body just moments after the shooting. In 1997 it was revealed that McCullough had been a CIA agent since at least 1974. Loyd Jowers, in 1993, did admit that he had been hired 25 years before to find a man to kill King – and the man he hired was *not* James Earl Ray. When an ABC TV reporter later called the CIA and asked to speak to McCullough, the latter admitted that he *did* know Jowers. When told the call was about the MLK assassination, McCullough slammed the phone down. McCullough today denies being MLK's assassin and claims he did not join the CIA until *after* the killing.

Jailed killer Jules Ricco Kimble, who in 1963 had a PO box in the same New Orleans building as JFK assassination suspects Oswald and Ferrie, once boasted of his involvement in the King murder, saying that James Earl Ray was involved too but only as an unwitting fall-guy.

After making their own extensive inquiries, Martin Luther King's family joined in the campaign for a re-trial of James Earl Ray. They no longer believed Ray was guilty of killing their most famous family member. Unfortunately, and, perhaps, conveniently, Ray died before a re-trial was permitted.

After releasing the 'Lady Madonna' single and decamping from the Indian base of the Maharishi guru – Lennon famously blasting him for trying it on with some young female followers – he and McCartney appear on America's NBC *Tonight* show, partly to explain the concept behind the Beatles' latest venture, Apple Corps. Before the interview is through, Lennon raises eyebrows by telling host Joe Garagiola that continuing US involvement in the Vietnam War is "insanity". The solution to American political injustice is, Lennon continues, "to change the establishment", a comment later echoed by various counter-cultural gurus (Don't hate the media, *become* the media!).

A week later Lennon changed his own establishment. After 18 months of discreet flirting with Yoko Ono, a woman who'd sent him messages and postcards on a weekly basis, he finally invited her to his Weybridge home (wife Cynthia was away at the time). "I played her all the tapes that I'd made," Lennon said years later, "some comedy and stuff and some electronic stuff. She was suitably impressed and said 'Let's make one ourselves!' So we made 'Two Virgins'. It was midnight when we started and dawn when we finished and then we made love at dawn. It was very beautiful."

Two months after King's assassination young America's last hope for '68, Bobby Kennedy, was shot dead. The presidential candidate, aka RFK, died at LA's Ambassador Hotel, within minutes of hearing he'd won the Californian Democratic primary. His murder, so soon after King's, stunned a blood-soaked America.

His alleged killer was Sirhan Sirhan, who fired a handgun eight times from between two and six feet away from Kennedy. As there were dozens of witnesses Sirhan was soon bundled away and charged with the murder. As far as the LAPD were concerned it was case closed – Sirhan wasn't crazy (despite the later 'lone nut' stories) he was seen in the act, and he was alone.

But the LAPD's story, and that of their SUS (Special Unit Senator) investigators, didn't hold up, despite the support of the FBI. For a start there were too many bullets. RFK was hit three times and a fourth shot ripped his clothes. At least five other people took bullets and there were four more bullet-holes in the door frames. That total, of *thirteen*, was five more than the eight that Sirhan's gun could hold. Even if the door frame bullets were somehow ricochets, that still left 11 shots from an 8-shot handgun.

Then there was the awkward fact that the official coroner, Dr Thomas Noguchi, later revealed. The fatal shot had been fired into RFK's ear from *behind*, from less than two inches away. Effectively at point blank. And yet, at all times, Sirhan had been between two feet and six feet away *in front* of Kennedy.

Sirhan himself behaved curiously. He had gone on firing his gun even when being beaten by six people, receiving extensive bruising to his eye, scratches, a badly-sprained ankle and smashed finger. Such a beating would fell an ox, yet the slight Sirhan kept plugging away, his eyes "beautifully peaceful" according to witnesses. He seemed to other witnesses to be "in a trance".

Afterwards, in custody, Sirhan had the chills, despite the summer heat that was drenching everyone else in sweat. Months later these chills were to be repeated in prison, immediately after hypnosis sessions with a Dr Diamond. When asked why he'd killed RFK, Sirhan didn't seem to know, though, after discussions with his defence attorney, he later claimed it was in solidarity with Arab nationalism, after Kennedy had supported the sale of US jets to Israel. Yet RFK hadn't made public his jets-to-Israel statement until days *after* Sirhan had filled his own dairies with the endless slogan: 'RFK Must Die! RFK Must Die! RFK Must Die Before June 5th!'

The police and FBI ignored all this, ignored those who'd seen a security guard with a drawn gun behind RFK and ignored the other accomplices seen with Sirhan on the night, and at previous RFK meetings and later at a rifle range.

When the press picked up on the infamous girl with the polka dot dress – later found to be an Iranian whose father was linked to American intelligence – the LAPD response was to browbeat the two main 'polka dot' witnesses into withdrawing their testimony. They and several others had all seen the 'polka dot girl' running away with a young man seconds after the shooting, the girl happily shouting, "We've shot Kennedy!"

Sirhan's bullets were more problematic. How could between 11 and 13 shots be sprayed out from a handgun that could only hold eight? The SUS/FBI answers were simple. It was decided that, of Sirhan's eight bullets, three of them were 'magic bullets', which bounced round all over the place, nipping in and out of walls and causing exactly the right amount of injury and damage. The bullets in the door frames had, by now, disappeared anyway, since the LAPD had had the frames ripped out and destroyed, a strange way to treat the forensic evidence in an important murder case.

All this manipulation of evidence still left the problem of the firing distances. Sirhan's gun being between two and six feet away in *front*, and the fatal bullet coming in from less than two inches from *behind*. Again the official response was crude but effective – the RFK autopsy report was simply withheld from the defence team until after the trial had already started. A confused Sirhan later pleaded guilty anyway and the case was, for the moment, uneasily closed.

Many researchers, however, believed that the real killer must have been one or more of the security guards. There were no police present at the time of the shooting, only security guards. And only the security guards were armed, only they were close enough, only they were right behind RFK at the time of the shooting.

Sirhan's post-assassination proclamation: "We are all

puppets", hardly constitute the words of a man who had acted alone. In fact, this sentence uneasily echoed those of Lee Harvey Oswald in 1963, "I'm just a patsy in all this."

On the other side of the Atlantic, in 1968, Labour leader Harold Wilson found himself increasingly under fire from critics on the right. Under Wilson, Labour had done away with the death sentence and legalised abortion and homosexuality for adults over 21. They had also passed the Race Relations Act, outlawing racial discrimination, and increasing the pressure on both of Africa's biggest 'racist' states, South Africa and Rhodesia. To add insult to injury, as far as the establishment was concerned, Wilson had also refused to send British troops to fight alongside the Americans in Vietnam, even though a fellow Commonwealth country, Australia, had already done so.

Late in the year there were at least two secret meetings attended by several BBC governors, British Army chiefs and members of MI5 and MI6. Such was the establishment's panic, that the possibility of a military anti-Labour coup was seriously discussed – a piece of paranoid treason no doubt prompted by the less-than-rational belief of many CIA and MI5 high-ups that Britain's prime minister was really a Russian agent. Wilson was also unaware of the fact, recently revealed by the *Daily Mail*, that MI6 had put listening devices throughout his official residence at Number 10 Downing Street. Wilson was not told anything about this until 1975; by then he was regularly dropped hints that the UK's security services were plotting against him and he was widely accused of paranoia by almost the entire British press. Wilson had won four general elections up till this point in 1975, a post-war record, but he resigned the next year and the Labour Party were not to win another election for over 20 years. The establishment plot against Labour would seem, eventually, to have succeeded.

As 1968 wore on, musician Mick Farren and his rock band the Pink Fairies were stopped twice on England's M1 motorway. Farren and company were astonished to find that the police weren't interested in drugs. They were actually looking for guns. Official Cold War paranoia now embraced the counter culture too.

That summer had seen the Beatles recording demos at George Harrison's house, ostensibly for a new album. They had such a wealth of material after their Indian trip, however, that the single album became an epic double set that was some 94 minutes long, almost three times the length of some of their first LPs. Amongst the gems were Lennon's ethereal 'Dear Prudence' – written about, and for, Mia Farrow's shy sister – his chilling 'Happiness Is A Warm Gun' and the soulful 'Julia', about, of course, his long dead mother. Lennon also added the avant-garde 'Revolution 9' and the more conventional 'Revolution', a song – recorded in a blisteringly tough rock'n'roll style – that demanded change but stopped short of condoning violence ('count me out'). It also contained a side swipe at those young militants who thought carrying Chairman Mao's little red book was somehow cool and subversive.

These notions – anti-violent change and anti-Maoism – were to bring an array of 'sell out' claims from the extremists of the new Left, all aimed at Lennon. Although he would later sing more extreme versions of the same song, the lyric on the take released has stood the test of time. How many people today would defend the late Mao, now revealed as the murderer of millions? Years later, at the height of his New York radical phase, Lennon himself would don a Mao badge for a few days; a gesture that contained both an overly strong rejection of his pop past and, it has to be said, a touch of kitsch irony – not that the latter was appreciated at the time.

McCartney's contributions to the album were less

contentious but they were bright enough – the bounding ska reggae of 'Ob-La-Di Ob-La-Da', the ironic but, for eastern Europeans, welcoming, 'Back In The USSR' and the discreetly frantic 'Helter Skelter'. Throw in Harrison's shimmering 'While My Guitar Gently Weeps', which came with a poignantly beautiful guitar solo from Eric Clapton, plus over 20 other tracks, and you had a brilliant, if somewhat overlong, set.

Although this double album sold in excess of a breath-taking 20 million copies – the biggest US hit of the entire Sixties, selling almost 19 million Stateside – its recording, packaging and release date paradoxically showed how much the four band members were drifting apart. It had taken six months to finish and issue it – some of their first albums had taken just days – and the group simply couldn't agree on a name, let alone a cover image. In the end *The Beatles* became its simple title, while it was ultimately issued with a plain white sleeve featuring an embossed version of the band's name (hence its commonest nickname, 'The White Album').

Though the tumultuously honest *Let It Be* – a warts-an'-all album, and film – was to be The Beatles' last official release, *Abbey Road,* the *White Album*'s follow-up, was the real end. And, just like the music hall entertainers that McCartney had been referencing since *Sergeant Pepper*, they saved the best till last. *Abbey Road*, named after the EMI recording studio in north London where it was cut, opened with Lennon's sumptuous, pulsing 'Come Together' – a title that had obvious cultural, political and sexual overtones – a powerful atmospheric track that still sounds contemporary nearly half a century later. Harrison was now increasingly finding his own voice as a songwriter and his *Abbey Road* pieces were the joyful 'Here Comes The Sun' and the romantic 'Something', loved by everyone from Jim Morrison to

Frank Sinatra. Both are classics in their own right and are still the subject of endless cover versions.

Aside from the middle eights, backing vocals and suggestions that he sometimes added to the others' songs, McCartney's contributions were more diverse – and, on closer examination, more ominous. The slick, sick 'Maxwell's Silver Hammer' was edged with schoolboy humour, even as it hinted at Macca's minor obsession with death (perhaps understandable for a man who, like Lennon, had tragically lost his mother while still in his early teens).

His sour'n'sour 'You Never Give Me Your Money', like Harrison's 'Taxman' before it, showed how hung up the boys were becoming with the one thing they no longer had to worry about – money. In fact, the materialistic nature of this cut has always disappointed the more idealistic commentators with the late, great Ian McDonald – author of the definitive Beatles' track-by-track book, *Revolution In The Head* – declaring 'You Never Give Me Your Money' to be the real end of the sharing, caring spirit of the Sixties.

As if to demonstrate the point that such cash obsessions were not really relevant, *Abbey Road*, although not quite reaching the heights of the White Album, went on to sell a thumping 12 million copies in the US alone, the majority of these sales coming in the last three months of 1969.

In the mid-1950s when Britain's first rock'n'roll star, Tommy Steele, had asked for a Hawaiian guitar during a recording session, not one could be found the length of Shaftesbury Avenue, Charing Cross Road, nor even in London's 'Tin Pan Alley', Denmark Street. Some of the studio engineers hadn't even *heard* of Hawaiian guitars and had no idea how they sounded. Such was the numbing level of isolated parochialism in the British music industry circa 1956.

By the end of the Sixties, however, virtually every major British studio would have access to instruments, and ideas, from all over the world. From Chicago blues to Jamaican reggae, from Indian sitars to Greek bouzoukis, to Mexican marimbas, to Tibetan prayer bells. This internationalism, this huge transformation – a transformation that was a big, authentic growth in possibilities – is down to the 'England Swings' phenomenon, which made Britain in general, and London in particular, the cultural centre of the earth for a few years. And at the heart of the tumult of Swinging London was the new music, and at the heart of the music was, of course, The Beatles pop group, and their founder and leader, John Lennon.

Musically, the Sixties ended in Britain for the Lennons with a gig by the Plastic Ono Band. The latter 'band' basically being John and Yoko plus whatever Beatle-friendly musicians happened to be free. This time the line-up included George Harrison, keyboard king Billy Preston and The Who's legendary drummer Keith Moon. The chosen venue was the large Lyceum theatre, round the corner from the east end of London's West End Strand, with all proceeds going to UNICEF, the worldwide children's charity.

The Lyceum then was a magical place to view concerts. Often it would stay open until four or five in morning, virtually the only venue in London to do so then, before the ageing, sliding roof would grind open. Young Londoners would then get a glimpse of the stars above before the dawn bleached them all out. Although, like the other concert halls, it stopped serving alcohol well before midnight, the Lyceum was still an amazing place for a teenager to visit in its 1968-74 heyday.

The Lyceum was amazing too during the Plastic Ono Band gig, with Lennon saturating the Vic-wardian hall with feedback and wild, driving rock. Throw in Yoko's wailing vocals and some of the best guitarists in England, including Harrison and Eric Clapton, and you had a night to remember. Lennon himself regarded the Lyceum event as being influential, the first really 'heavy rock' night in Britain and in all the most important senses – volume, spectacle and attitude – he was probably right.

The man who was still, technically, at least, a full member of the Beatles, was now sporting a crew cut since, he said, long hair had become virtually meaningless. There was 'nothing' in the increasingly complicated music and lyrics of late Sixties rock that the original rock'n'rollers of the Fifties hadn't said in a more simple direct way, Lennon told *Rolling Stone*, in an interview that seemed to predict both his 1975 *Rock'n'Roll* album, and the rise of punk. Young punks Glen Matlock and the late Joe Strummer are both said to have been teenage visitors to the Lyceum in this period, several years before they respectively kick-started the Sex Pistols and The Clash, although Matlock, now a successful solo artist who still tours with the reformed Pistols, was a heavy drinker for a time and has no definite memory of seeing the Plastic Ono Band at the Lyceum, a venue the Pistols themselves were to play in 1976.

As the Sixties finally wound up, Britain's biggest commercial television network named the world's three *Men of The Decade* in a special hour-long programme. The trio ITV named were the late President Kennedy of the USA; Chairman Mao Tse Tung, the leader of 600 million Chinese citizens and the largest army on earth. The third man of the decade was a musician, a Liverpudlian musician, called John Lennon.

CHAPTER ELEVEN

CONCERT SECURITY

Source advised police officers patrolled only on the outside.

FBI memo December 1971

John and Yoko got married in March 1969, enjoying the most public honeymoon in history by inviting the world press to a series of 'Bed-Ins for Peace' in Amsterdam and Vienna. Middle-aged journalists present at these events are angry, in some cases to the point of apoplexy, accusing the Lennons of "cynically exploiting" their fame for peace. Many of the disappointed reporters had actually expected the 'bed-ins' to feature sex, or at least some nudity. The bed-ins also produced the 'Ballad of John & Yoko', a Number 1 single done in an early rock'n'roll style. It was, officially, a Beatles track, though its lyrical concern was entirely about the Press's hounding of the couple. The subject matter alone made its success in Britain a surprising indicator of just how much affection there still was for Lennon. Banned for blasphemy by Australia's ABC broadcasting corporation, and given little airplay in many US states, it was to be the last Beatles Number 1 in the land of their birth.

The bed-ins also gave us the classic anti-war single, 'Give Peace A Chance'. The latter was a Lennon composition that was his first solo effort to chart, a Top Ten hit that he produced himself, and the track itself, a great singalong, had a curious, if not unattractive, beat that seemed to be heavily echoed, perhaps because of the hotel room's acoustics. Years later John confessed that he'd added reverb to cover up the fact that some of the amateur vocalists were mistakenly clapping on the off-beat. His next 1969 hit, the searing rocker 'Cold Turkey', was another confession, of a much heavier kind. After hearing Yoko describe her New York heroin experiences as being 'not too bad', Lennon had taken the drug, ostensibly to deal with the torrent of criticism the couple were now living under (he for daring to leave his first wife and child, she for being the foreign *femme fatale* who was starting to break up the much-loved Beatles). The heroin was, of course, a wrong move and Lennon's fight to get off the drug was bitterly chronicled in 'Cold Turkey'.

This last recording, like The Move's menacing 'Night of Fear' single, was bizarrely seen as being part of rock's pro-drug stance, despite obviously taking the opposite position. The establishment, and its media, was then obsessed with the idea that any discussion of 'illicit substances' was tantamount to promoting those same drugs. But with the gradual collapse of moderate religion, and the rapid rise of sensation for its own sake, it was increasingly obvious that drug use, even of the strongest types, would mushroom (no pun intended) in modern society.

It was, *is*, the humanitarian duty of those experienced in potentially dangerous subjects to issue some kind of warning about them. Yet when this occurred in the past, as with 'Cold Turkey', the establishment media seems to have deliberately mistaken the warning lights for alluring neon adverts.

Later in the year the Lennons had also met the parents of James Hanratty, a small-time burglar who had been hanged – most experts believed wrongly – for the 1961 A6 Murder. The Lennons listened sympathetically to the Hanrattys' story and later gave them money for a film to fund the re-opening of the case.

There were bigger, brighter – and darker – things happening in 1969. As half a million 'hippies' gathered peacefully for the headline-grabbing Woodstock Festival, Roman Polanski's wife Sharon Tate, and several of her friends, were murdered by the Charles Manson gang in LA; a savage set of killings that Manson allegedly claimed was sparked off by The Beatles' songs 'Helter Skelter' and 'Piggies'.

This was sinister enough, yet even more disturbing was Manson's possible connection to Operation CHAOS. The violent CHAOS campaign was, in part, Hoover's plan for the FBI and CIA to work together to divide the so-called New Left opposition: Black Panthers, peace groups, activist groups and pro-cannabis organisations. This division and destabilisation was done through assassination, drug planting, harassment, bugs and surveillance. The Panthers alone saw over 200 of their leaders killed, mostly under dubious circumstances, in the seven bloody years that Operation CHAOS was secretly running, at a cost of millions of dollars and with some 60 full-time agents employed.

Female radio presenter and researcher Mae Brussell, was a friend of the Lennons. She was also the woman who broke the Watergate story months before Woodward and Bernstein had persuaded the *Washington Post* to run with it. Brussell is now convinced that the Manson murders were part of Operation CHAOS, since the whole CHAOS project went into a mysterious, ultra-secret 'no-paper, no-files' state immediately before the Manson Family murders began and others have since claimed that Charles Manson had indeed been a police informer "for years" before the killings. Manson was also a man who, it has been alleged, had been introduced to mind control techniques just before leaving prison, and about the same time that he met Sirhan Sirhan's lawyer, according to

Brussell, when Manson was duly presented with credit cards, as well as a black Volkswagen bus.

It seems far-fetched and yet, the plain fact is that the actions Manson took did *all* fit in with the aims of Operation CHAOS, i.e. trying to provoke a race war within the 'New Left', associating 'hippie protest' with murder, blackening the Beatles by linking their name, and their songs, with the Manson gang's murderous actions. The Fab Four were, Manson claimed to believe, the four long-haired angels mentioned in the biblical Revelation 9.

Sirhan's lawyer later wrote the book *Helter Skelter* which, in its theories and very title, once again cemented the unpleasant Beatles-Manson connection. The lawyer in question, Vincent Bugliosi, produced another book, years later, about the JFK assassination, a book which cleared the CIA of all blame and instead defended the Oswald-acted-alone "nut with magic bullets" theory.

Writer David Malmo-Levine later pointed out that, when George Bush Senior was trying to become head of the CIA in 1975, he went out of his way to reassure the Senate Committee on The Armed Services that, under him, the Agency would "not harass American citizens, like in Operation CHAOS".

One final point about CHAOS; a page of one of John Lennon's FBI files, half of it blacked out, has the sub-heading 'CHAOS'. And on one of the few Lennon CIA files ever seen – a secret 'restricted handling' teletype from Agency Director Richard Helms to FBI boss Hoover, dated 10 February 1972 – the name Richard Ober appears. Richard Ober is quite an important figure in all this, for he was the man in charge of the CIA's Operation CHAOS.

Either way, whether the Manson-CHAOS connection is solid or not, the fact is that, even as the flower children partied at Woodstock, in the foothills above LA, Manson's knife groupies hammered a bloody full-stop on

to the end of the Sixties; the decade of change; the decade
The Beatles had made their own. It was a dark omen, and
a grim end to a great golden age of optimism, the last real
decade of hope.

airtel. 4/23/70

To: Special Agents in Charge (SACS), New York, Los Angeles.
From: Director, FBI/
JOHN LENNON (next words blanked out)
GEORGE HARRISON (next words blanked out)
PATRICIA HARRISON (next words blanked out)
INFORMATION CONCERNING (next words blanked out)

*On 4/22/70 a representative of the Department of State advised
that the American Embassy in London had submitted
information showing the captioned individuals planned to
depart from London, England on 4/23/70 via TWA Flight 761,
which will arrive in Los Angeles at 7.15 local time. These
individuals are affiliated with the Beatles musical group and
Lennon will be traveling under the name <u>Chambers</u> while the
Harrisons are using the name <u>Masters</u>.*

*Lennon and the Harrisons will remain in Los Angeles
until 5/6/70 for business discussions with Capitol Records and
other enterprises. They will travel to New York City on 5/7/70
for further business discussions and will return to London on
or about 5/16/70.*

*Waivers were granted by the Immigration and
Naturalisation Service (INS) and the Embassy was to issue
visas on 4/22/70. In this case waivers were necessary in view
of the ineligibility of these three individuals to enter the US
due to their reputations in England as narcotic users.*

(next words blanked out)
Airtel to New York

Re: John Lennon, George Harrison, Patricia Harrison.
While Lennon and the Harrisons have shown propensity to
become involved in violent antiwar demonstrations, each
recipient remain alert for any information of such activity on
their part or for information indicating they are using
narcotics. Submit any pertinent information obtained in form
suitable for dissemination.

On 23 April 1970 – two months after John had paid the
£1,344 fines imposed on Scottish anti-apartheid
demonstrators (over £15,000 in today's money) – the
Lennons, George Harrison and Harrison's wife Patti
Boyd had indeed flown from London to Los Angeles.
Although J Edgar Hoover's above airtel – an internal FBI
message that must be sent the day it's written – doesn't
mention Yoko Ono, the trip was mainly her idea, so that
Lennon, now her third husband, could undergo gruelling
Primal Therapy at Arthur Janov's Primal institute in LA.

There had, of course, been previous American
complaints about John and Yoko's 1968 album *Two Virgins*
for, under the sleeve's brown paper wrapper, the couple
had appeared nude on the cover. There were even nine
pages in Lennon's FBI files concerning it, though four of
these were letters from congressman, all along the lines of
'must we fling this filth at our pop kids?' Most of the rest
were about a student demo at the University of Hartford,
Connecticut where the students were complaining about
the suspension of the campus newspaper over an editorial
decision to run the *Two Virgins'* sleeve.

But the April '70 airtel from the FBI's boss was the
first time, officially, the Bureau had begun to generate its
own paperwork on John Ono Lennon. By then John
Lennon was hardly alone in his anti-war stance; protests
had been growing since 1965 and marches half a million
strong had taken place the year before. And even the

airtel admits that neither Lennon nor the Harrisons had shown any 'propensity to become involved in violent antiwar demonstrations'.

Lennon, like the Harrisons, was a British born subject. He was also, at that point, a British-based subject who was merely visiting the US for a few days; a strange subject for the FBI, the domestic wing of American intelligence. Why were the LA and NYC FBI offices alerted? In case of the unlikely event of Lennon inviting arrest and imprisonment by taking drugs publicly? It would have to be public since there is, after all, no mention of surveillance – electronic, telephonic or otherwise. Or were these field offices contacted in case the Beatles' founder suddenly reversed the philosophy of a lifetime, ignored his 'non-violent propensity', and physically attacked a police officer at a peace demo?

Despite this being a Freedom of Information Act (FOIA) release – issued over 18 years after it was sent and some 16 years after Hoover's death – there are still a few words that FBI staffers have blanked out. What are these? the names of informers? Just who amongst the US Embassy's Department of State workers – or Britain's showbiz establishment – was keeping tabs on Lennon before he had even left England? And why?

The very next day, 24 April 1970, brought Hoover a couriered airtel from Ottawa, Canada, that later resulted in an FBI 'triumph'. The message, from the FBI's Ottawa Legat concerns a 'PEACE STATION NETWORK, IS – MISCELLANEOUS (NEW LEFT – FOREIGN INFLUENCE – CANADA).'

After 1969's successful Toronto Peace Festival, featuring John and Yoko, Eric Clapton, Chuck Berry and Bo Diddley, the Lennons had suggested setting up a 'loose organisation' of radio stations promoting both peace and the 3 July – 5 July 1970 Mosport Peace Festival; a 'youth orientated' event at which the Lennons and others would again play live.

Ritchie Yorke and John Brower had taken it upon themselves to coordinate and promote the festival and their Toronto-based Peace Station Network had approached a Canadian radio station WJWL.

After refusing to air a five-minute PSN peace programme, the station's conservative manager Edward Marzoa was lobbied by a local youth delegation determined to hear what they had been missing. Marzoa agreed to at least listen to the programme before making a final decision, but he then contacted the Royal Canadian Mounted Police on 18 March, as he suspected the subversive worst about the young people behind PSN.

I would like to know who their officers are; what their purposes are; how they are financed; and why the Canadian base. I have my suspicions. The (airtime) decision is of course mine, I would appreciate however, something more concrete than my intuition to support whatever that decision may be.

On 21 April the RCMP's Superintendent Chisholm acknowledged receipt of Marzoa's letter concerning the '5-minute 'peace' programs' but regretted that the RCMP were:

... unable to supply you with the information which you requested as government policy requires us to liaise with the Federal Bureau of Investigation in matters related to enquiries of this nature. We therefore suggest you redirect you enquiry to the Federal Bureau of Investigation.

It's an astonishing reply really; a police officer of the sovereign state of Canada telling one of the nation's subjects to write to the foreign Federal Bureau of Investigation about a Canadian-based radio network – before the same letters are anyway secretly forwarded to the FBI. Was Chisholm aware of an FBI file on PSN? Or was Lennon's FBI file – barely ten pages at this point and, officially at least, virtually dormant – actually far larger and already highly active? Had Chisholm already been told to send any Lennon-related material to the FBI?

Whatever the answer to the latter question, the FBI eventually got what they wanted from their Canadian correspondence. The Mosport location for the peace festival was vetoed by Ontario's Municipal Board, while the PSN got very few Canadian radio broadcasts – and Lennon never again played north of the border.

In December 1970, Lennon's one-time hero Elvis Presley met President Nixon at the White House. The meeting was about Presley wanting to 'reach' the kids who were drifting into drugs. The man whose hip-swivelling stage act had sold rock'n'roll to the world, now wanted, 'to restore some respect for the flag which was being lost'.

Nixon listened attentively as Presley explained that part of the problem was The Beatles who "had been a real force for anti-American spirit, they had come to this country, made their money and then returned to England."

Nixon nodded in agreement then indicated that he felt that those taking drugs were also those in the vanguard of the anti-American protests. It was curious how being against the Vietnam War seemed, in Nixon's mind, to automatically make someone 'anti-American'. It was as if, mentally, he was still on McCarthy's witch-hunt against 'UnAmericans'.

Presley, after a few more expressions of loyalty, then asked the President to meet a couple of his 'Graceland mafia' cronies. Nixon agreed and, after a few minutes, both the hangers-on and Elvis were on their way out of the White House. At the meeting it was Nixon – not the slightest bit over-awed, of course – who warned Elvis about losing his credibility by being too closely associated with the 'government squares'. Presley himself – depressed, pilled-up and with his marriage going wrong – was too busy trying to save America from Lennon's Beatles to worry about damaging his own fading career.

Neither Presley nor Nixon bothered to mention the biggest news story of the moment – the mass bombing of North Vietnam, US air-raids which had recently resumed after a two-year break, killing thousands of civilians. One bombing wave was so severe it left an entire school, of hundreds of children, permanently deafened.

In London, one Beatle was about to drop his own bombshell. On 30 December Paul McCartney launched a High Court suit to permanently end The Beatles' business partnership. The rift between himself and Lennon had widened since the 1969 recording of *Let it Be*, when cameras had captured McCartney's attempt to become band leader. Many of his suggestions were valid but the scenes where he harassed Harrison made uncomfortable viewing. Lennon had brought Yoko to the sessions – again – and bringing 'birds' to the studio had been a no-no as far as the band were concerned, particularly McCartney. He put up with it, but was later enraged when, after the sessions had formally ended, Lennon allowed Wall of Sound producer Phil Spector to drench certain tracks with strings. Macca's 'Long and Winding Road' was the principle victim. It is still an outstanding ballad but the feud between the twentieth century's premier songwriters had just gone up a notch.

January 1971 saw the release of Lennon's honest, at times harrowing, *John Lennon/Plastic Ono Band* album. It contained a beautifully crafted love song, the much-covered 'Love', but the essence of the album was, after the Janov sessions, all about soul-baring. On *God* he dismissed all his figureheads and heroes – from Dylan, to

141

Jesus, to the Beatles – being willing to affirm his belief in nothing more than Ono and himself, as a couple. In 'Working Class Hero' he pin-pointed the age-old bittersweet dilemma, at school – as with the office junior and the factory apprentice – the powers-that-be hated defiant intelligence and yet 'despised' those who were mere foolish yes-men. The same song touched on the sad fact that once anyone from the working class, or even the lower middle class, gained any representative power they immediately became isolated from their peers.

The opening and closing tracks – 'Mother' and 'My Mummy's Dead' – dealt with the raw rejection and sorrow of his interrupted relationship with the late Julia Lennon; the woman who'd had John though he felt like he'd 'never' had her, as if he'd never had a mother. These were shatteringly personal themes that no major musician had ever dealt with before so honestly and so publicly. To May Pang, then a teenager who was a 'mere' office junior at the New York music corporation ABKCO, Lennon's "painfully truthful" album was a fascinating piece of work that "made it impossible not to care for him" as both an artist "and a human being". She had no illusions though; in her position at the business-like ABKCO she'd be very lucky to glimpse one of Lennon's contracts, let alone ever see the man himself.

At the end of that year, on 11 December 1971, Lennon's official FBI file ground into life again. Two months after issuing his second solo album – *Imagine* with its classic universal brotherhood title track that some took to be 'Communistic' – the former Beatle had performed live at the 'John Sinclair Freedom Rally' at the Crisler Arena in Ann Arbor, Michigan on the day before.

His first live US gig in five years was a radical benefit concert played with Yoko – and proceeded by Stevie Wonder, Bob Seger, Commander Cody, David Peel and

Phil Ochs – before an audience of over 15,000. Black Panther Bobby Seale, poet Allen Ginsberg and 'Yippie leader' Jerry Rubin were all there too, speaking onstage with the latter MCing the event.

Lennon wound the night up with songs like the freshly-penned 'John Sinclair'. Although the lyrics to this soon appeared amidst the sleeve notes of Lennon's forthcoming *Sometime in New York City*, the FBI deemed the words 'confidential' and withheld the document from public scrutiny for years.

The subject of the event, John Sinclair, was the former manager of rock radicals the MC5. He was also a leader of the anti-racist White Panthers, a Yippie type radical who'd helped disrupt Mayor Daley's grotesque Democratic National Convention of 1968, when anti-war protestors, young Democrats and even passers-by were randomly beaten and gassed by the Chicago police. Sinclair had been sentenced to a staggering ten years in jail for the heinous crime of selling two small cannabis joints to an undercover police officer.

And it was because of the forthcoming Republican National Convention (RNC) that the FBI were watching Lennon. At the RNC President Nixon's pro-war stance was to be rubber-stamped as he was to be re-nominated to lead the Republican party into the November 1972 US election. The Bureau were convinced that Lennon's Ann Arbor benefit was merely a taste of things to come, a forerunner of a nationwide radical rock tour that would culminate at the RNC in San Diego in August.

The speeches at Ann Arbor – secretly recorded and then transcribed word for word by the FBI g-men – certainly showed hostility both toward Nixon, his drugs policy and the status quo he represented.

Radical lawyer William Kunstler was busy on another case and so sent a tape to broadcast through the PA – a tape which was then, of course, taped in turn by the FBI. He began by talking about Sinclair's imprisonment:

JOHN [Sinclair] is in jail for two essential reasons; first of all he is a political person who calls into question the validity of the super-state which seeks to control all of us and destroys those it cannot readily dominate. Secondly, his harsh sentence dramatizes the absurdity of our marijuana laws which are irrational, unjust and indefensible. Recently the National Institute of Mental Health submitted to the Congress its 176 page report 'Marijuana and Health' which comes to the conclusion that, quote, 'For the bulk of smokers, marijuana does not seem to be harmful,' end quote. Yet it is made a crime in every state with penalties ranging in severity from life to six months in jail. On the other hand, conventional cigarettes can be legally sold as long as they bear a legend on the package that they can cause serious illness or death.

Another, unnamed speaker, who may be Jerry Rubin or MC Bob Rudnick, cranks the political rhetoric up a notch:

It's the only way we are going to attack Capitalism. To expropriate from that Capitalistic system the goods, the technology etc, to put it down in the poor oppressed communities, all of us, the people that are oppressed and us too and everybody processing it and giving it away free. It's the only way I know [to] start attacking the monster of Capitalism. A monster of charging people money for everything they get, we're saying the music is free, the life is free, the world is free and if it ain't free, let's start getting our chains off now. The psychology chains and the chains of oppression, if we don't have the chains off of us they are going to annihilate us.

They are going to annihilate us by polluting this earth, the Capitalists and Fascists they are going to do this here. We [are] saying the universe belongs to the people, Mars belongs to the people, and the people belong to the people, all power to the people. Thank you very much, Right on, Power to the people."

Rubin, surprisingly articulate, then raged against the President, and all his works, while speaking about the Lennons as the previous speaker had, before, one suspects, it had actually been confirmed that they had turned up.

It's really incredible that JOHN and YOKO are gonna be here tonight, and [we] should really think of what that meaning is. Cause it's really a committed act by people who are very involved in music, who are identifying to the culture you and I are part of. The family you and I are part of and for them to come on this stage, and for JOHN and YOKO to sing a song about the IRA and Attica State. It's really incredible. It shows that right now we can really build the movement all across the country. (applause)

It's like a whole cultural renaissance is about to begin and if JOHN and YOKO can come here we really have to go back to high school and college and communities and rebuild the movement, to rebuild the revolution because all the people who say the movement and revolution is over should see what's going on right here, because it doesn't look over to me.

But there are, there are a lot of problems, for example the amount of heroin and dope that is smoked in the black and white youth communities. Heroin is poison and you know it get its source from South-east Asia, Laos, and then it's shipped by the CIA back to the US as a poison to poison us, so we don't make a revolution, that's why they are pushing all this heroin into us. (applause)

... we want JOHN SINCLAIR out of prison, we want him out of prison to help us organize the music at San Diego. (applause)

... NIXON's program is not for winding down the war but for winding down the anti-war movement, it's the most cynical appeal to us, to say it doesn't matter that more people are being

killed today than there were last month, it doesn't matter that
there are more people killed last month than there were under
JOHNSON, as long as they are Asians [dying], as long as they
are not Americans.

... Now one last point, I also came to hear JOHN and YOKO
sing a song to the liberation of JOHN SINCLAIR and the other
prisoners. We have the power, we have the strength if, like the
Vietnamese and the Cambodian and the Laotians, we do not allow
the government, visible or invisible, to pacify us, if we do not
allow them to convince [us] that we are weak and impotent and
nothing we do will matter. Ever since 1964, the Press, the dove
press, mind you, and the government has been saying the war is
ending and the anti-war movement is dead, but it has never been
through, and it is not through today, the war will not go away by
itself, and JOHN SINCLAIR will not get free by [himself].

Despite ending in rousing applause, the event was slated
by *Detroit News* reporter Bill Gray, a writer billed that day
as 'News Amusement Writer'. While admitting it was the
Lennon name that brought most of the 15,000 listeners to
the Crisler Arena, Gray attacked Yoko for her inability to
stay on key before finding Lennon's contribution, of three
new songs, similarly disappointing.

The new material was, Gray said, not up to the former
Beatles' 'usual standards' and Gray found him
insufficiently star-like, a man who was flippantly playing
the working class hero.

Although he didn't play the demanding diva, thus
failing to placate the local press, Lennon *did* go down
well singing 'John Sinclair' – reading the lyrics off papers
taped to the mic stand. He didn't, in the end, sing any
songs dedicated to the IRA. He was, however, initially
sympathetic to the Irish Republican cause, at least until
the wave of bombings that shook Northern Ireland and
mainland Britain between 1972 and 1974.

Such sympathies, like some sections of the above speeches, are easy to condemn with 20/20 hindsight. But some of what was said that night still rings true, and much of the passion, the hope and the lingering innocence of the Sixties were shown to be still alive and kicking as the tape reels of the 'invisible government' turned.

And Rubin was right in one sense for, messy and OTT though much of that evening was, it *was* something new for a world famous entertainer to be standing on a stage alongside barefoot radicals, demanding an end to war – and an end to the harsh imprisonment of those who were merely being a little reckless with their own health.

It was, it seems, an effective night too. For less than three days after Lennon had topped the bill at the 'Free John Now Rally' the Michigan Supreme Court had indeed released Sinclair from prison as they declared the state's own statutes on cannabis to be unconstitutional. Here was proof positive of the power of both modern celebrity and of John Lennon, the power to force society to focus on injustice. And the power to force that society to do something about it.

The initials SM and IS appear on these particular FBI documents – SM standing for Security Matters and IS for Internal Security (the leading captions are 'SM – New Left' and 'IS – White Panther Party'). The first informer has his name blanked out, while the second is identified as the 'Intelligence Unit of the Michigan State Police'.

Seven different FBI field offices received between two and five copies of this nine page document – along with the 'WFO', another blanked out recipient and the National Student Association. The latter was a supposedly independent group but, in actuality, it was a CIA-supported front that worked nationwide.

So at least 17 copies were sent out initially – plus those letter head memo (LHM) copies that, like all of

Lennon's FBI LHMs went out to the CIA, the Secret Service, US Army Intelligence, US Naval Intelligence, the State Department and the INS.

Much of this document was withheld after its initial Freedom of Information Act release. Confusion also reigns over the page numbering – page 2 is crossed out and numbered as 3, page 3 is crossed out and numbered as 4 etc. Page nine is missing in its entirety.

More disturbingly still, one of the half pages that was withheld for a dozen years shows a strange fascination with the event's – and therefore with Lennon's – offstage security.

Source advised 10 off-duty Ann Arbor police officers patrolled the area near the rally hall. Source advised the services of the off-duty police officers were obtained and paid for at a cost of $150.00 by the WPP at Ann Arbor, Michigan. Source advised police officers patrolled only on the outside of the rally hall and were not permitted to enter the rally.

Source advised the entire portion of the rally hall was patrolled by so-called WP Rangers.

Why are these matters of such import to the informants? The informants presumably being in this case the officers of Michigan State's Intelligence Unit who had dutifully noted down all of the above details.

Why was the recording of these details hidden by the FBI for as long as was legally possible? Is it just another long hidden FBI red herring, like the careful hiding of the long public 'John Sinclair' lyrics? Or something more sinister?

Were these security matters important because, at some point, the FBI or CIA – or paid trouble-makers – were aiming to violently disrupt such events and thus needed to know how the organisers would police them?

Or did it go beyond disruption into an area that's far more deadly? It was, after all, a security guard who many researchers later came to regard as the real assassin of Robert Kennedy just three years before.

The fact that few such Lennon 'protest' concerts ever took place, and no major ones reached 1972's Republican National Convention, is neither here nor there. No one in the US intelligence community could possibly have foreseen that at the time. And the systematic mugging, beating, kidnapping and deporting of peace demonstrators at the RNC was seriously suggested a few months later to Nixon's Attorney General John Mitchell.

This incredibly irresponsible idea came from Nixon trouble-shooter Gordon Liddy and his ex-CIA agent associate E Howard Hunt, a man with his fingers in many pies. Hunt was a close friend of both Richard Helms and Allen Dulles, the former being CIA deputy director until 1965, director until 1973 and US Ambassador to Iran 1973-1976. Helms was also the creator of the CIA's MK-ULTRA mind-control project and its South-East Asian assassination programme, while Dulles – brother of John Foster Dulles – was CIA director until sacked by President John F Kennedy in the aftermath of the 1961 Cuban Bay of Pigs fiasco.

Dulles later served on the Warren Commission – alongside Earl Warren and Republican politician Gerald Ford – supposedly investigating JFK's assassination with rigour. Hunt himself had been the political officer for the Bay of Pigs operation, a failed invasion that was planned, in part, by Richard Nixon during the dying months of the 1952-1960 Eisenhower administration when he, Nixon, was still Vice President. Hunt is also alleged to have forged cables falsely blaming Kennedy for ordering the killing of South Vietnamese President Diem.

In the end, Nixon's Attorney General Mitchell rejected Hunt and Liddy's first plan too. Mugging and hijacking protesters at the 1972 RNC just wasn't on. It wasn't the illegality that worried America's senior law enforcement official, it was just the excessive financial cost.

But Mitchell did agree to listen to Liddy and Hunt's alternative suggestion. The latter idea was another criminal action, a plan to break into the Democratic Party HQ in Washington DC's Watergate complex, there to photograph documents and plant listening devices so Nixon would know the Democrats' plans in advance.

CHAPTER TWELVE

INSANITY
APRIL-MAY 1972

*We've got to get Nixon out, we've got to stop the
automated war in Vietnam. It's power if we vote
together, we ought to go to both Conventions, and,
not violently, make our presence felt. If we do
anything any other way, we'll be killed.*

Jerry Rubin, 1972

Christmas 1971 had seen the Lennons repeat their 'HAPPY
XMAS! WAR IS OVER (IF YOU WANT IT)' bill-board
poster campaign, though they still didn't have a finished
record to go with it. But this campaign did pioneer the
now huge overlap between concept art, music media and
advertising. The difference between these independent
works and the much-sponsored efforts of today's concept
artists is similarly huge. The Lennons were, after all, first,
and they were also trying to save Vietnam's peasantry
from extermination, a higher aim, one would have
thought, than the petty greed and ambition that motivates
most of today's post-Saatchi art groupies.

Perhaps because of this campaign, 12 January 1972
saw one of the more threatening FBI Lennon documents
brought into play. A Special Agent – name deleted –
reported the fairly banal fact the John and Yoko had
appeared with Jerry Rubin at a press conference shown
on citywide New York television channel WABC-TV.
After noting that only Lennon himself had been
interviewed by the TV reporter present – and that "Rubin
appeared to have his hair cut much shorter than

previously shown in other photographs" The SA had written in huge, underlined capitals, *'ALL EXTREMISTS SHOULD BE CONSIDERED DANGEROUS.'*

Remembering that this is being written about 'peacenik' John Lennon makes it seem that much more startling. And ominous.

On 25 April 1972 an FBI agent sent a confidential teletype to the 'Honourable H.R. Haldeman, Assistant to the President, The White House, Washington DC'. The document stated that John Winston Lennon – 'a British citizen and a former member of the Beatles singing group' – had been convicted in London of 'possession of dangerous drugs'. These 'dangerous drugs' consisted of around 200 'grains' of cannabis hashish, that were allegedly found in Ringo Starr's Montagu Square flat when Lennon and Yoko had replaced Jimi Hendrix as temporary tenants there in October '68. Lennon always denied the hashish was his, saying he had 'cleaned the place up' after *Daily Mirror* reporter Don Short had warned him the previous month that Detective Sergeant Pilcher and certain other officers in the Drugs Squad 'were after Lennon'.

Although believing that the cannabis had been planted, Lennon still entered a guilty plea and paid the £150 fine to prevent the fuss a not guilty plea might have caused, a fuss that could have led to Yoko Ono's deportation from the UK. Such a 'crime' today would not even lead to an arrest in most parts of the UK, Holland and northern Germany – and on 8 November 1972 the alleged 'drug-planter', Detective Sergeant Pilcher, was himself charged with conspiracy to pervert the course of justice.

Despite this heinous outrage and his 'apparent ineligibility' Lennon had, the agent noted, somehow obtained a US visa in 1971 and entered the States. The agent then informed Nixon's assistant that during:

February 1972, a confidential source who has furnished reliable information in the past, advised that Lennon had contributed $75,000 to a newly organised New Left group, formed to disrupt the Republican National Convention.

The visas of Lennon and his wife Yoko Ono expired on February 29th, 1972 and since that time Immigration and Naturalisation Service (INS) have been attempting to deport them. Their attorney stated that Lennon felt he was being deported due to his outspoken remarks concerning US policy in Southeast Asia, the attorney requested a delay, then read into the court record that Lennon had been appointed to the President's Council for Drug Abuse (Nat. Comm. on Marijuana and Drug Abuse) and to the faculty of New York university NYC. A second confidential source who has furnished reliable information in the past, advised that Lennon continues to be a heavy user of narcotics. On April 21st, 1972, a third confidential source advised that there was no information available indicating that Lennon had been appointed to the National Commission on Marijuana and Drug Abuse.

Although this teletype didn't classify Lennon under 'Security Matters – Revolutionary Activities' as previous FBI memos had, and although it conceded that New York University had indeed offered Lennon a temporary teaching post of sorts, it still ended on a chilling note:

This information is also being furnished to the Acting Attorney General. Pertinent information concerning Lennon is being furnished to the Department of State and INS on a regular basis.

It was criminal, really. There were Nazis, child-molesters and heroin dealers that had been given American 'green cards' (the right to stay in the US) – and now the Lennons were being denied them purely on the basis of a single, suspicious cannabis bust. The green card denial was even more outrageous in Yoko's case; she had no criminal convictions at all. Apparently just being a friend or relative of John Lennon was enough to get you blacklisted in 1972.

Four days earlier FBI agent R.L. Shackelford informed bureau superior E.S. Miller that "New York City Police Department currently (is) attempting to develop enough information to arrest both Lennons for narcotic use."

Despite this hoped-for arrest there was, however, "a real possibility that the subject will not be deported from the US in the near future." Shackelford then baldly stated that:

Subject's activities [are] being closely followed and any information developed indicating violation of Federal laws will be immediately furnished to pertinent agencies in [an] effort to neutralize any disruptive activities of subject. Information developed to date has been furnished, to INS and State Department, also been furnished Internal Security Division of the Department.

In other words, the FBI, the State Department and the SD's own Internal Security Division were all trying to lean on the immigration service in an attempt to get the Lennons deported. Republican Senator Strom Thurmond had already written to the attorney general complaining about Lennon's presence. The letter had the scrawled footnote 'can we keep him out?'

The next day, 22 April, John and Yoko defiantly joined the National Peace Rally in New York protesting against the USA's increased carpet bombing of North Vietnam – both of them addressed the 20,000 strong crowd, as well as the FBI agents who were also present.

The couple had initially flown to New York to try to find, and win custody of, Yoko's eight-year-old daughter Kyoko. In December 1971, in Houston, Texas, they had come close to achieving that goal and Ono's ex, Anthony Cox, had even been jailed for five days for refusing to let her see her child. In March '72 Yoko finally won the case, legally at least, and a Houston court awarded her custody of Kyoko, but Cox grabbed the child and disappeared into the night. The search for them continued, fruitlessly at first. John and Yoko had previously spent thousands chasing Cox halfway across the world, via Spain and Trinidad, but the sincerity of even this maternal quest was to be questioned after the Lennons had dared attend the National Peace Rally.

On 1 May, John and Yoko appeared in New York City court to try and obtain an injunction against the INS proceedings. INS representative Vincent A Schiano told the court that John's UK drugs conviction was 'not likely to be overturned' and though Schiano admitted that there had been a large volume of mail opposing the Lennons' deportation, he also claimed that there was a similar amount of correspondence supporting the action.

Lennon's lawyer Leon Wildes read a letter from Mayor John Lindsay, publicly requesting that the INS proceedings be dropped as the couple in question were 'distinguished artists in the music field and are an asset to us', they were only being treated this way by the INS because they were 'outspoken' on the 'major issues of the day'.

The court made no decision beyond postponing the hearing until 9 May. This postponement was itself postponed to the 17th. By that time Lennon had appeared on the *Dick Cavett's TV Show* and told the stunned audience that he and his lawyer's phones were being tapped and that he was being followed by government agents. Lennon spoke out after hearing clicks, feedback and conversation fragments – the usual evidence of pre-digital phone tapping. "Guys would always be standing on the street opposite. If I got in a car they'd get in cars and follow me, blatantly. They wanted me to know I was being followed."

Photographer Bob Gruen, a close friend of Lennon's, had also noticed. "I was taking pictures of John in a recording studio one day and after I'd left I noticed this car tailing me for miles, right back into town. I was a little freaked and so I called John. He said, 'Oh yeah, they've been following me for weeks'."

But, as Lennon knew, the media sometimes has a little power of its own. "The day after the [Dick Cavett] TV show, there was nobody standing outside my place."

The night before the hearings of 17 May, the FBI's NYC office once again wired their Acting Director – the temporary replacement of the recently deceased J Edgar Hoover – on the subject of 'John Winston Lennon'. The teletype revealed that Schiano had told the FBI he was going to use three key arguments in his battle to evict John and Yoko Lennon from US soil.

Firstly, he was going to allege that the Lennons' 'claim' that Cox had abducted Yoko's child was untrue, that the couple were actually 'party to keeping the child hidden as a tool of delaying deportation hearings'.

The second reason is five and half lines long, it cannot be revealed what that reason is, for even the released FBI document still has those five and a half lines blacked out.

When a single line of text is blacked out that is only to be expected on occasion. The names and addresses of informants must, sometimes, be withheld for their own safety. When line after line goes missing it is usually connected with something much more sinister. Even now, decades on, the truth is hidden from the public whose taxes paid for such surveillance.

The third reason stated is disturbing enough in itself, 'INS will request mental examinations of Lennon at later date.'

Here was proof positive of the attitude behind the infamous John Dean memo of August 1971, wherein President Nixon's legal counsel had gleefully stated that the machinery of government could be used 'screw' political enemies. Here too was the hypocrisy of the Nixon regime laid bare. Having attacked the Soviets for using psychiatry to silence dissent, the US government was now suggesting that 'mental examinations' could help deport a couple, a couple whose only real 'crime' had been criticising America's war in Vietnam.

There is something else interesting about this teletype. It, like many others later, specifically mentions that one of the FBI personnel to receive it is one E S Miller. Miller was Head of the Domestic Intelligence Division and he was later to be one of the first two FBI agents ever convicted of crimes committed while on official FBI duty.

At the end of the hearings of 17 May, Lennon said, "I don't know if there's any mercy to plead for but, if so, I would like it for both us and our child." A definite decision was again postponed but the Lennon's were given leave to stay while this was happening.

On the following Saturday there was a 'Candlelight Vigil & Procession For Peace' in Duffy Square, New York. 'Stop The Blockade Now!' 'Stop Them Bombing Now!' 'U.S. Out Of S.E. Asia Now!' read the flyers. Among those 'legally and peacefully' registering their opposition to 'Nixon's latest and most dangerous escalation' were satirist Jules Feiffer, actors Ben Gazzara, Viveca Lindfors, Eli Wallach, Lee Grant and Peter Boyle, writers Arthur Miller, Kurt Vonnegut Jr., Anais Nin and John Lahr, and, of course, John Lennon and Yoko Ono.

Sci-fi writer Vonnegut read out a statement which concluded, 'at this critical time, we believe it is important to share some time and peace and feeling for peace.' In the small print of the previous day's news stories – the actual headlines were reserved for John and Yoko – lay the reason Nixon had resorted to ever more long range bombing; both the US troops in the field and those at home were starting to rebel. Even the US Servicemen's Fund was announcing a list of anti-war demonstrations at Fort Dix, while New York's 23rd annual Armed Forces Parade had already been cancelled for fear of GI protests.

Before the Lennons went back to their small Bank Street apartment that night they chatted to another celebrity who'd joined the protest – actor Robert Ryan. He was about to start working on *Executive Action*, a new feature film he was appearing in alongside Burt Lancaster, Will Greer and John Anderson. It was being directed by David Miller and was based on Donald Freed and Mark Lane's best-selling book of the same name; a factional piece about the American intelligence services assassinating a popular liberal figure, namely President John F Kennedy.

The following week the FBI's Acting Director contacted his Houston office and boasted of the 'progress' being made in:

… developing excellent coverage (of the) subject's activities, however, aspects of investigation relating to subject's appearance at INS hearings and possible perjury involved in false statements made by subject strictly responsibility of INS.

When it came to proving that the Lennons had lied about Kyoko's whereabouts in Houston:

In view of possible court proceedings, active investigation by FBI in this area could result in FBI agents testifying, which would not be in Bureau's best interest and could result in considerable adverse publicity.

The FBI didn't mind bugging and following the Lennons, going through their trash and trying to prove them liars, they just didn't want the public to know what they were doing, in case of 'adverse publicity'. The Kyoko-in-

Houston line of attack was all to be in vain anyway. The teletype of 25 May, despite having some 16 lines completely blanked out, ends mournfully, 'no further inquiry being made by Houston Division.'

Meanwhile, a thousand miles away in the deep south of Atlanta, Georgia, a lonely 17-year-old continued to nurse his biggest love – an obsession with the music and lyrics of one particular musician. Mark David Chapman had not enjoyed his childhood. His father had been, in Chapman's opinion at least, cold and distant. His parents argued, sometimes violently, while his mother would shelter in Mark's room as he got older. This undoubtedly helped feed young Chapman's narcissistic tendencies – he was the equal, the helper of adults – as well as making him wary of male-female relationships. He was later to admit that he found the sexual act with women unappealing.

Chapman had taken strong LSD at 14 and been arrested the same year. He'd then run away to Miami for two weeks the next spring. After returning home, penniless, he'd enjoyed an intense but brief flirtation with religion. But even though he joined a Christian music group and organised special events for his local church, he continued to occasionally smoke dope and drop acid.

By 1972 the teenager's main – some said his only passions – were drugs and the music of one man. Not John Lennon, but one Todd Rundgren. For it was the latter, an acerbic Philly-born singer-songwriter and producer, who was Chapman's real hero. Rundgren, who'd had no success with his self-produced band Nazz, did clock up a Top 20 solo hit in 1970 with 'We've Gotta Get You A Woman' which appeared on Albert Grossman's Bearsville label.

Chapman had saved up and later bought that hit single, then the *Runt* album it came from, and then the follow-up set ('The Ballad of Todd Rundgren'). Chapman was even said to have the *Straight Up* album Rundgren had produced for Badfinger, the Welsh band who'd once been on The Beatles' Apple label. In '72 Chapman's most treasured possession was Rundgren's double LP *Something/Anything?* Its smorgasbord of musical styles – soul, semi-acoustic, heavy rock and pop – had a special appeal for a young man whose own life seemed to have been similarly scrambled.

CHAPTER THIRTEEN

WATCHING THE DETECTIVES

An address book containing 395 entries was found.

FBI memo, May 1972

Although the now ailing FBI boss Hoover had told Nixon on 12 April 1972 that Lennon was only staying in the US in order to disrupt the forthcoming Republican National Convention, Lennon had actually abandoned such plans by then – he was too busy fighting deportation. Lennon's partial withdrawal from frontline politics was no doubt one intended side effect of the CIA-FBI-INS crusade. It was an intense legal battle Lennon faced and even extreme radicals like Jerry Rubin understood Lennon's less involved position in the anti-war campaign, "there was a child involved, after all".

A coded FBI teletype was sent to the Director from the Bureau's New York field office on 3 May '72. It stated that the British Government had 'advised' that Lennon's 1968 drugs conviction would not be overturned, no matter what, despite the subsequent prosecution of the arresting office Detective Sergeant Pilcher for perverting the course of justice. Normally when a police officer is arrested, charged and convicted for breaking the law, all the previous cases he or she was in charge of are reviewed to see if any innocent person has been wrongly convicted.

After being tipped off about Pilcher's interest, Lennon had emptied the Montagu Square apartment of drugs, a clear-out witnessed by Yoko Ono. Pilcher planted drugs there and was himself later jailed for dishonesty. So why wasn't Lennon's drugs case reviewed?

On 12 May the INS had tried to divide the Lennons by granting Yoko, and Yoko alone, the right to stay longer. She should have had this from the start, as she hadn't been charged after Lennon's '68 London bust, the official reason for keeping her husband out of the US. To Lennon it must have seemed a provocation. Whether he thought so or not, Lennon took to the streets the next day, supporting a New York anti-war march and leading choruses of his 'Give Peace A Chance'.

The day of 18 May saw the sending of an FBI memo from SAC – Special Agent in Charge of – Field Office San Diego to SAC NYC. It speaks of the arrest of an unnamed – well, name deleted – anti-war activist for:

Conspiracy to Injure Government Property and Trespassing for the Purpose of Injuring Government Property during demonstrations against the Vietnam War. An address book containing 395 entries was found in his possession.

Of the following three pages, which end with John and Yoko's address, of these released Freedom of Information documents, virtually three quarters have been blanked out by the FBI on the grounds of 'national security'.

On 23 May an urgent teletype to the FBI's Acting Director still claimed that Lennon intended 'to travel to the Republic and Democratic convention this year.'

Later an unnamed officer of the 3rd Narcotics District, NYC "advised that his department had been unable to make a narcotics case on the Lennons. NYPD continuing."

In spite of all the lurid talk, and FBI memo references, the NYPD's narcotics division had been unable to 'bust' Lennon for a single joint, let alone a stash of serious drugs. If the NYPD were serious about catching law-breakers, perhaps they should have been looking elsewhere. Perhaps in Washington DC.

A week later press copies of Lennon's *Sometime In New York City* album were issued, an abrasive collection of radical comments on the big issues of the day – Lennon later admitted that "the politics got in the way of the poetry". Although tracks like 'Woman Is The Nigger of The World' do break new ground – and rockers like 'New York City' still sound strong – it is, in many ways, just like the newspaper the cover parodies, artistically a snapshot of a man on the run.

Astonishingly, just weeks later Nixon's Attorney General Mitchell did agree to the illegal E Howard Hunt and Gordon Liddy scheme – to break-in and bug the Democrat HQ within Washington DC's Watergate complex. It was to be charged to CREEP – the Committee to Re-Elect The President. Barker was put in charge of the burglary and took along Hunt, Sturgis and two others on the evening of 16 June 1972. But it all went wrong – the Watergate burglars were apprehended and arrested by 'over-efficient' local cops. Initially, however, the media did not emphasize the link between the men and Nixon's White House.

Some two weeks later, with talk of the Watergate burglary just starting to raise a few awkward questions, John Lennon met several 'radical journalists'. He is said to have offered both encouragement and money to aid their attempt to expose the Nixon links with the Watergate burglars. The details of exactly when and where the meeting took place now seem to be lost but it is a known fact that Lennon was intensely interested in the Watergate case and did actually attend at least one of the Washington DC Watergate hearings – on 29 June 1973.

Several months later, as *Washington Post* reporters Woodward and Bernstein fought editorial indifference and got closer to the heart of the Watergate story, their inside source, 'Deep Throat', told them that their lives were now in danger. On 8 December 1972 E Howard Hunt's wife, another woman linked to US intelligence, died after the plane she was on blew up when it was several miles over Chicago airport. Earlier in the year Hunt had refused a request, from Nixon aide Charles Colson, to break into Arthur Bremer's house after Bremer had attempted to assassinate rightist presidential candidate George Wallace of Alabama.

The 21-year-old Bremer had fired five shots from a .38 handgun at Wallace at close range. Within seconds he was overcome and arrested; the subsequent wounding of Wallace prevented him running for the 1972 presidency, thus giving Nixon the entire centre-right, right and far-right vote – guaranteeing him a victory that had been on the cards since RFK's death. In May 1972, at Nixon's express request, the FBI had sealed Bremer's residence, preventing local police from investigating further.

On 8 December 1972, the New York SAC sent an airtel, SUBJECT; JOHN LENNON, to the acting Director, copies of which were to go on to the US Legat in London. It baldly stated that:

In view of subject's inactivity in Revolutionary Activities and his seemingly rejection by NY Radicals, captioned case is being closed in the NY Division.

In event other information comes to New York's attention indicating subject is active with Revolutionary groups, the case will be re-opened at that time and the Bureau advised accordingly.

With Nixon successfully re-elected, the Vietnam War still on and Lennon still busy struggling against deportation, the FBI decided, officially at least, to close the John Lennon file.

The fact that only four CIA John Lennon documents have ever been seen publicly – when it is known there are dozens, perhaps hundreds, more – is not exactly reassuring, however. Nor is the fact that over a dozen of the available FBI pages are mostly or completely blacked out. Others have two or thee line deletions and others still have hard-to-find 'white-out' deletions that are even more difficult to see or track down. At least one other has even its date censored and could have been sent at any point between 1968 and 1981. It is a 'Foreign Government Information' document, one that relates to the country of the former Beatle's birth – Great Britain.

And yet, all in all, it is likely that the FBI *did* relax their surveillance of Lennon a little after Nixon's November 1972 election victory, as the December airtel outlines. Exactly how long that stand-down actually lasted no outsider really knows.

CHAPTER FOURTEEN

THE LOST WEEKEND

*I'm in favour of it all, booze or religion, whatever
gets you through the night.*

Frank Sinatra

On US election night '72, as state after state voted for
Nixon, an increasingly depressed Lennon began to hit the
bottle like a man on a mission. By 9.30 he was openly
flirting with other women in front of Yoko, by midnight
he was groping them. A bad year was coming to a bad
end. The Vietnam War continued in all its bloody
savagery, and John's arch-enemy, war-monger Nixon,
was going to be re-elected. The Lennons still hadn't got
John's green card, nor had they got a hit album – *Some
Time In New York City* had failed to reach the US Top 40
after selling a 'mere' 164,000 copies – and nor, more
crucially, did they have the full-term pregnancy Yoko had
been trying to get for over three years.

New Year 1973 seemed to continue the trend, the
couple quarrelling while Yoko's ground-breaking
Approximately Infinite Universe album failed to reach even
the Top 100. The pressure of fighting eviction from the
US, a battle now well over a year old, was starting to tell
on the couple. Early March, however, saw Lennon having
a little fun unofficially producing Ringo Starr's new
album in LA. George Harrison dropped down later, at
Lennon's invitation, and for a few care-free hours there
was almost a Beatles reunion happening.

The party mood ended abruptly on 23 March 1973,

when Lennon was given a 'full and final' order to leave the United States of America within 60 days, or face arrest and forced deportation. Lennon's wife was given permission to stay indefinitely. She and John then hired the shy Chinese-American beauty May Pang as an in-house assistant. She had finally met John and Yoko when they'd visited the ABKCO offices at the end of 1971. ABKCO represented The Beatles' Apple label in the USA and its President was the ruthless Allen Klein, the same Allen Klein whom Lennon had chosen to negotiate for the group against the wishes of Paul McCartney who'd preferred Lee Eastman, the father of his wife Linda. McCartney may have had a point; at the same time that Klein was effectively managing the affairs of the Beatles and the Stones, he was involved in 51 law suits, he was being investigated by the Securities & Exchange Commission, and he was being pursued by the Inland Revenue Service. The New York Stock Exchange had suspended all the shares in his Cameo Parkway record label and his own Cameo stock-holders were suing him for many thousands of dollars.

Ms Pang had then been a glorified runner and on-the-spot administrator, in the making of several of John'nYoko's films, principally the glorified album promo *Imagine*, the more surreal *Up Your Legs Forever* – wherein 365 celebs, and non-celebs, had their lower limbs filmed from toe to thigh 'for peace' – and Yoko's *Fly* which mainly consisted of an insect crawling over a naked, and quietly stoned, woman.

In late February 1973 the Lennons moved into the gothic Upper West Side Manhattan building known as the Dakota. Actor Robert Ryan, then dying of cancer, had first introduced them to the exclusive apartment block on 72nd Street just a few weeks before.

The Dakota is divided into four sections, A, B, C and

D, each with its own entrance and its own service entrance. The Lennons' new home was in Section A. The Dakota is the building of which the movie star Richard Burton once remarked, "Anyone who moves in there must think there's someone after them" because it's built "like a fortress".

With John's 'final' deportation from the US just weeks away, John Lennon's attorney Leon Wildes managed to win yet another postponement. Although Lennon would sometimes, privately, crack jokes about his legal status in America, the struggle to remain there was affecting him. After the crushing claustrophobia of early Beatlemania and the London drug bust, and the general hostility that he felt Yoko had received there, Britain was not an option. One of the most talented men in the entire rock industry was increasingly feeling like a refugee, a somewhat bewildered refugee. As May Pang was to later tell me, "John took the immigration battle seriously, he just didn't understand why the United States government thought he was so important."

It seems that the author of 'Nowhere Man' still hadn't understood his own lyrics, or importance. He didn't seem to know that the world was, in some ways, his 'to command', potentially at least. This potential was, however, something that the authorities were fully aware of.

At the end of June, John and Yoko made one of their last public political gestures – joining a demonstration at the South Vietnamese Embassy in Washington DC to protest about the Saigon regime's imprisonment of a female Buddhist peace activist. A photo of the Lennons at the South Vietnamese Embassy was copied to the FBI Washington Field Office file on Lennon that summer. If the FBI had definitely closed Lennon's file, as they later were to officially claim, then this was a strange way of showing it.

The next day, whilst still in DC, the Lennons attended

the Watergate Hearings, now in full flow as Nixon and his cronies fought to keep the power they had so blatantly abused.

A 25 September 1973 FBI missive headed 'ELECTRONIC SURVEILLANCE' claims that, after studying records concerning captioned individual Lennon, it had been discovered that he was 'not the subject of a direct electronic surveillance, nor were any of [his] conversations monitored by an electronic device of the FBI.'

Which isn't to say that, even if this were true, local police intelligence units couldn't have carried out similar wire-taps. So could the CIA and so could other pan-State agencies. The letter half acknowledges this by blandly ending, 'It is suggested that other Federal investigative agencies be contacted to determine if they had coverage of the subject(s).'

There is no evidence that the suggestion was acted on, or that any such checks took place. Federal bugging of the Lennons *had* happened – far too many other callers had heard the clicks and conversation replays that were then the hallmarks of phone bugging – but now it was being discussed in public, no one in authority was anxious to find a smoking gun. Especially if it might turn out to be in their own pocket. Such a result would be bad, to say the least, for US intelligence 'unity'.

But John and Yoko's own united public front couldn't last, however. Tired of the misbehaviour of the last year, Yoko was said to be thinking of dating musician David Spinozza as Lennon recorded the uneven *Mind Games* album – an artistic failure by his own high standards despite the melodic and lyrical strength of the title track. After finishing it at New York's Record Plant, Lennon took off with a new lover the same month as the FBI's mealy-mouthed surveillance letter was dispatched.

John's new lover was May Pang, an affair that began,

allegedly, at Yoko's suggestion. If this bizarre story is true, and it may well be, then perhaps it happened that way because Mrs Lennon felt they needed a break and believed too that the man she'd seen screaming and sobbing his way through Janov's sessions could not be trusted to find a kind, 'safe' lover on his own. There were too many hustlers and gold-diggers that would zero in on an ex Beatle, even one who, like Lennon, had most of his monies tied-up in legal limbo.

Pang was barely 22 years old, sweet and, seemingly, over-awed by Yoko. If the latter ever wanted Lennon back it would, apparently, not be too difficult.

For, despite some limited success, it was still Lennon's royalties, or rather the promise of them, that financed both the Dakota and Yoko's recording and art projects. How much practicalities may have influenced what happened is now impossible to judge, but the plain fact is that, according to all those who witnessed these events, both May and Yoko loved Lennon; the former passionately, the latter with some of the distance that could only be expected from someone whose roots lay in the privileged Tokyo of the 1930s. Someone, moreover, who was an artist as well, something that couldn't help but make her consider Lennon a rival as much as a partner through much of their first years together.

According to May, during Lennon's time with her – the 15 months up to February 1975 – he didn't worry about the FBI at all. "He was well aware of his immigration status, but he didn't think he was being followed [then]. John loved being in the studio, but he felt safe virtually everywhere," she insists.

This is undeniably true – with Nixon tied down by the Watergate scandal, and with the FBI and CIA under increasing political and journalistic scrutiny, the plain fact is the Lennon was probably under little or no surveillance during this period. Nor was he stalked by Chapman or anyone else.

"John was very down to earth and he didn't project any energy that might be negative," May said in 2003. "At most, he'd have to sign an autograph, shake a hand or pose for a picture, which he gladly did when he either arrived or left the studio, prior to December 1980, I don't believe any rock star felt really 'at risk'. People were very cool, very friendly to both of us and gave us our space. Nor did I ever feel I was in danger".

But there was some danger for May Pang during her time as Lennon's lover. It came, mostly, from John himself. "During our time together, he was enjoying life and making music," she said decades later and this is indeed true, but it is not the whole truth. Having an affair with a beautiful young woman whom he greatly liked and desired, undoubtedly gave Lennon a great deal of pleasure. The fact that May loved rock'n'roll, even the early stuff, almost as much as the ex Beatle himself, only added to their simpatico, as did the fact that Ms Pang's own Catholic childhood was a little disturbed too – her cold Chinese father had stereotypically despised female children, including May.

Yet the gap between May and John was far wider than the decade that separated their birthdays. Lennon was, by then, old before his time, yet quite immature. As all the post 1967 pictures of Lennon showed – and the same applied to Harrison, Starr and even McCartney – these men in their twenties and early thirties had lived several lifetimes already. Liverpool, Hamburg, London, Paris, Manila, San Francisco, New York, tours, films, TV shows, albums, books, unlimited access to fast cars, fast women, cigarettes, alcohol and then soft drugs and even, occasionally, hard drugs. And all this at high speed. The pressure, the semi-permanent jet-lag, the lack of financial brakes, the natural paranoia – which new 'friends' were really just 'after them' for their money? – had all added incredible turbulence to their lives.

As the one with the most shattered childhood, and as the one who'd experimented with the most drugs, Lennon – the one who'd always been the leader – was of course the most vulnerable. He also had the added pressure of the never–ending fight against deportation and the FBI. This struggle ensured that, aside from occasionally giving funds, Lennon did not have the time or energy to indulge in any kind of politics – an effect that the process was no doubt designed to have.

Taking Yoko's seeming rejection of him as another personal affront, Lennon – infantilised by both his background and the pampered rock star lifestyle – began to drink excessively when under pressure, or when in the wrong company. May Pang wasn't a heavy drinker, and she avoided drugs throughout most of her time with Lennon, but her calming influence could be easily swamped by a Phil Spector or a Harry Nilsson. May successfully kept Lennon away from heroin and also got him to face meeting his son Julian again. She managed, too, to get him to actually enjoy the experience, something that the nervous Lennon had been dreading. "He was very happy re-establishing ties with Julian," she rightly insists – but the nights of recording with Spector soon became problematic.

After one night of endless takes during the *Rock'n'Roll* oldies sessions, and after endless drinking with the gun-toting Spector, Lennon suddenly exploded, wrecking the LA house he and May were staying in with the strength of ten men. Windows, chairs and door frames were all damaged before he trashed several gold records, smashed the remaining furniture and screamed abuse at all and sundry. Spector and his bodyguard finally tied him up and then fled. Lennon broke lose, snapping his bonds and pursuing May into the street. The lovers' idyll had turned into a nightmare with May being "too frightened" to sleep on several occasions.

Recording the *Rock'n'roll* album at the A&M studios with Phil Spector, just got wilder and wilder, however, with Lennon drunkenly trashing Lou Adler's memorabilia collection, while Spector locked people in the studio and shouted groupie insults at Joni Mitchell and her stunned beau Warren Beatty. The recording sessions themselves quickly ground to a complete halt after the Wall-of-Sound king fired live bullets into the ceiling before, reportedly, taking a dump in one of the studio elevators.

Spector then disappeared into the night with the tapes and was unavailable for months. Lennon sobered up – he was always unreservedly contrite and apologetic after any of his booze outrages – and started to plan an album of new material. All would probably have gone smoothly had not the hard-drinking Nilsson showed up, desperate for Lennon to produce his *Pussycats* LP. Drunken nights soon followed with Lennon, a Kotex sanitary towel plastered on his head one night, getting thrown out of clubs and even getting into an angry street fight on the infamous occasion he heckled the Smother Brothers at The Troubadour club. Such nights would usually end with a screaming, threatening row with the bewildered May. Evenings like this were the exception, not the rule, but they must have still been a disturbing experience for a trusting young woman barely in her twenties.

On 1 March 1974 Lennon appeared before the INS again to appeal against the latest US government deportation order, then flew back to May Pang in Hollywood. There Elizabeth Taylor introduced him to her new acquaintance David Bowie. Despite the worst fears of both, the Man Who Fell to Earth and the Former Beatle actually got on well, despite Lennon's gentle mickey-taking (calling Bowie 'Dave' and enquiring about the name of his tailor). Bowie, then still seen as a young rebel – he'd called Jagger 'a mother figure' just a couple of years before – seemed to have some genuine respect for Lennon. Bowie liked May too whilst quickly becoming firm friends with Liz Taylor.

There were soon more drunken high jinks with Nilsson, and Ringo, and a permanently half-naked Keith Moon. These nights were not as wild as the 'Spector evenings' and May even developed a kind of friendship with Moon, one of the few celebrities around LA who didn't ignore her when Lennon was absent. Lennon himself returned to New York on 18 July 1974, in time for the INS to slap another 'final 60-day' quit order on him. He returned to court on 31 August to claim that he'd been denied the right to stay in the US purely on political grounds, because Nixon feared that he would campaign heavily against the President in the run-up to the '72 election. With Nixon having been forced to resign over Watergate just three weeks before, there finally seemed to be a slight chance that Lennon's 'green card quest' might yet succeed.

It was at this time that John Lennon had his one and only meeting with Malcolm McLaren. It was in a late night Manhattan bar and McLaren's association with the New York Dolls, and the Sex Pistols, was months in the future. The Londoner was just in the Big Apple to promote the risqué clothes' range that he and Vivienne Westwood had developed – a blend of zoot suit trousers, rubber jackets and tight cropped t-shirts.

He was with photographer Bob Gruen, who knew Lennon, and so was pleased to introduce the music superstar to a fellow Brit. It could, and should, have been a memorable encounter between the avant garde street fashionista and future Sex Pistols' Svengali and the ex

Beatle. Unfortunately, the latter was being a little too drunk and aggressive. And, before McLaren had barely opened his mouth, Lennon had taken one look at his stylish zoot suit and snapped, "I want that suit!"

That's great, McLaren had breezed happily, "I'll get them to send one over from London. What's your size?"

"No, I want *that* suit now!" Lennon repeated, tugging at the jacket Malcolm was wearing.

"But what would I wear?" McLaren had asked; he didn't want to annoy a future potential customer, especially one that he had a sneaking respect for. But he couldn't spend the rest of the night in the bar clad only in his underwear. *"I want that suit!"* an increasingly lairy Lennon had insisted. The Mexican stand-off between the two men was finally resolved by the suggestion that Bob Gruen go back to McLaren's hotel to fetch him a change of clothes. In the meantime, John would finally get 'his' zoot suit as McLaren waited in the toilet, in his boxer shorts, for Gruen's return. Whether Lennon ever bothered to customise that suit – he was a different size from McLaren – or whether it was drunkenly tossed aside later that same night, nobody seems to know. Another lost item during the so-called 'lost weekend'.

During the rest of that 1974 mayhem Lennon recorded and released an album of new songs. The single from it became his first big solo hit in the US – the piano-pounding, breezy 'Whatever Gets You Through The Night'. The title was taken from one of Sinatra's throwaway lines when he was with Mia Farrow, "I'm all in favour of it, either booze or religion, whatever gets you through the night", and it came complete with choruses and keyboard work from new superstar on the block Elton John. The 45 reached the Number 1 slot in November just as Lennon's new *Walls and Bridges* album managed the same feat. It remains a strong yet mixed album, 'Old Dirt Road' and 'Nobody Loves You (When You're Down And Out)' saw him singing the blues – the latter in a crooner style – while 'Scared' saw him in naked, confessional mode again.

Lennon was pleased with the LP's warm reception – and also a little shocked. "He was very proud of his [solo] success," May Pang asserts, and it was a success she had played a hand in. She was studio veteran by now, a supportive veteran, and it was probably her presence that allowed John to relax enough to let young Julian Lennon – over for a short visit – play drums on one of the tracks. *Walls And Bridges* was his biggest post-Beatles hit, proving that – for all their undoubted talent – he didn't need a Paul McCartney, a Phil Spector or a Yoko Ono when it came to recording a hit.

This minor triumph pleased him and yet didn't overly inflate the Lennon ego. To May the occasional flashes of total self-confidence that he did show were usually humourous and for public consumption only, "He was a humble man and it actually surprised him, having his first Number One single and album."

Fulfilling an old promise, Lennon appeared onstage at an Elton John gig before 20,000 fans at New York's Madison Square Gardens, where he and Elton performed Lennon's current Number 1 plus 'Lucy In The Sky With Diamonds' and 'I Saw Her Standing There'. Lennon and Yoko chatted backstage afterwards – their first face-to-face for many months.

New Year's Day 1975 found Lennon with a hangover ringing in his head as he went to court yet again, but this time to be told by Judge Richard Owen that he should be allowed to interview INS officials and even to inspect their files on him in order to see whether political considerations had played any part in their persecution of him.

A fortnight later Lennon accepted Bowie's invitation

to join the sessions for the *Young Americans* album. Lennon was mainly there as an observer but he contributed to an interesting cover of The Beatles' 'Across The Universe' before, with Bowie and guitarist Carlos Alomar cooking up a 'clunky yet funky' guitar riff – "Worra great riff, wow, worra great riff that is," Lennon eulogised, before suggesting the title 'Fame'. The latter became one of Bowie's finest tracks, with the Thin White Duke's lyrics dissecting a subject Lennon knew all too well; the problems and pressures of fame.

In February Morris Levy released *Roots*, a TV-advertised mail order album that was basically rough mixes of the *Rock'n'Roll* set. That Lennon actually had no legal recording contract with the American song publisher was just one of many complications. The source of Morris' master tape was swiftly found to be Lennon himself. He had naively given his new 'pal' Levy a mix tape when they'd had friendly discussions about the minor dispute between them. It dated back to a line from the Beatles' 'Come Together', which had been borrowed from an old Chuck Berry composition that Levy had published. To end the row, John had agreed to cover three old rock'n'roll numbers on the eponymous album.

EMI-Capitol then promptly rush-released *Rock'n'Roll*, with a wonderful black and white cover that Lennon had picked, a 15-year-old photo of him – a be-quiffed rocker – standing in a Hamburg doorway. To add to the nostalgia, the album had the tag-line, 'You Shoulda Been There'. Musically it was a fair collection of covers with its stand-out points probably being a heartfelt 'Stand By Me' and a blisteringly tight version of 'Slippin' And Slidin'. On hearing news of the album's release, Levy immediately sued for a staggering $42 million dollars. It was all settled eventually, and almost amicably, but it was another reason why Lennon was now getting through a pack or two of cigarettes virtually every day. At this point Yoko contacted him about a new anti-smoking cure she felt he should try. It had worked for her she said. Lennon went to visit his estranged wife at the Dakota for an hour. The hour turned into two days and within weeks he had left the heart-broken May to be reunited with his wife. And soon after, following the adoption of a diet suggested by a Chinese acupuncturist, Yoko was pregnant. After all John's guilt about abandoning Cynthia and little Julian, here was a second chance to be a 'proper father', a second chance to 'start over'.

A few weeks later one of the Lennons' New York friends, TV presenter, Geraldo Rivera shocked America with 26 seconds of 8 millimetre film screened on his NBC *Good Night America* show. The Zapruder home movie footage was of the JFK assassination, the only clear film that the FBI or Warren Commission would admit existed of the killing. Outside of the FBI and Warren Commissioners, only amateur cameraman Abe Zapruder and CBS TV reporter Dan Rather had seen the footage. Rather had described it as showing JFK being knocked *forward* as he is killed. Selected frames printed in *Life* magazine appeared to support this – *Life* had bought the film rights from Zapruder – all of which seemed to confirm the 'lone nut theory', that Lee Harvey Oswald had killed Kennedy alone, firing three shots from behind the President, shots that had knocked JFK forward.

But *Life* was published by Henry Luce, whose wife Clare Booth Luce was an anti-Castro fanatic who had little time for Kennedy. And both *Life* and Rather had *not* told the whole truth. After photo-analyst Bob Groden had given a Zapruder film copy to Dick Gregory, the entertainer and civil rights activist who was another Lennon pal, the latter had persuaded Rivera to screen it live on network TV.

And so, for the first time, the America public got to

see the footage that the federal authorities had been hiding for over a decade – colour film which clearly showed JFK's fatal wound coming from the *front* as it knocked his head *back*. *Life* magazine had cheated the film frame sequence and Oswald had obviously not acted alone. America's intelligence services had been lying for years – there *had* been a conspiracy, after all.

In March 1975, one committed right-wing Christian, 20-year-old Mark David Chapman, used a YMCA international scheme to apply for a visa to visit the Soviet Union. It seemed a strange choice. Why go somewhere that you do not like or approve of? When this Russian visit fell through – though Chapman did now speak Russian it wasn't, it was felt, to a sufficiently high standard – he had then picked the potential trouble-spot Beirut, which had seen shootings and massacres for months. Chapman *could* have chosen to go Jerusalem, Bethlehem or Nazareth, ancient Holy Land places of great interest to anyone with a spiritual bent, let alone a self-proclaimed Christian. Yet he chose Lebanon's capital Beirut and he was at that city's YMCA in June 1975 during the first few bloody weeks of the Lebanese civil war. Later, after he and the other YMCA visitors were pulled out, Chapman played his friends audio tapes he'd made of the gunfire. He also wrote a letter to the YMCA's South De Kalb Board of Management. In the letter he admitted to being thrilled by his little excursion.

None of this is logical if Chapman is merely an innocent traveller. A Christian tries to visit the Soviet Union, then goes to the Middle East but avoids the Holy Land? And all in preference for a trouble spot that had became a war-zone? He wasn't doing any charity or medical work in the Lebanese capital. So why go there?

There are two other points about all this. In Philip Agee's book *Inside The Company: CIA Diary*, the ex CIA agent admitted that the YMCA was then often used as a front for CIA activities. The second point about Chapman's Lebanon visit is equally chilling – its capital Beirut was a major base for CIA and US Naval Intelligence right up until the 1980s. Beirut was also for years said to have been the home of one of the CIA's top secret assassination training camps.

On 23 April 1975 the South Vietnamese regime finally crumbled, as desperate Southern officials tried to hold on to the US helicopters taking off from Saigon's rooftops. Within hours the Americans were gone and the Vietnam War was finally over. Most Western reporters fled as well, fearing that the North Vietnamese, and the few surviving VC, would instigate a massacre. Their fears turned out to be groundless. Despite some harassment of 'collaborators' there was no huge bloodbath as the two Vietnams finally become one.

Five days later Lennon gave his last major TV interview, with lawyer Leon Wildes and host Tom Snyder on NBC. On 9 June '75 Lennon filed suits against both Richard Kleindienst and Nixon's former Attorney General John Mitchell – his suits claiming that both men deliberately blocked Lennon's US visa application for purely political reasons.

With the Zapruder assassination film out in the open, and following the Watergate and Vietnamese 'defeats', pressure grew for an inquiry into America's intelligence services. The Frank Church Committee and House Select Committee on Assassinations freed thousands of documents revealing numerous FBI and CIA crimes, lies and distortions. Acoustic experts conducting tests on Dallas sound tapes of 22 November 1963 concluded on behalf of the HSCA that at least four shots were fired. Even when the HSCA was 'neutered' by new chairman Robert Blakey its official conclusion was still front page news –

there *was* a conspiracy to kill John F Kennedy. But Blakey's committee refused to point a definite finger of blame at anyone, beyond vague murmurings about the Mafia.

After Oliver Stone's 1992 movie *JFK* showed the Zapruder film again, amidst much new 'factional' detail, there was a further demand for information. The government's subsequent JFK Act allowed thousands of pages more to become public, including some that showed that the Fifties and early Sixties' income tax records of Lee Harvey Oswald, and one of his relatives, were classified as 'state secrets' of the highest order.

There were also two other individuals whose Fifties and early Sixties' income tax records were considered so important that they too were now state secrets of the highest order. In fact, these individuals were – *are* – so important to the US state that, almost 40 years later, the public is not allowed to know *even their initials* let alone their full names. Researchers who had previously been sceptical about conspiracies in general, and the Oswald lookalike theory in particular, were forced to think again. Who were these unnamed two? And why did their secret tax records *exactly* shadow, day by day, the tax records of the Oswalds?

The year 1975 ended on a high for the Lennons – as Bowie got his first US Number 1, with the Lennon co-composition 'Fame', the INS were finally forced to give some ground as a federal court, on behalf of the New York State Senate, cancelled the original John Lennon deportation order and insisted that the INS reconsider Lennon's request for full resident status. The elusive green card had moved a few inches closer.

Lennon was still smiling two days later when, on his own birthday 9 October, Yoko gave birth to Sean Taro Ono Lennon. The couple's joy was mingled with fear over Yoko's health following the traumatic Caesarian birth but, after two weeks, she and the child were thought well enough to be allowed home to the Dakota Building.

At the same time, Mark David Chapman finished several months of working with Vietnamese refugees at the camp in Fort Chaffee, Arkansas. He had been flown there a few weeks after returning from his three week trip to Beirut.

But then for John Lennon, the New Year started bleakly – his old friend, and much-loved Beatles aide, Mal Evans was shot and killed by LA police officers after allegedly threatening his girlfriend with a gun. On hearing the news Lennon wept.

Three months later another Lennon friend was the target, as fellow rock star David Bowie was involved in a major police drugs bust in New York State. Unfortunately for the Westchester police, all they could find amongst the possessions of Bowie and his entourage was a small amount of marijuana. But Bowie and two of his friends were still arrested and charged. He was then bailed for thousands of dollars and had to appear before the same court in March 1977, but by then the Nixon-Ford years were finally over and Democrat Jimmy Carter was in the White House. The Bowie prosecution was quietly dropped.

On 27 July 1976, as *Melody Maker* hailed the new English punk bands whom writer Caroline Coon claimed would 'inspire' a third generation of rockers, Lennon's five-year legal battle reached its conclusion.

The hearing was at New York's Immigration Bureau. After opening statements, Lennon, supported by the likes of writer Norman Mailer, actress Gloria Swanson and TV personality Geraldo Rivera, took the stand and was asked a series of questions by Wildes.

Leon Wildes: Have you ever been convicted of any crime, anywhere in the USA?

John Lennon: No.

LW: Have you ever been a member of the Communist Party or any other organisation that may seek to overthrow the US government by force?

JL: No.

LW: Do you intend to make the US your home?

JL: I do.

Minutes later Norman Mailer took the oath.

"I think John Lennon is a great artist who has made an enormous contribution to popular culture," said the man then regarded as America's finest living novelist. "He is one of the great artists of the Western World. We lost T.S. Eliot to England and only got Auden back."

After the Bishop of New York called Lennon "a gentleman of integrity," Gloria Swanson spoke up as well, praising the ex-Beatle for his 'anti-junk food' attitude – she'd met him in a health food store chasing after macrobiotic fare – a positive notion which she thought he could help spread to a wider public.

After 90 minutes Lennon was at last told he would be given his own green card, except that, like most 'green' cards back then, this one was actually blue. Judge Ira Fieldsteel announced the verdict and the Lennons smiled as the rest of the court-room spontaneously burst into applause. Now the Dakota's most famous resident could come and go – and remain within – the US indefinitely.

"It's great to be legal again!" a smiling Lennon told TV reporters afterwards. "The Immigration Service have finally seen the light of day. It's been a long and slow road but I'm not bitter. On the contrary, now I can go and visit my relatives in Japan and elsewhere." Will you now go on and become a full US citizen, one journalist asked. "I wanna enjoy the advantages of holding a green card before I make up me mind on that point. The main thing is I can travel now. Until today my attorney wouldn't even let me go to Hawaii for a vacation in case I couldn't get back in. Whenever I flew to Los Angeles I was paranoid in case the plane was diverted to Toronto on the way."

When asked why he'd chosen to live in New York anyway, Lennon swiftly replied, "If I had lived two thousand years ago I would have wanted to live in Rome. New York is the Rome of today, now I'm going home to crack open a tea-bag and start looking at some travelogues!"

He could also have said, as he did both before and after, that he loved the exhilarating buzz of New York – Greenwich Village and SoHo and the sights that Yoko had first discovered as a teenager, a city where the people in the street didn't ever hassle you, although it was in New York that Lennon first started to dream about a stranger who asked for an album to be autographed then returned later, angry and with a loaded gun.

The very last question Wildes had asked Lennon that day was to the point: "Do you wish to continue your work here?" To which Lennon had replied, "Yes, I wish to continue to live here with my family and to continue making music."

But this wasn't quite the case. For the next three and a half years there would be precious little music made by either Lennon or Yoko and none for scheduled release. Nor would his relatives 'elsewhere' – Aunt Mimi and the others back in Britain – ever receive another visit. Lennon would not live to see England again.

In January 1977 Chapman arrived in Hawaii. Some later claimed he'd gone there to commit suicide, others that he just wanted to get away from his family and friends – and still others said he was feeling just fine at that point.

The Hawaiian islands were then, and to a large extent still are now, a tropical paradise, with extinct volcanoes providing the perfect backdrop for endless sun-kissed beaches fringed with palms. The islands bristle with golf courses, exclusive clubs and four and five star hotels.

They are also home to a US Naval Intelligence complex and at least seven US Naval and Army bases.

And Hawaii, like Chapman's other old stomping ground Beirut, is also – according to, amongst others, Daniel Sheehan of the Christic Institute – the site of a top secret assassination training camp, owned and used by US intelligence.

After arriving at Honolulu airport Chapman checked in to the expensive Moana Hotel, money again seemingly no object. After a few weeks he returned to Georgia, then flew back and stayed in the local Honolulu YMCA.

A year of dead end jobs led to Chapman's alleged suicide attempt. Whether it was a genuine effort or not, he had soon checked into the psychiatric wing of Castle Memorial Hospital. Soon Chapman, his suicide 'attempt' all but forgotten, was observing mentally ill patients as he began work for the Castle Doctors. This incredible transition, from psychiatric patient to psychiatric staffer within weeks, is one of the fastest turnarounds in medical history. The fact that no officials remarked on this at the time, and virtually none have since, is remarkable in itself.

In July 1978, after arranging a complex itinerary with his travel agent, a pretty Japanese-American girl called Gloria, Chapman takes off on a world tour. It is an amazing trip for a college drop-out without money, encompassing as it does the most expensive cities on earth – Tokyo in Japan, London in England and Geneva in Switzerland.

Then there are the weeks he spent in India and Nepal, plus Bangkok in Thailand – even then a favourite holiday destination for sex tourists of all appetites – plus Hong Kong, Korea and two Communist destinations.

Vietnam and China had just started to allow a few Western tourists in at that point and so Chapman became one of the very first to see both Red China and unified Vietnam. Perhaps it made up for his failed attempt to get into Soviet Russia in 1975? He then flew on to Iran.

These were just some of the countries Chapman visited while he snapped away with his camera – taking over 1,200 Kodachrome colour slides, another hobby that, at that level of use, then cost many thousands of dollars. On the way back to Hawaii, Chapman changed planes and flew to Atlanta so he could call in on his old police friend Dana Reeves.

When Chapman finally got back to Honolulu on 20 August, travel agent Gloria Abe was waiting for him at the airport. They would be wed within the year.

CHAPTER FIFTEEN

WATCHING THE WHEELS – 1979

When I did 'Woman is the Nigger of the World' I was a feminist in theory, only later did I really become one.

John Lennon

A Love Letter From John And Yoko To People Who Ask Us What, When, And Why:

The past ten years we noticed everything we wished came true in its own time, good or bad, one way or the other. We kept telling each other that one of these days we would have to get organised and wish for only good things. Then our baby arrived! We were overjoyed and at the same time felt very responsible. Now our wishes would also effect him. We felt it was time for us to stop discussing and do something about our wishing process: The Spring Cleaning of our minds! It was a lot of work. We kept finding things in those old closets in our minds that we hadn't realised were still there, things we wished we hadn't found.

As we did our cleaning we also started to notice many wrong things in our house: there was a shelf which should never have been there in the first place, a painting we grew to dislike, and there were the dingy rooms, which became light and breezy when we broke the walls between them. We started to love the plants, which one of us originally thought were robbing the air from us! We began to enjoy the drum beat of the city which used to annoy us. We made a lot of mistakes and still do. In the past we spent a lot of energy trying to get something we thought we wanted, we wondered why we didn't get it, only to find out that one or both of us didn't really want it.

One day we received a sudden rain of chocolates from people round the world. "Hey, what's this! We're not eating sugar stuff, are we?"

"Who's wishing it?" we both laughed.

We discovered that when two of us wished in unison, it happened faster. As the Good Book says – Where two are gathered together: It's true. Two is plenty. A Newclear Seed.

More and more we are starting to wish and pray. The things we have tried to achieve in the past by flashing a V sign, we try now through wishing. We are not doing this because it's simpler. Wishing is more effective than waving flags. It words. It's like magic. Magic is simple. Magic is real. The secret of it is to know that it is simple, and not kill it with an elaborate ritual which is a sign of insecurity. When somebody is angry with us, we draw a halo around his or her head in our minds. Does this person stop being angry then? Well, we don't know! We know, though, that when we draw a halo around a person, suddenly the person starts to look like an angel to us. This helps us to feel warm towards the person, reminds us that everyone has goodness inside, and that all people who come to us are angels in disguise, carrying messages and gifts to us from the Universe. Magic is logical. Try it sometime.

We still have a long way to go. It seems the more we get into cleaning, the faster the wishing and receiving process gets. The house is getting very comfortable now. Sean is beautiful. The plants are growing. The cats are purring. The town is shining, sun, rain or snow. We live in a beautiful universe. We are thankful every day for the plentifulness of our life. This is not a euphemism. We understand that, we, the city, the country, the earth are facing very hard times and there is a panic in the air. Still the sun is shining and we are here together, and there is love between us, our city, the country, the earth. If two people like us can do what we are doing with our lives, any miracle is possible! It's true we can do with a few big miracles right now. The thing is to recognise them when they *come to you and be thankful. First they come in a small way, in everyday life, then they come in rivers, and in oceans. It's goin' to be alright! The future of the earth is up to all of us.*

Many people are sending us vibes every day in letters, telegrams, taps on the gate, or just flowers and nice thoughts. We thank them all and appreciate them for respecting our quiet space, which we need. Thank you for all the love you send us. We feel it every day. We love you too. We know you are concerned about us. That is nice. That's why you want to know what we are doing. That's why everybody is asking us What, When and Why. We understand. Well, this is what we're doing. We hope that you have the same quiet space in your mind to make your own wishes come true.

If you think of us next time, remember, our silence is a silence of love and not of indifference. Remember, we are writing in the sky instead of on paper – that's our song. Lift your eyes and look up in the sky. There's our message. Lift your eyes again and look around you, and you will see that you are walking in the sky, which extends to the ground. We are all part of the sky, more so than of the ground. Remember, we love you.

John Lennon and Yoko Ono
May 27th 1979
New York City

Although at times banal to the critical eye, the Lennons' May '79 advert-stroke-letter to the *New York Times* does have a certain spaced-out charm all its own – a missive that's a blend of proto-type New Age mysticism and rock rebel royalty tips, affectionately passed on in maturity to those who might not know. Superficially at least, it comes across as a gentle letter of resignation both from music and any kind of political involvement. The line 'when you think of us' almost begs to be followed by the words, 'please remember the good times.' But there's happiness there too – a genuine celebration of little Sean. In terms of perfect domestic bliss he may have arrived six or seven years behind schedule, yet it's always better late than never with a child – and there seems a real joy about the couple's words after he's mentioned.

The talk of magic and prayer was also appropriate. The man who'd sung about there being 'no heaven' was now a firm believer in an after-life. "You do go on," he'd said to several friends and acquaintances. "It's just like changing your suit or your car, it's a change but you *do* go on." He seemed quite certain about it.

For the three years following the 1976 court victory Lennon had stayed in. He wasn't quite the hermit of legend – he still sometimes strolled to the coffee shop round the corner and there were also quick visits to Japan, Spain and – some claimed – South Africa. But though he doodled with songs there were no serious, full-on recording sessions. He even let his recording contracts lapse. For the first time in 18 years he had no record label.

"I think he'd genuinely got to a point in his life when he was happy," says Roy Carr, an occasional New York visitor in the days before 1980. "He wasn't out partying. You used to have to phone there and leave a message for 'Johnny Rhythm'. And then an hour or two later he'd usually call you back at your hotel and say, 'C'mon, come on over', and he'd be sitting there, asking if you'd seen any good Beatles gear, watching the news or The Beatles cartoons – he loved those cartoons. Having got out and survived it, I think he'd got it all in perspective by then. He could look back and see that there had been plenty of good times."

A serious Beatles re-union still seemed to be a no-no though. "What would we do, play 'Twist and Shout'?" Lennon said dismissively, "The Beatles were only really the Beatles in Liverpool and Hamburg anyway. After that it was just showbiz."

To all intents and purposes Lennon had retired, John happy to play the house husband while Yoko did deals on real estate and re-releases.

On 4 November 1979 the post-Shah Iran finally erupted against the symbol of the country that had most blatantly supported him and his hated secret police. The US Embassy was stormed by militant students and dozens of US officials were taken hostage. The officials' last few hours' work – shredding thousands of State Department and CIA documents – was later undone as the young Teheran radicals swiftly set up special 'de-shredding' centres where, on the floors of gyms and basketball pitches, most of the papers were painstakingly re-assembled, pieced together over a period of weeks by carpet weavers.

The exiled Shah had flown to New York for medical treatment just ten days before – the loss of 'his' country no doubt aggravating his cancer condition.

But 1979 was a bad year all round for dictators. The genocidal Stalinist regime of Pol Pot, although still discreetly backed by the US and subsequently recognised by the UN, collapsed in Cambodia. The final straw for his Khymer Rouge regime had been when Vietnam – angered by years of border incidents – ordered a full scale incursion (the successful invasion revealed the full horror of Pot's 'killing fields' for the first time – over a million civilians have been murdered there, their skulls heaped up into two storey high pyramids).

Nicaragua's hated 'el jefe' Somoza had killed thousands of opposition activists but he and his National Guard thugs were eventually forced from power that same year by the leftist Sandinistas – the latter started a new government that contained businessmen, poets and priests, but elements within the US media and Congress still immediately condemned the new regime as 'Communistic'.

Central African Islamic dictator Jean-Bedel Bokassa – infamous for the armed 'woman hunts' he went on with French officials – and Uganda's cannibal President Idi Amin, were both ejected from power in popular revolutions.

In post-Franco Spain Adolfo Suarez became the nation's first elected prime minister for 43 years and civilian rule was restored to Nigeria.

But it wasn't all one way – before the year was out, the colonels in El Salvador had killed 60 civilian demonstrators and launched another coup. Meanwhile, thousands of miles away, the Russians responded to the growing, CIA-sponsored chaos in neighbouring Afghanistan by sending in an invasion force. In Washington a leading member of President Carter's cabinet, Zbigniew Brzezinski, is said to have cheered at the news, glad that the Soviets had taken the bait, "Now we can give 'em [the Russians] their own Vietnam!"

CHAPTER SIXTEEN

WALKING ON THIN ICE

It's up to all of us to make what we can of the Eighties.

John Lennon

On 29 September 1980, *Newsweek* broke the story that had been an open secret in the US music industry for almost a week – John Lennon's comeback was official. A new album, *Double Fantasy*, was mentioned, as was the forthcoming single, '(Just Like) Starting Over'. These recordings, credited to both John and Yoko, were mostly started in Bermuda in June 1980. Others were based on sketches begun years before, though this doesn't necessarily mean, however, that the Lennons' talk of a totally fresh album was hyperbole: the completion of the songs, the end production, the ultimate arrangements and the final flourishes were all new, as were, of course, the mixes (and mixing and production are, since *Sergeant Pepper*, a key part of most audio releases).

Sneak previews of the recordings were, like the finished reviews later, mixed. But the album did contain work as good as anything Lennon had ever recorded. Apart from the jaunty, Fifties parody 'Starting Over' and funky 'Clean-Up Time', other highlights included the moody 'I'm Losing You', the touching 'Woman' and the superb, uncluttered 'Watching The Wheels' – the latter perhaps being the perfect pop single, even though it broke some of the rules that Lennon himself had helped to write (the first chorus doesn't come in until the song's halfway through).

Ono's contribution is more problematic for most critics, though 'Beautiful Boys', her ode to her son and

193

husband, shows her ability – rarely used it must be said – to marry both Western and Japanese musical traditions to great effect. It is a true family album, an authentic marriage of different genres, cultures, styles, poems, egos.

Lennon's own song dedicated to four-year-old Sean, the similarly titled 'Beautiful Boy' is superbly produced, with its discreet 'vocoded' backing vocals on the chorus and Lennon's paternal whispers. The line about there being nothing to fear as the 'monster' was gone, is 'on the run', is almost certainly a reference that Sean could never have understood at the time, a reference to the man who'd tried hard to divide and deport the Lennons, Richard Nixon. The song ends happily on the beach, complete with atmospherics, and is intensely poignant. Within a month of its release it was to become even more so.

According to his post-December 9th recollections, Mark David Chapman decided that Barbara Graustark's *Newsweek* story of 29 September revealed Lennon as 'phoney'. The disillusioned 'life-long fan' then, he later claims, plays all his old Beatles and Lennon records. To Chapman, they showed Lennon's 'hypocrisy' at its most obvious. The fanatically 'devout' fan suddenly becomes Lennon's enemy – though murder had not yet entered his mind, he says.

All of which would be fine, except for several key points. Graustark's story was not even remotely hostile to the Lennons. And besides all that, Chapman had never, ever been a real Beatles or Lennon fan.

To the Reverend Newton Hendrix, who'd been in the high school choir with him, Chapman never expressed any comment at all about the band or Lennon. Nor did Hendrix ever hear Chapman sing, "Imagine if John Lennon was dead!", the perverted rewrite of 'Imagine' that Chapman was alleged to have sung over and over again at Hendrix's prayer group meetings.

Nor were any of Chapman's few original songs done in a style that even vaguely resembled anything done by The Beatles or Lennon.

Captain Louis Souza of the Honolulu police spent the period between mid-December 1980 and mid-January 1981 thoroughly investigating Chapman and his background. He was later to tell barrister and journalist Fenton Bresler that Chapman was *not* a Lennon fan. As far as Souza and his officers could discover, Chapman hadn't put forward any opinions whatsoever about Lennon. In fact, as discussed earlier, the only musician that Chapman had ever really expressed any admiration for, from way back in 1972, was Todd Rundgren, whose work had sometimes moved him to tears.

Chapman's Beatles and Lennon 'collection' is never photographed or catalogued and the 14 hours of cassette tapes that some reports later claim Chapman had with him are never produced, for the simple reason that they do not exist.

When, between 20 and 22 October 1980, Chapman wants to listen to Lennon records, he has, by his own admission, to go the Honolulu Public Library to hear them!

When, within 24 hours of this, he wants to hear some Beatles' tracks, he has to dig out some of his wife's Beatles' albums since, again, Chapman has none of his own. Admittedly, the Chapman family had once owned a copy of *Meet The Beatles* but then so had over 5 million other American families. And all this was over 15 years before, back in the fall of 1964, when Chapman was barely nine years old. And it was the only, feeble, connection with what was supposed to be the biggest thing in his life.

This point just *cannot* be over-stressed, despite all the subsequent press hype, the plain fact is that Mark David Chapman, the supposed 'John Lennon obsessive', the 'fan of fans', did not own a single one of Lennon's records until he bought a copy of *Double Fantasy* during the last weekend of Lennon's life in December 1980. Before then he did not own one Lennon single, book or album. Not *one*. Some fan. Some obsession.

On 2 October 1980, at Washington DC's L'Enfant Plaza Hotel, an Iranian said to be an intermediary for the new Teheran regime met three officials from the campaign team of Republican Ronald Reagan, presidential candidate. This is no press conference – the meeting is top secret. Two weeks later Reagan's men meet more Iranians, this time in Paris. Although Reagan is leading Democrat President Carter in virtually all the opinion polls, the men behind the right wing Reagan are taking no chances. They know that one of the key reasons for Carter's unpopularity is his inability to get the American hostages in Iran home.

The Reagan men need this 'hostage-crisis' situation to continue until Reagan's presidential inauguration. So they then, it is alleged, offer the Iranians a deal – over $3 million cash (approx $20 million today) and the promise of resumed US arms sales to Iran after Reagan's electoral victory. But if, and *only* if, Teheran delays the release of the American hostages until January 1981. The Iranians say the offer is acceptable.

There appear to be no surviving records of either of these meetings, but both Carter's CIA Director Admiral Stansfield Turner, and Carter's White House press secretary, Jody Powell, are just two of many who are absolutely convinced that they took place.

On 23 October 1980 Chapman signs out of his security guard job for the last time, signing out as 'John Lennon', then hurriedly crossing the words out. He then sends a postcard to an Italian friend mentioning a 'mission' he has to undertake in New York. The return address on the postcard is Lennon's Dakota home.

On the 29th Chapman flies from Honolulu to New

York, carrying with him a .38 handgun. He stands outside the Dakota for much of the next day and for the following five but the staff continue to tell him Lennon is away.

On 4 November, with the US hostages still stuck in Iran, Ronald Reagan defeats the incumbent President Carter. The day after Reagan's electoral victory Chapman, having discovered he cannot buy bullets in NYC without a permit, flies off to Georgia where his longtime associate Dana Reeves, an Atlanta police officer, has no qualms about supplying him with five deadly hollow point 'dum-dum' bullets. Mutual acquaintances have since described Reeves as being a 'bad influence' on Chapman and the latter seems to have been intimidated by him; a single glance from Reeves apparently being enough to make him 'freeze in his tracks'.

On 9 November Chapman takes yet another plane – money again seemingly no object for the unemployed former security guard – and arrives back in New York. He returns to his Dakota vigil for three days, then, after allegedly wrestling with his mysterious 'kill Lennon compulsion', he phones his wife before flying back to Hawaii on the 12th.

On 28 November John Lennon, as part of the legal effort to stop the stage show *Beatlemania*, signs an affidavit stating that the four former Beatles *have* agreed to reunite for a concert during the next five years.

December 1980 started with a pleasant surprise for some Japanese-American workers involved in a strike against their food-importing employers on the West Coast, where the bosses were insisting on paying them less than their white American co-workers. A supporting telegram arrived from New York.

We are with you in spirit. Both of us are subjected to prejudice and abuse as an Oriental family in the Western world. Boycott it must be, if it is the only way to bring justice and restore the

dignity of the constitution for the sake of all citizens of the US
and their children.

Peace and love,
John Lennon and Yoko Ono,
New York City, December 1980

But, to the workers' astonishment, they discover that the Lennons aren't just going to support their boycott of the companies in question, they are coming over – John, Yoko and little Sean – in mid-December to San Francisco. The Lennons are actually going to march alongside the strikers and their families.

There were now even rumours that the former Beatle would attend an anti-nukes demo in the New Year. John Lennon wasn't just back on the music scene, he was starting to re-enter street politics again – and damn the fact that Reagan was now President-elect.

Reagan's electoral victory had been a major slap in the face to most American liberals – and to the vast majority of Europeans. Reagan's main political mentor had been his father-in-law, who'd constantly raged about the pernicious influence of 'niggers' and 'kikes', and similar attitudes lurked amongst some of his kitchen cabinet. Reasonable people asked how could Reagan, the man who'd supported McCarthy over the red witch-hunts in the Fifties, Goldwater over the Vietnam War in the Sixties and Nixon over Watergate in the Seventies, how could that man now be President-elect of the United States of America?

Reagan's victory was partly, of course, down to Carter's failure to get the US hostages out of Iran. Although Carter, to be fair, had tried almost everything, including a military helicopter getaway that had gone wrong in very bizarre circumstances – chopper after chopper crashing into each other as if sabotaged, leaving over a dozen US personnel dead.

Whoever was to blame it still left Reagan – the man

who'd once compared JFK with Hitler, the man who'd held a cocktail party the weekend of Kennedy's funeral – as leader of the free world. A man in his seventies, many of whose supporters believed in 'the rapture' – wherein born-again Christians would be suddenly 'raptured'; taken out of this sinful 'half-Communistic' world and placed in the next world. Others, higher up the Republican right's hierarchy, now believed in the once-dead concept of a 'hot' Cold War, of a winnable nuclear war. It was a frightening new government for many and even some of the Republicans' natural allies – Europe's Conservatives and Christian Democrats – felt more than a little uneasy.

With Reagan's election now in the bag, both the CIA's hawks, and the Latin American police states they supported, decided they were virtually untouchable. On 27 November 1980, Salvadoran security officials stood aside and deliberately allowed right-wing gunmen to kidnap 20 members of Salvador's FDR democratic opposition who'd been holding a press conference in a Jesuit high school. The mutilated bodies of six of the FDR men are dumped on the outskirts of San Salvador the next day. One of the dead victims is actually that of FDR leader Enrique Alvarez Cordova.

On 2 December, after leaving San Salvador airport, four US churchwomen 'disappear'. The American nuns had long been regarded with suspicion by Salvadoran security officials, who saw them as potential witnesses to state crimes.

The same day Mark Chapman boards yet another jet plane. This time with both his .38 handgun and the deadly hollow point ammunition, and this time he leaves Honolulu to fly to Chicago. Although he has a grandmother in Chicago it's extremely unlikely that the armed Chapman really spends three days and nights alone with her.

The suspicion that he was *not* with her, but involved in something far more sinister, is heightened by the fact – revealed by lawyer Fenton Bresler – that the air-ticket later found in Chapman's New York hotel room had been doctored to make it *look* as if he flown straight to New York from Hawaii on 5 December, a falsification of the ticket that omits the Chicago stop-over. Someone, for some reason, does not want Chapman's Chicago visit to be investigated.

On 4 December 1980 the mutilated bodies of the missing US churchwomen are found in a shallow unmarked grave near San Salvador's airport highway. To the American public's horror, it is revealed that Ita Ford, Dorothy Kazel, Maura Clarke and Jean Donovan had all been raped and tortured before being slowly killed. Salvadoran security officials made no attempt to hide their contempt both for the dead nuns, for other death squad victims, and for the US press. Before the month was out, Salvadoran Treasury Police would be linked to the permanent 'disappearance' of another American citizen, reporter John Sullivan.

Outgoing President Carter suspends economic and military aid to El Salvador as his Ambassador Robert E White stands by the women's graveside and thunders a warning to the murderers, "This time they won't get away with it!"

But he was wrong, those who ordered the women's death squad killing were never brought to justice and within weeks aid is restored to the bloody Salvadoran regime – and days later it is the outspoken Ambassador White who is dismissed by the new US President, former actor President Reagan.

During 1981 the US sent the Salvadoran government $30 million as that regime presided over the deaths of another 10,000 of its own civilians, including women and children, most of them murdered by the Salvadoran military or its death squads. Nineteen eighty-one was also the year when musician, and former actor, John Ono Lennon would finally become eligible for full US citizenship, a citizenship which also included the right to run for public office, to become a city mayor or even a state governor.

After at least one night in the YMCA on 63rd Street, Mark David Chapman moved into the expensive Sheraton Hotel on 7 December. He hires an upmarket call girl for the night, but despite spending 100 dollars on getting her to his room, he does not have sex with her. The unemployed Chapman later explains his seemingly endless supply of money for such extravagances by saying that he had sold his Dali and Norman Rockwell paintings. Even if this were true, where did the 25-year-old Chapman, who never had a single well-paid job in his life, get the money to buy Rockwells and Dalis in the first place?

On 8 December Chapman rose early, checked his new copy of J.D. Salinger's *Catcher In The Rye*, then built a little shrine of his possessions in his hotel room.

All his life, John Lennon had had a quiet obsession with the number nine. He believed it was his lucky number, luckier and more 'magical' than any other. And, whether by happenstance or destiny, the number did seem to crop up with, on, and around him, time and time again. He was born at 6.30pm on 9 October 1940. Brian Epstein first saw The Beatles at the Cavern club on 9 November 1961 and he later managed to secure The Beatles an EMI recording deal on 9 May 1962.

'She Loves You', 'Can't Buy Me Love', 'Day Tripper', 'We Can Work It Out', 'Give Peace A Chance' and 'Happy Xmas (War Is Over)' were all singles that charted in the UK on the ninth day of the month. The Beatles created a record TV audience of 73 million in the USA on 9 February 1964 and Lennon first met Yoko Ono on

9 November two years later at the start of her 9-day show.

The release of *Walls & Bridges* – with Lennon in a Number 9 shirt on the sleeve – came 9 years after The Beatles' debut in Paris. That day, a few hours before the first French gig, John had received a neatly typed note. It contained just 9 words, *"I Am Going To Shoot You At Nine Tonight"*. Over and over again the number would crop up at key moments.

Through the early evening of 8 December 1980, the Lennons continued to mix 'Walking On Thin Ice' – a stridently powerful piece of funk flavoured rock that had been written, and sung, by Yoko. The plan was to issue it as a single, probably credited to Yoko, in the New Year. It was undoubtedly influenced by Lennon but it still made obvious – for most people for the very first time – what he had always maintained; that Ono possessed a streak of sheer musical genius. It's atmospheric, energetic *and* dramatic – nothing before or since has sounded remotely like it. From its squealing intro, through its pulsing verses, it just builds and builds, possessed of a relentless strength all its own.

Yoko's contrasting vocal is a sweetly sung narration on life and love, that's then balanced with a doomy clanking riff and her strident manic barks. Four minutes in, it reaches a plateau, the quiet in the eye of the storm, and the beat arrangement drops back a little as Ono, in confessional mode, starts to relate the story of the naive girl who tried to walk across thin ice. The tale ends as glacial synths surround the singer. The beat kicks back in, the track's hammer-edged riff carrying us away into a world of ruthless destiny. The shouting barks then return – it may be just the way they're recorded, but the shouts sound like 'hai', the Japanese word for 'yes' – as the guitars crank up even further and chase the fade.

Unsettling and emotional, to be sure, and as uneven as a mountain pass, but then, Ms Ono has never wanted or claimed uniformity. It is undoubtedly a classic, brilliantly spanning both the rock and dance genres – not with ease but with a manic intensity all its own.

Curiously, 'Walking On Thin Ice' also came across, even then, as being autobiographical, as if Yoko somehow fully understood just how fragile life could be. But she didn't fully understand that fragility, not then, not at that exact moment – not quite. That revelation was yet to come.

At 8.05pm photographer Paul Goresh decided to leave the sidewalk outside the Dakota. Although he was now in a unique position for a paparazzo – on speaking terms, almost friendly even, with his favourite pictorial target – he'd already snapped John Lennon several times that day. It was time to go home. The cold and hunger were beginning to get to him and there was the drive back to New Jersey to think about as well – North Arlington just isn't that close to Manhattan.

Chapman asked him to stay a little longer, as he turned the conversation back to Lennon and the picture of him signing the *Double Fantasy* album for Chapman "It was just a ruse," Chapman later admits. "I wasn't there to take his signature, I was there to take his life."

Goresh agreed to develop the film that night – Chapman offered $50 cash for a print of him with Lennon. He asked whether Goresh would think about "shooting Lennon again" that night. Goresh replied that he was too tired, that he could photograph Lennon almost anytime. "But what if you never see him again?" Chapman asked abruptly and then, as Goresh walked away, he spoke up again, "What if something happens to him?"

In the recording studio a beaming John tells Yoko that 'Walking On Thin Ice', "is really great … it'll be a Number One … in the disco charts at least." Ono manages a tired smile in reply – unaware that the musical partnership that began over a dozen years before is now over. They will never record together again, for John Lennon only has minutes to live.

The Lennons leave Record Plant East at 10.30pm, telling everyone that they're going to grab a bite to eat at the Stage Deli restaurant. Six years before, on the *'Rock'n'Roll'* album's cover of Lloyd Price's 'Just Because' – John's last solo recording before his 'retirement' – Lennon can be heard jokingly bidding farewell to Record Plant East. He later admitted that, even as he spoke, at the back of his mind he was actually asking himself a serious question, "Is this my goodbye to the music business? Is this my goodbye?"

In the limousine the Lennons decide to forget eating at the Stage Deli and opt to go straight home instead.

In British terms – Greenwich Mean Time – it is now well past midnight. Back in Liverpool and London it is already the ninth – 9 December.

John and Yoko Lennon arrive back at the Dakota Building at 10.49pm Eastern Standard Time. Rather than order their driver to get them into the courtyard, the Lennons get out of the white limousine, get out on to the sidewalk. As the limo pulls away from them they walk the last few yards to the Dakota's entrance.

Mark David Chapman steps from the shadows, the loaded .38 handgun clutched in his hand, deep in his coat pocket. Yoko walks past him, giving a tired, barely perceptible nod in answer to Chapman's blank smile, Lennon follows, a pair of cassette tapes in his hand.

Lennon's eyes meet Chapman's briefly. Neither speaks. Lennon goes on walking past him, on Chapman's right. Chapman has the gun out of his pocket but it is still hidden amongst the folds of his coat.

Lennon is still less than ten feet away. Chapman later says he hears a voice within endlessly repeating two phrases "I Want This! I Want This!" and "Do It! Do It! Do It!"

Lennon is now a little further away, while Yoko is almost out of sight.

"Mister Lennon?"

John Lennon slows, starts to turn but as he does so Chapman snaps into a combat pose like a hardened pro' – both hands on the gun – and fires five times at Lennon. At least four hollow point shots hit him in a neat cluster, the bullets slapping into his body so close together that pathologists will later have trouble marking out the different entry points. If all of these shots have come from Chapman it is a miraculous piece of shooting – in fact, if *any* of them have it is miraculous. For Chapman was standing on Lennon's right and, as the autopsy report and death certificate later make clear, all Lennon's wounds were in the left side of his body.

Once inside the victim's body, the hollow points shatter in all directions with evil force, shredding Lennon's internal organs.

Yoko says later that, as the shots rang out, she thought that a 'guerrilla' war had just begun. It was a telling remark, for the peasantry of El Salvador the 'war' was already months old and their suffering would soon be replicated by fresh victims in Angola, Mozambique, Afghanistan and Nicaragua, as Reagan's backers determined to force back the clock, no matter how high the cost, no matter how bloody the task.

To Chapman's amazement, a determined Lennon somehow keeps walking, stumbling on towards the Dakota, on towards his family.

Lennon enters the Dakota. He even manages to speak, "I'm shot, I'm shot!" He then collapses as Yoko tries to help him.

Chapman's gun is shaken out of his hand. Chapman makes no effort to resist losing his only weapon. The .38 handgun skittles along the ground past John Lennon's blood-stained glasses. "Do you know what you've done?" Jose the doorman allegedly asks Chapman.

"Yes," Chapman allegedly replies, "I just shot John Lennon."

He is told to flee, "Just get away from here!"

But after a moment of quiet reflection, Chapman merely answers the question with a question of his own, "But where would I go?" He then drops his hat and coat and casually leans against the Dakota wall. He then pulls out his latest copy of *Catcher In The Rye*. As the seconds tick by he makes no effort to leave, although two roads, a subway, and Central Park all beckon. In this he stands almost unique in modern criminal history, a man who has killed a non-relative, a celebrity, and then made no attempt whatsoever to escape.

After some three and half minutes the NYPD arrive. They find a strange sight – the alleged killer, unrestrained and still on the scene, strolling up and down as he casually reads a paperback book. The cops handcuff him as two others carry the bloodied Lennon to their squad car, gingerly placing him in the back. Chapman looks on unconcerned; this particular twentieth century 'Chapman' has seemingly delivered his fatal message, a message from which the bloodied dream-weaver before him will never recover.

One of the cops carrying Lennon mutters angry obscenities at Chapman. In a kind of reply, Chapman asks arresting officer Steven Spiro not to let anybody hurt him. After Spiro's reassurances the prisoner volunteers his first real statement to the police, a statement almost as strange as his refusal to try and escape. "I acted alone," Chapman says, in answer to a question that no one has even asked him yet, "I acted alone, I'm the only one."

Minutes later John Lennon is dead.

In the darkened projection room the screen suddenly

bleaches white with the intensity of an atomic flash. With the top projector reel now empty the last seconds of film snake through the gate. And then they are gone. Without the restraining tension from the top reel, the lower one accelerates wildly out of control – no sprockets or film to hold it – spinning faster and faster. The last few feet of celluloid snap loose against the projector stand; this happens time and time again as the full spool whirrs round and round. The snapping noises sound like gunshots. Pieces of film start to fly off – two frames here, half a dozen there – before floating gently down to the carpeted floor.

The images are split-second snapshots of a strange, explosive life; the sad smile of the shy, hurt boy child, a traumatised boy who now has no father; the defiant jaw-jutting grin of the heavy drinker, fists clenched; the quiet bespectacled poet; the proud grinning father; the puzzled guitarist threading his way through a sea of wheelchairs; the onstage superstar bathed forever in Klieg light as thousands scream; the actor who stares down at his own bloody uniform before he slowly looks up at us, bewildered accusation in his eyes; the man with the smart suit and loosened tie – and a dazzling blonde on his arm; the street marching militant in scuffed army fatigues.

Then there is a spray of private moments, first with one Oriental woman, then with a second, younger, Asiatic female. Then our subject is alone with the first woman again. A small child is with them in the next clip. The boy child grins, embarrassed, as his parents try to make him wave at the camera. They give up and, beaming, just wave themselves. Their hands are still in motion when the abbreviated clip abruptly ends. As the lights go down the last image we see is of a shy, hurt boy child, a traumatised boy who now has no father.

CHAPTER SEVENTEEN

WHISPERS

*And when they saw him afar off, even before he came near
unto them, they conspired against him to slay him. And they
said to one another, Behold this dreamer cometh. Come now
therefore, and let us slay him, and cast him into the pit and
we will say, 'Some evil beast hath devoured him.' And then
we shall see what will become of his dreams.*

Genesis 37.18-37.20

I never wanted to hurt anybody, my friends will tell you that.

Mark David Chapman

Just before 11pm, Lennon arrives at Roosevelt Hospital
on 9th Avenue. Despite being diagnosed DOA – dead on
arrival – the doctors try vainly to get some response from
Lennon's shattered body.

But with at least five pints of blood already lost, it's
all in vain. As with Kennedy years before, the hollow
point bullets have efficiently done their deadly work.

At 11.15pm – according to some accounts it's nearer
to 11.30 – Doctor Stephen Lynn and the rest of the
Roosevelt's exhausted Emergency Service Team finally
give up the unequal fight.

Lennon's wife, now with label boss David Geffen,
tries again to see Lennon. This time, finally, she is told the
terrible news in full and succumbs to hysteria, asking,
"Do you mean he's asleep? Asleep?"

May Pang hears the bad tidings on the radio and
screams. She hurries to be with others who knew Lennon.

Distraught, she spends the agonising hours till dawn weeping as she talks incessantly to David Bowie and his secretary Coco. Bowie, the 'Cold Thin White Duke', is himself in tears. Dozens of fans start to gather outside the Dakota, then hundreds. By late the next day they number in their thousands.

As the news hits England in the morning, Roy Carr, then a senior *New Musical Express* editor, takes it like a stomach punch, "I was speechless, lost for words for a minute. I just couldn't believe it. Neil Spencer, he's now at *The Observer*, he was in my office at the time and he was absolutely convinced it was a conspiracy. He kept saying so over and over again, 'No way were they gonna let him come back and go on strikes and marches and stuff, no way. They killed him, didn't they? *They* killed him.'"

Upon arrival at the station-house Chapman is given a strip-search. Although the temperature is mild it's found that he has on – under the fur hat, heavy duty coat and thick full length shirt – long johns and a thermal vest. As the night is very mild he's asked why he's so over-dressed. Chapman says it's because he hates the cold, because he's from Hawaii – a comment that makes it sound, wrongly, as if he was born there.

The NYPD's Lieutenant O'Connor then questioned Chapman. When asked the key question, of why he'd killed Lennon, Chapman gives the same reply over and over again – he just *had* to. John Lennon "had" to die. John Lennon "had" to die. Had to.

To O'Connor the suspect seems calm yet absent, as if he might have been programmed to kill. Arresting officer Spiro, and others, are similarly impressed with Chapman's tranquil manner, especially when he takes a phone call from his wife Gloria. Only at the end of the call, after her tearful declarations of love, does Chapman show any kind of human emotion.

These unusual signs are, however, rapidly ignored. In late 1980 the NYPD was, in many ways, overwhelmed. Violent crime was edging up and tens of thousands of man-hours had been expended on the so-called 'Phantom of the Opera' killing. It was, officials later claimed, a period of desperate 'fire-fighting' – a time best captured in Daniel Petrie's 1981 feature film *Fort Apache, the Bronx*, starring Paul Newman, Pam Grier and Ed Asner. Asner's own, very popular, TV show *Lou Grant* was to be cancelled the very next year. US sponsors including Vidal Sassoon pulled the plug after Asner dared to go on a march protesting against US support for El Salvador's death squad government – one more sign of the growing divisions within the Reagan era.

With this pressure on the city police, the Lennon case is effectively closed when Chapman signs his confessional statement less than two hours after reaching the station. Chapman's version of the actual killing is backed by the Dakota Building's doorman, after all. A man is shot dead, someone confesses, and another witness pretty much backs up the immediate sequence of events. End of story.

But this was the assassination of the controversial John Lennon, a world famous superstar, a Beatle – *the* Beatle – now the male half of the (in)famous John and Yoko team, a partnership that had garnered more column inches than any other couple in recorded history, including the Reagans, the Kennedys and the Royals.

Lennon's killing was a case that, at least one NYPD detective later claimed, was pursued with incredible vigour, with no detail being too small to overlook. Everything was, it was claimed, checked again and again.

Yet Chapman's bizarre post-killing calm is *not* questioned, Chapman's behaviour is *not* checked with a drugs test, Chapman's "programmed" state is *not* investigated, Chapman's previous movements are *not* thoroughly looked into, Chapman's seemingly endless cash supply is *not* analysed, nor is his ability to speak Russian, nor is his time in Vietnam, nor his time in Beirut, nor his visit to China nor his 'missing' three days in Chicago, nor why documents have been altered to cover those three missing days.

And when Chapman's wife refuses to be interviewed, this surprising rejection – which can, of course, be overruled by the police in a murder case – is casually accepted. *Chapman just killed John Lennon but his wife doesn't want to discuss it? OK, fine, let's just leave it at that then, shall we?*

And then there was motive. Chapman was *not* insane and he later wasn't found to be insane. So why had he killed a man he'd barely met? The police knew he wasn't a serious Beatles or Lennon fan – there was only the one day-old *Double Fantasy* album in his possession, or at his house. The police also knew he wasn't a deranged autograph-hunter. For a start, he didn't even seem to possess a single autograph book.

And Chapman wasn't a loner who killed out of loneliness, since he had an attractive young wife back in Hawaii, who was constantly telling him to come back home.

If he was an attention-seeker then why did he turn down the chance of a full trial? It would have been the 'trial of the decade' according to some newsmen. Others disagreed and felt it would have been bigger – the 'the trial of the century'. By pleading guilty, Chapman missed all of this attention he was supposedly seeking. Again, why?

Put simply, the authorities' investigation, or lack or it, into the John Lennon assassination was shockingly slack. With hindsight, it actually beggars belief.

The statement the NYPD took from Chapman, early on the morning of 9 December 1980, reads as follows –

I never wanted to hurt anybody, my friends will tell you that. I have two parts in me. The big part's very kind, the children I've worked with will tell you that. I have a small part in me that cannot understand the big world and what goes on in it. I did not want to kill anybody and I really do not know why I did it. I fought against the small part for a long time. But for a few seconds the small part won. I asked God to help me but we are all responsible for our own actions. I have nothing against John Lennon or anything he has done in the way of music or personal beliefs. I came to New York about five weeks ago from Hawaii and the big part of me did not want to shoot John. I went back to Hawaii and tried to get rid of my small part but I couldn't. I then returned to New York on Friday 5th December, 1980. I checked into the YMCA on 62nd Street. I stayed one night. Then I went to the Sheraton Center 7th Avenue. Then this morning I went to the bookstore and bought The Catcher In The Rye. *I'm sure the large part of me is Holden Caulfield who is the main person in the book. The small part of me must be the devil. I went to the building, its called the Dakota. I stayed there until he came out and asked him to sign my album.*

At that point my big part won and I wanted to go back to my hotel, but I couldn't. I waited until he came back. He came in a car. Yoko passed first and I said hello, I didn't want to hurt her. Then John came, looked at me and passed me. I took the gun from my coat pocket and fired at him. I can't believe I could do that. I just stood there clutching the book. I didn't want to run away. I don't know what happened to the gun. I just remember Jose kicking it away. Jose was crying and telling me to please leave. I felt so sorry for Jose. Then the police came and told me to put my hands on the wall and cuffed me.

Signed: Mark David Chapman.

Although most of the basic facts in the above 'confession' are more or less correct, with hindsight Chapman's words are most startling for what they don't say, for what they leave out. His statement contains none of the boasts that emerged later – "I killed the Sixties!" – nor does he refer to his mind's 'little people', or his alleged hatred of John Lennon's 'phoniness'. Nor does he at any point claim to be a huge Beatles or Lennon fan. The only possible reference to being a fan comes in the line about buying the album and getting Lennon to sign it. These are indeed are possible indications of being a fan, but over seven million people were to buy that album and dozens had it autographed. None of the others stalked the Dakota day after day with a gun. And even this purchase of Chapman's didn't come until some three and half weeks after *Double Fantasy* had actually been released. In fact, it was a purchase that only happened after two real Lennon fans outside the Dakota had *suggested* it. As Chapman himself later admitted, buying the album and getting it autographed was merely a "ruse".

The 'Lennon obsession', the hate for the 'phoney', his mind's 'little people', Chapman's talk of becoming a 'somebody', his smug boasts – these statements are all to come later, in some instances years later. They are to arrive long after the incarcerated Chapman has been in custody, long after he's taken, and made, many outside phone calls and long after he's enjoyed many extensive discussions with his various lawyers, and others.

Yet even what he does say in his original statement is curious enough. Apart from a seemingly obvious attempt at sketching out a schizophrenia or insanity plea for any future court case – the 'big part and the little part', the wait to be arrested – there is a strange flavour to it all. He "never wanted to hurt" anybody, let alone John Lennon. He had, he freely admits, "nothing against John Lennon" and, another curious addition this, "I have nothing against anything he has done in the way of music or *personal beliefs*"(my italics).

Why did Chapman stress beliefs? And why did he really kill Lennon? What made him do such a thing? And what was later to compel his wife Gloria to tell a public press conference – later screened on American TV to an audience of millions – that she was so "sorry that John Lennon *had* to die" (my italics). Why did Lennon *have* to die?

Part of Mark Chapman's compulsion seems to have been triggered by J.D. Salinger's bitter-sweet doomed youth novel *The Catcher In The Rye*. But again, for what possible reason? Why should Salinger's sad coming-of-age book lead to murder? There's nothing in it that suggests that murdering a celebrity would be of any help to anyone. There's only the hero's vague hostility to 'phoneys', along with a lot of other things that he despises with equal disdain, everything from swing bands that do bad cover versions, to sales clerks that short-change his mother. Why didn't Chapman start shooting salesmen in sports stores?

It only makes the slightest glimmer of sense if *Catcher In The Rye* was part of Chapman's hypnotic programming, a trigger that could be 'fired' at him by a few simple key words. A trigger that could be 'pulled' long distance, by a cassette tape message, by a telex, a telegram or even by a mere telephone call. A trigger that could get him to act and then, when the trigger was used again, could get him to discuss, to *expose*, that very same trigger. All it needs is a message, or series of messages, that he could easily receive at home in Hawaii, or later in a New York hotel room – or even later, under arrest in a police cell.

If, as increasingly seems the case, Chapman was a 'fall guy', a programmed 'patsy' – like Sirhan Sirhan – then it appears that his programmers had learnt something since Sirhan had allegedly 'assassinated' RFK single-handedly. For it was noticed that Sirhan had post-killing chills despite the blistering heat of LA that June of

'68 – chills are one sign of deep hypnosis, a sign Sirhan repeated when he was hypnotised in his cell by Dr Diamond. These chills were written about and they helped feed the 'programmed Sirhan' theory (a theory that looks more and more like fact as time passes).

When Chapman was arrested this problem was overcome, despite the mildness of the weather – it was over 45 degrees Fahrenheit in New York on the evening of 8 December 1980 – by the fact he was wearing a heavy shirt, equally heavy trousers, a full thick overcoat, a fur hat, plus thermal long johns with a thermal vest. No wonder Chapman didn't replicate Sirhan's chills that night.

When he was asked by the police why he was so heavily dressed, Chapman told the NYPD it was because he was from tropical Hawaii. But he wasn't from Hawaii, he'd just lived there for a few years. He was, in fact, born and raised in the continental USA.

Then there was the Beirut incident – why had a serious, committed Christian gone to the Middle East, yet avoided the Holy places in 1975? It was a strange anomaly that someone must have noticed – perhaps one of Chapman's US intelligence 'handlers' – for it was dealt with some three years after his first visit. At the very end of his 1978 world tour Chapman squeezed in a couple of days in Israel and there he gave a couple of the Holy sites a cursory glance.

It was nothing compared to the weeks he'd just spent elsewhere – in India and Thailand, for instance – but it did make up for his earlier 'oversight' and now that box could be ticked off. *Holy sites – not avoided. Been there, done that.* If anyone were to ask Chapman he could now honestly say he *had* visited *some* of the Christian shrines during his time in the Middle East.

Two years later and street shrines were appearing in New York, all clustered around one dark block, and all dedicated to a confused yet brilliant artist.

John Lennon was important and of course his resurgent rock career and returning street activism would have undoubtedly embarrassed the incoming Reagan regime. In the weeks leading up to his death, nothing Lennon said or did undermined his anti-establishment stance. He *did* distance himself from hard drugs and from the far Left/New Left position of Jerry Rubin *et al* – as he had for years – but this only made him more subversive; the rebel who was off the bottle, off the needle and away from the 'lunatic fringe'. But he was still an anathema to America's hard Right.

The letter indicating his intention to march with striking workers, his comments supporting Punk and New Wave, the anti-nukes demo rumour – all these added to the Right's already burgeoning paranoia about him. Even his December 1980 statement about Elvis Presley's death three years before was hardly MOR stuff; "When Elvis died people were harassing me in Tokyo for a comment," he told BBC Radio One's Andy Peebles. "We [John and Yoko] were making no comment. Well, I'll give it to you now – Elvis died when he went into the army, that's when they killed him, that's when they castrated him. The rest of it was just a living death."

Add to this the growing hysteria of the US right during 1979-80 and then, equally important, add the possibility of the CIA entering another successful entry in their MKULTRA programme. And so, with one stroke, an annoyingly popular, radical irritant has been removed, just when he needed to be, as the Republicans usher into power a former actor in his seventies. And the man who helps with the killing is a hypno-programmed fall-guy, who calmly accepts the consequences for actions which are not his own. And if any blame does trickle down then – as with Oswald, Ray and Sirhan – there are the various Phase One, Two and Three fullbacks, 'lone nut', 'stalker', 'schizo fan' which many media pundits will happily peddle till the subject is off the front pages again.

Of course, professional hypnotists have usually maintained that no one can be made to do things under hypnosis that they would not normally do in real life. Yet, while there is some truth in this, it does not apply to everyone. It does not apply to those who already have a mildly disturbed background, or that 17 per cent of the population who are especially susceptible to hypnosis, or those who have been simultaneously treated with drugs, to induce, say, model psychosis.

Nor would it apply to those hypnosis subjects who have also been paid large sums of cash – and promised even more – to voluntarily undergo such treatment as part of a special 'patriotic mission'. Under deep hypnosis, blocks can be introduced – the subject can remember absolutely nothing, not even when asked to recall such things under 'normal' hypnosis. To get at the truth can then take months or even years of follow-up sessions, as well as complete cooperation.

Oswald, the man who'd dreamed of being a spy as a teenager, underwent hypnosis so he wouldn't give away his real role. He was only in Russia to reveal the truth about America's U2 spy plane and its secret flights over Soviet airspace, to thus drive a wedge between the increasingly close leaders of the US and USSR.

Sirhan underwent his hypnosis sessions so he could complete his 'secret mission' and earn the $80,000 he'd been promised, the $80,000 he continually wrote about in his diaries (a sum worth over $1.5 million today). In those pages he even added the cover-up words '*I have never heard* please pay to the order of ... this or that 80,000 ...' (my italics).

And it was Sirhan who answered all questions instantly when he was under hypnosis in custody – all, that is, *except* questions about a conspiracy to kill Robert Kennedy – and then his suddenly slow answers were delayed by up to five seconds, significant pauses in such circumstances.

Chapman underwent his hypnosis so he could fulfil the 'special training' that had taken him round the world, principally into danger areas like Vietnam, Beirut and China. Training that was to give him money and prepare him for his ultimate action, action that was to be triggered by a simple phrase – or a line from a book (like, say, *Catcher In The Rye*).

At some point his handlers had been forced to let him know he stood a good chance of getting caught. But his training had prepared him for this. For his training included observing the treatment he got following his fake unwitnessed 'suicide' attempt in Hawaii, and the subsequent months he spent actually working in the same psychiatric wing of Hawaii's Castle Medical Center, observing the patients. This was all perfect preparation for 'acting up' enough to cop an insanity plea and stroll out of a mental hospital just a couple of years later, a leaner, freer and richer man.

Of course, he'd have to change his identity in order to avoid revenge attacks but, his handlers had no doubt assured him, if Mafia informers, Nazi war criminals and important witnesses could be given a new identity, then so too could Chapman, once he'd spent a year or two being analysed.

And to Chapman it must have seemed to be working at one point. Several of the psychiatrists who analysed him before sentencing talked about 'schizophrenia' and mental disturbance, at one point he appeared to be almost halfway to a successful insanity plea.

The 'breakdown' Chapman underwent before sentencing was possibly genuine, at least in part – for there is a big difference between getting 20 months in hospital and 20 years to life in a maximum security prison. Some things cannot be prepared for, not 100 per cent. But even here, during his 'breakdown', there were parallels with past alleged assassins – a berserk Chapman climbed the high bars of his cell like a monkey, just as Sirhan had a dozen years before, when the latter was in one of Dr Diamond's hypnosis sessions.

In the late 1980s Dr Herbert Spiegel, a leading medical hypnotist, researched the RFK case and then expressed his belief that Sirhan *had* been subjected to 'hypnotic treatment'.

Even if one wishes to disregard all of the above, there are quite a few other, factual, cases of hypnosis being used to commit crime by proxy. In Denmark in 1951 hypnotist Bjorn Nielsen put Palle Handrup into a deep trance and ordered him to rob a Copenhagen bank and shoot dead anyone who tried to stop him. The crime *was* carried out and after Nielsen had grabbed the cash a bemused Handrup was rapidly jailed. In prison, however, Handrup began to recall details about Nielsen and the final hypnosis session. There were, however, still some 'blocks' on what he could recall. A psychiatrist with experience of hypnotic technique finally got the full story after almost a year of 'unblocking' Handrup. The latter was eventually pardoned and freed as the police sought Nielsen.

Thirty years later Dr Dorothy Lewis, then a research professor of psychiatry at New York University School of Medicine, and also a clinical professor of psychiatry at Yale, examined Mark David Chapman and declared her belief that he might have been acting in response to a "command hallucination" the day John Lennon was killed.

In April 1994 Mexican presidential candidate Colosio was assassinated apparently by 'lone nut' assassin Aburto. The latter said he had 'no intention' whatsoever of killing Colosio until the candidate came close and then a command hallucination, a voice within, ordered him to shoot him. The local Chief of Police did not believe Aburto had acted of his own free will – nor did he believe that Aburto was the only gunman shooting at the victim that day. His investigations came to an abrupt halt, however, when 'persons unknown' shot and killed the Chief of Police himself. The Mexico government's official inquiry concluded that Colosio *had* indeed been assassinated – probably with the help of 'mind control' experts – a killing carried out by well-supported conspirators whom the Mexican police have been unable to trace.

In Rome, in 2008, a 'strange bearded man' used hypnotism to send cashiers into a trance as he stole thousands of euros. CCTV footage showed him strolling over to a supermarket cashier and seemingly hypnotising her before walking out with wads of cash. The same criminal was responsible for robbing several banks. One experienced bank cashier stated that the bearded man came over to her, leaned over and asked her to look into his eyes. Moments later he was gone as she began to notice that her till was now empty. A third cashier gave him almost 1,000 euros the same month after, she said, she'd became mesmerised by him. Local 6 News announced that the cashiers didn't recall any of the actual thefts, only that everything that happened, including their own actions, seemed completely natural at the time.

And then there are these quotes – all by men found *sane* by the legal system, all of them talking with respect and even affection about the men they allegedly assassinated:

"I'm not a malcontent, nothing irritated me about the President [Kennedy]." – Lee Harvey Oswald speaking after he'd allegedly assassinated JFK.

"I liked [Robert] Kennedy, he stood up for the little guy." – Sirhan Sirhan speaking after he'd allegedly assassinated RFK.

"I didn't mean to hurt anybody, I like John Lennon." – Mark David Chapman speaking after he allegedly assassinated John Lennon.

These men were all found to be sane by courts of law. If they had *not* been 'hyno-programmed' then why did these sane men supposedly kill the leaders they had no grudge against? Leaders that, in some cases, they said they actually admired?

There was another startling incident in 2008 that, although it did not concern crime, did reinforce the power of hypnotism. In Brighton, on England's south coast, a hypnotist induced his own trance to endure a complex hand operation without anaesthetic. Alex Lenkei, 61, could hear the surgeon chipping and cutting away a walnut-sized growth, then manipulating a tendon on his arthritic hand. Lenkei, a hypnotist for over 15 years, said that he put himself under in less than a minute and wasn't aware of any part of his body "apart from my arm, I could feel them manipulating, then the bones cracking. I'd have said if I was in pain. I told them to zap me immediately if I cried out."

Surgeon David Llewellyn-Clark said Lenkei's pulse and respiration remained constant throughout the operation at Worthing Hospital, a procedure that lasted over 80 minutes. Orthopaedic surgery is known to be incredibly painful, especially when dealing with such sensitive areas as the hand.

There is one final point on hypnosis. Despite many people proclaiming it to be just harmless fun, without any dangerous applications, the fact remains that no major television network anywhere in the world has *ever* permitted a 'to camera' broadcast of a full hypnosis session. It has always been considered far too dangerous.

On 20 January 1981 Ronald Reagan was inaugurated as President of the United States of America. Within hours word came from Iran that, after 444 days, the American hostages had 'suddenly' been released by Iran and put on a plane home. On hearing the news, the recently defeated Jimmy Carter and his former Vice President, Walter 'Fritz' Mondale, both broke down and wept angry tears.

Five years later – with Republican activists trying to get the US Constitution's 'Roosevelt amendment' changed so the still popular Reagan could run for a third term – his government was abruptly shaken by the Irangate-Contragate revelations. The heart of these revelations was that the US had secretly been selling arms to Revolutionary Iran, the hostage-takers – as a pay-off for some unnamed favour to the Reagan regime – despite the fact that this was the same Iran whose agents had blown up hundreds of US Marines in Beirut. Those US officials involved had then used the cash generated to illegally fund Nicaragua's right-wing Contra terrorists (notorious for attacks that used rape, mutilation and murder, in one case beheading a baby just a few months' old – tactics that didn't prevent America's far right, and Britain's Federation of Conservative Students, from offering the Contras their full support).

The prime mover in the Irangate affair was National Security Council adviser Colonel Oliver North, the same US Marine who'd helped get an acquittal for Randy Herrod, patrol leader during the 1970 Southang massacre of South Vietnamese civilians. But in the fall-out from the Irangate-Contragate scandal, Oliver North was forced to resign from the NSC. He later tried to enter Congress and failed, and all talk of Reagan being allowed a third presidential term was quietly, finally, dropped.

CHAPTER EIGHTEEN

CONSPIRACY FACTS

We can use the available political machinery to screw our political enemies!

John Dean, legal counsel to President Nixon, August 1971

If anything happens to me and Yoko it will not *be an accident.*

John Lennon 1972

In the wake of his death, both the news-stands and the charts were besieged by Lennon specials and Lennon recordings. Every major newspaper and music magazine in the world dedicated pages to it, some entire issues. Coverage and tributes even extended into the Eastern Block, with papers in Moscow, Poland, Hungary and Yugoslavia mourning his passing. Three young female fans of Lennon's took their own lives and dozens more attempted suicide.

The '(Just Like) Starting Over' and 'Imagine' singles sold millions and reached Number 1, then 'Woman', 'I Saw Her Standing There', 'Happy Xmas (War Is Over)', Yoko's 'Walking On Thin Ice' and 'Watching The Wheels' all became hits too, the latter just after Roxy Music's cover of 'Jealous Guy' reached the top spot. This was swiftly joined in the charts by a Lennon tribute from fellow Beatle George Harrison, 'All Those Years Ago'. Right up until July 1981, over seven months after his assassination, the records kept selling, staying on the listings continuously as the grief kept pouring out.

Within weeks of his death Lennon had sold over two million records in the UK alone, within a year, sales of the *Double Fantasy* album approached seven million.

And it still wasn't over. A rash of Sixties' nostalgia hits, mostly cover medleys, kept coming right up until the end of 1981: 'Stars On 45', 'Beatles On 45', 'Stars on 45 II', 'Beach Boys Gold', 'Back To The Sixties' – these recordings themselves going on to sell millions.

In Liverpool four roads and the main international airport were re-named after John Lennon whilst in another unprecedented step the borough of New York set aside over three acres of Central Park for the Strawberry Fields memorial gardens in honour of him. The gardens were opened in 1985, half a decade after the fatal shooting.

In its depth and longevity this huge public reaction dwarfed even the stunned receptions that had greeted the deaths of James Dean, Marilyn Monroe and Elvis Presley. Only Princess Diana's death, some 17 years later, was to match it. John Lennon, the self-proclaimed 'Nowhere Man' was much more loved and, in terms of cultural-political influence, much more powerful than he'd ever guessed.

It is a mainstream commonplace that the assassinations of JFK, Malcolm X, MLK, RFK and John Lennon are actually far too 'big' to have any official involvement. How can it be true? How could 'they' possibly dare? And yet the big lie has a long-running, if dishonourable, history, in every corner of this planet. If the lie is big enough then, as the Nazis secretly proclaimed, people will probably believe it. And it was the Nazi's own SS killers who time and again told their victims, as millions were beaten and murdered all around them, "It doesn't matter if you alone somehow manage to survive all this. It won't matter, for no one will ever believe this ever happened anyway. No one will ever believe you."

This evil cry has had many echoes down the years – by Rwanda's genocidal Hutu killers, by Pol Pot's Khymer Rouge torturers, by El Salvador's Army of the 1980s and its death squads, by Milosevic's concentration camp guards. *No one will believe you.*

And thousands, perhaps millions, do not believe the victims. There are still those who insist that most of the above holocausts or massacres did *not* happen, or were, at worst, a small aberration, on a tiny scale.

Such duplicity had always lurked within people and those of intelligence have always recognised this fact. The day in April 1945, for instance, that the Nazi concentration camp at Bergen Belsen was liberated, a senior British officer present insisted that one of his men write down the names of every soldier present – when asked why, the CO replied it was because one day someone would deny that such a crime had ever been committed.

Richard Dimbleby recorded a radio programme the same day he arrived at the same camp, but the BBC refused to believe his account about tens of thousands of civilian inmates starved and murdered – *how could Dimbleby make such claims? The Nazis weren't Communists after all, nor were they Russians.* The BBC subsequently refused to broadcast it. Eventually Dimbleby Senior had to threaten to resign before the corporation would reluctantly transmit what he, and hundreds of others, had witnessed with their own eyes.

Photographs? Witnesses? Memos? Reams of circumstantial evidence? Full confessions even? Not good enough. To some it doesn't matter how much proof is ever offered. For their own emotional, or financial, reasons they will deny the evidence of everything, even the evidence of their own ears and eyes. *No one will believe you.*

Could it all possibly have been the random work of madmen? Madmen so 'clever' they could endlessly fool hundreds of psychiatrists and psychologists? The odds are clearly against this – by trillions to one – and then there is also the other obvious fact that when a genuine madman, a real 'lone nut', attempts an assassination, the botched hallmarks are obvious. When deranged woman Violet Gibson, who believed her moods could change the weather, attempted to kill Mussolini, it was a messy fiasco. Il Duce came away from it with nothing more than a scratch on his nose that only required a single plaster. When several of Charles Mansion's acid groupies tried to act without him – firing shots at President Ford – their bullets missed by miles, and when a paranoid schizophrenic attacked George Harrison he was hurt but not killed.

When the professionals – like elements within the CIA or their proxies – hit an individual, they stay hit. Dead. Period. The fact that the CIA can utilise elements of the Mafia, the FBI, the DIA, the DEA and US Naval Intelligence, can only make committing such crimes easier. The fact that some local police forces, much of the legal establishment and even some sections of the media can then be pressurised into quickly accepting the official verdict, can only make 'covering up' a virtual formality in certain circumstances.

No one is perfect, of course, and mistakes do lead to clues which can slip out. And connections between apparently unrelated people do, after a time, slowly slip to the surface. So then, what are the connections between Nixon, the mob, the FBI, the CIA and the assassinations? And what of the assassins of John F Kennedy, Robert F Kennedy, Martin Luther King and John Lennon? Are there really more than one or two faint links between Lee Harvey Oswald, James Earl Ray, Sirhan Bishara Sirhan and Mark David Chapman? What are the conspiracy *facts*?

Below is a brief run-down of the connections between the alleged killers, the authorities and the 'big shots'.

It is not a definitive list by any means, respected American assassination experts such as James DiEugenio, Lisa Pease and Mark Lane could, if they wished, produce even more links. But the following *does* at least give a flavour of what has slowly become public knowledge, much of it over the last few years.

CONNECTIONS

THE ILLICIT ESTABLISHMENT

– Richard Nixon, Jack Ruby, E Howard Hunt, Bernard Barker and Frank Sturgis all supported or worked with red-baiter Senator Joe McCarthy in the Fifties.

– Nixon employed Ruby, Hunt, Barker and Sturgis during his political career.

– Nixon, Ruby, Hunt, Barker and Sturgis all worked on planning or implementing the failed 1961 invasion of Cuba, the Bay of Pigs fiasco.

– Nixon, Ruby, Hunt, Barker and Sturgis all worked with the CIA – Nixon working with them for years as he was US Vice President.

– Nixon, Ruby, Hunt, Barker and Sturgis all worked in the American Deep South.

– Nixon, Ruby, Hunt, Barker and Sturgis were all present in Dallas on 22 November 1963 when JFK was assassinated. Barker has been identified by police officer Seymour Weitzman as being the so-called 'Secret Service agent' who prevented policemen and others from inspecting the grassy knoll in the seconds after the JFK shooting, while Hunt once went to court to try and prevent his presence in Dallas that day becoming public knowledge. He failed, the court ruling that he *was* present in Dallas that day.

– Nixon, Ruby, Hunt, Barker and Sturgis were all subsequently suspected of being involved in, or at the very least aware of, the plot to assassinate JFK.

– Hunt and Sturgis, as gunmen, have long been actual assassination suspects.

– Nixon, Hunt, Sturgis, Barker and Liddy all discussed the John Lennon case.

– Nixon and Hoover both had Lennon tailed and wire-tapped.

– Nixon, Hunt, Sturgis and Barker were all aware of the 1972 Watergate burglary before it happened.

– Hunt, Sturgis and Barker were all prosecuted over the 1972 Watergate burglary

– Barker was actually the leader of the Watergate break-in team and was later jailed for this.

– Nixon, Ruby, Hunt, Barker and Sturgis all finally came to grief over their involvement with the Watergate break-in.

– Nixon, after stalling for over two years, was finally forced to resign his presidency on 8 August 1974, over the Watergate break-in and the subsequent, failed, cover-up. During Nixon's active political career hundreds of virtual innocents had been ruined by his work with McCarthy while President Kennedy, Malcolm X, Martin Luther King and Robert F Kennedy had all later been assassinated. During Nixon's presidency the Governor of Alabama had been badly wounded in an assassination attempt, the democratically elected government of Chile had been violently overthrown and at least 25,000 American troops, plus over a million native civilians, had died in Vietnam.

Nixon, who'd been in charge of overseeing the CIA during his time as VP, had accumulated plenty of enemies, people who, with some justification, wanted their day in court, as well as some recompense for the very real losses they had suffered. People who wanted to know why, and for how long, he had employed Jack Ruby. People who wanted to know what words had been edited out of the so-called 'Watergate tapes' – and why.

Within a month of Nixon's resignation, however, the new Republican President, ex-Warren Commissioner Gerald Ford, enraged many commentators by giving Richard Nixon a full pardon. This presidential pardon effectively freed 'Tricky Dicky' Nixon from the possibility of ever being prosecuted or jailed for any of his long list of indiscretions. It also saved him from having to answer any questions about the legal, and illegal, activities of both the FBI and the CIA.

CONNECTIONS

THE ALLEGED ASSASSINS

– Lee Harvey Oswald, James Earl Ray and Mark David Chapman were all painted as loners yet all had partners, lovers or wives, as well as friends.

– Oswald, Sirhan Sirhan, Ray and Chapman all left damaging clues against themselves, despite all being of average or above average intelligence (clues included written evidence and the public or mail order purchase of guns and bullets that could easily have been bought anonymously in shops).

– Oswald, Sirhan and Chapman all consorted with religious extremists of the Christian far right. The 1976 Church Committee forced an admission from the CIA that the Agency had over 20 Christian 'missionaries' on its payroll, along with over 40 agents who liaised with local police forces in New York, LA and other US cities.

– Oswald, Sirhan, Ferrie and Chapman all showed confused sexuality or homosexual tendencies.

– Oswald, Ruby and JFK assassination suspect Ferrie were described as 'bedmates' by many witnesses.

– Oswald, Sirhan and Chapman all had Middle Eastern connections – all centred around Iran or Beirut, the latter being a centre of US Naval Intelligence operations throughout the Sixties and Seventies, as well as being the alleged site of an assassination training camp.

– Oswald, Sirhan and Chapman all travelled extensively, despite being, ostensibly, penniless. Oswald and Chapman going round the world, Chapman doing this *twice*.

– Oswald, Ray, Sirhan and Chapman all made blatantly crass and public anti-American statements which they did not believe and which were obviously done to attract attention (Oswald's insulting of US cars and ridiculous praising of their Soviet equivalents, Ray's attack on America's 'tolerance' of blacks, Sirhan's declarations of war against a 'corrupt' America, Chapman's laughter at the Pearl Harbour memorial ceremonies).

– Oswald and Chapman, despite public gestures to the contrary, were both heavily against Castro's Cuba.

– Oswald, Sirhan and Chapman all showed classic signs of being hypnotised and/or programmed.

– Oswald, Sirhan and Chapman were all described as being enormously 'calm' after the assassinations.

– Oswald, Chapman and Sirhan all spoke several languages, including Russian.

– Oswald and Sirhan both had their incredible 'marksmanship' officially explained by 'magic bullets' (Oswald apparently used one 'magic bullet', Sirhan three).

– Oswald, Ruby and Chapman all visited YMCA centres even when they had the money for hotels and/or companionship (and Chapman, seven years after being jailed, was still writing to YMCA directors).

– Oswald and Ruby both had contacts with both the FBI and CIA.

– Oswald and Ruby both had their own files with both the FBI and CIA.

– Oswald, Sirhan and Chapman were all the subjects

of official documentation that has been either altered or destroyed. Oswald's CIA and FBI files are much deleted, while his US Army file was completely destroyed in 1973; Sirhan's gun forensic files are both inaccurate and incomplete; while Chapman's YMCA employment file is missing and his crucial 5 December 1980 flight ticket has been altered to omit his time in Chicago – and his October 1980 postcard to an Italian friend that spoke of New York and a 'mission' was later returned to the USA as undeliverable. When it finally arrived the original posting date had been changed to 1981 and the word 'mission' had been carefully removed.

– Oswald and Chapman were both amongst the very first US citizens to visit Communist nations – Oswald with his short-lived defection to the USSR in 1959, Chapman with his visits to Vietnam and China in 1978, after he'd attempted to enter the USSR.

– Oswald and Chapman both made 'suspicious' suicide attempts. The latter's was not seen by anybody, while Oswald's was not taken seriously at all.

– Oswald, Sirhan, Ray and Chapman, despite all being described as 'lone nuts', 'schizophrenics' etc, were all found to be *sane* at the time of their arrest.

– Oswald, Sirhan, Ray and Chapman, despite all being described as 'lone nuts', 'schizophrenics' etc, were all found to be *sane* at the time of their arraignment.

– Sirhan, Ray and Chapman were all found *sane* by the courts.

– Sirhan, Ray and Chapman, despite all being labelled attention-seekers, all eventually pleaded guilty, thus rejecting the chance of world-wide publicity, the attention that full-length public trials would have given them.

– Sirhan and Chapman both chanted, or wrote, repetitiously before the assassinations – another classic sign of hypno-programming (Sirhan scribbling 'RFK

Must Die! RFK Must Die! RFK Must Die!' – this was written days *before* RFK publicly agreed with the US-Israeli jet sale, which Sirhan's lawyers claimed was the actual motive for RFK's death – while Chapman chanted, 'The Phoney Must Die Says The Catcher In The Rye! John Lennon Must Die Says The Catcher In The Rye.')

– Sirhan and Chapman both climbed the bars of their cells like monkeys, Sirhan after being ordered to do so in a hypnosis session and Chapman during one of his post-guilty plea 'breakdowns'. Dr Eduard Simson-Kallas, San Quentin prison's chief psychologist, observed Sirhan over many hours and to this day is certain that the prisoner had indeed been 'hypno-programmed'.

– Sirhan and Chapman both wrote, *'please pay to the order of ...'* in note-books over and over again.

– Oswald was shot dead before his trial but Ray died in a 'normal' prison for the sane.

– Sirhan and Chapman both made clumsy attempts to appear insane but only *after* heavy prison sentences loomed.

– Sirhan and Chapman, despite being labelled madmen, both today remain in 'normal' prisons for the sane.

... WIRE STORY ... WEDNESDAY SEPTEMBER 27TH 2000 ... LENNON ASSASSIN TRIES FOR PAROLE. The one-time Hawaiian resident Mark David Chapman who assassinated former Beatle John Lennon in 1980 will get his first parole hearing this coming Tues. (Oct 3rd). Chapman, currently serving 20 years to life at Attica Correctional Facility, Rochester, NY, worked with psychiatrists at the Castle Medical hospital in late 1977 thru' to 1979 before transferring to Castle's community relations unit.

He shot dead Lennon in NYC on December 8th 1980. Chapman speaking for the first time in nine years claimed that Lennon himself would probably want him freed.

Chapman has been reported for some small scale infractions while in Attica though he has since obtained work in the law library. He now says he feels some remorse for the Lennon slaying. It was, he said, 'terrible' that Lennon was dead.

Eliot Mintz, a spokesman for Lennon's widow Yoko Ono, said that she had sent a letter to the parole board but did not disclose the letter's contents ... STORY ENDS ...

... WIRE STORY: ... CHAPMAN UPDATE 4th OCTOBER 2000 – CHAPMAN, MAN WHO KILLED JOHN LENNON, DENIED PAROLE ... No further details yet available on parole failure of Mark David Chapman – now claiming, for the third time, to have discovered God – after Oct 3rd parole hearing. Chapman shot John Lennon Dec 8th 1980 and avoided trial by pleading guilty ... STORY ENDS ...

... WIRE STORY: ... JUNE 26th 2003 ... SIRHAN SIRHAN ATTORNEY DEMANDS RFK ASSASSINATION RETRIAL ... Thirty-five years after Bobby Kennedy's assassination, Lawrence Teeter, Sirhan Sirhan's lawyer, has forcefully argued that his client had been hypnoprogrammed and thus framed for the killing, possibly by a conspiracy set up by elements of the [US] government.

"The guy was set-up, he remembers nothing whatsoever of the shooting," Teeter told reporters. "There is an innocent man sitting in prison."

Sirhan is currently serving a life sentence in Corcoran State Prison after eventually pleading guilty to assassinating RFK, Senator Bobby Kennedy, then a 42-year-old presidential candidate, in LA in June 1968.

He has since been denied parole a dozen times – lastly in March 2002 – and Teeter now wants the whole case moved from LA to Fresno, since one of those who originally prosecuted Sirhan has since become a federal judge in the LA area thus making, in Teeter's eyes, a free and fair trial impossible.

"Those who wanted Robert Kennedy killed were those who

were not satisfied with his promise to end the Vietnam War," said Teeter who believes the 'military-industrial complex' is to blame. He maintains that Sirhan Sirhan was hypnotised into firing shots at RFK and that Sirhan was almost certainly using blanks rather than the real, fatal, bullets.

Either way, Sirhan could not have fired the actual shot that killed Robert Kennedy, since all the witnesses put him at least two feet away from Kennedy. RFK's fatal wound was fired in from behind, from less than two inches away. The case's original coroner Thomas Noguchi even admitted this at the time and has not denied it since. Sirhan's original defence team were only informed of this 'one inch – two feet' discrepancy once the original trial had already begun. The original jury were never told about it.

Also Teeter believes that prosecutors blackmailed Sirhan's original defence attorney into 'throwing the case' and that police and government intelligence agencies conducted the assassination investigation inadequately, disregarding and browbeating many key witnesses and ignoring the other men who were seen with guns around the scene of the crime that night (June 4th-5th 1968). This was done, Teeter and his team believe, purely in order to produce a 'whitewash' verdict.

Although she has not, at time of writing, answered any of Teeter's specific points, LA County DA Sandi Gibbons, who covered the first Sirhan Sirhan trial as a junior reporter, still said, "I don't think so, no. I think that the person who shot and killed Robert Kennedy was convicted and sentenced properly. Absolutely. And after a fair trial too, I think Sirhan killed him [RFK]. And he killed him alone."

Teeter is petitioning an LA federal court for a full public retrial. "The integrity of the [American] judicial process is at stake here," he said.

... RFK-SIRHAN 26/6/03 ... WIRE STORY ENDS ...

234

CHAPTER NINETEEN

NOT FADE AWAY

The mass of men serve the State thus, not as men mainly, but as machines, with their bodies. They are the standing army, and the militia, jailers, constables, posse comitatus etcetera – in most cases there is no exercise whatever of the judgment or of the moral sense; they put themselves on a level with wood and earth and stones; and wooden men can perhaps be manufactured that will serve their purposes as well.
Such men command no more respect than men of straw, yet such as these even are commonly esteemed good citizens. Others – as most legislators, politicians, lawyers, ministers and office-holders – serve the State chiefly with their heads; and, as they rarely make any moral distinctions, they are as likely to serve the Devil, without intending to, as God.
A very few men – as heroes, patriots, martyrs, reformers in the great sense, and men *– serve the State with their consciences also, and so necessarily resist it for the most part; and they are commonly treated as enemies by it.*

Henry David Thoreau, Civil Disobedience

It was a staggering moment when I heard the news. Lennon was a most talented man and, above all, a gentle soul. John and his colleagues set a high standard by which contemporary music continues to be measured.

Frank Sinatra

John took the [FBI] battle seriously, but he had great trust in the American justice system. I think he always knew it would turn out fine.

May Pang

235

Jon Wiener's quest, to free *all* of the John Lennon FBI files, seemed to have reached a dead end by the summer of 1997, stuck on the problem of the files pertaining to a foreign power, i.e. Britain. But the election of a New Labour government, ending 18 years of Tory rule, promised change. The incoming prime minister, Tony Blair, headed an administration pledged to achieving an unparalleled 'openness in government'.

There was even to be a new law which would replace the selective 30-year rule that had obtained in the UK since the Seventies. Finally, after centuries of obstruction, the British were to be allowed some kind of freedom of information act.

The renegade MI5 spy David Shayler gave his employers a nudge by revealing the fact that there were British files on Lennon – over his support for left-wing parties – as well as on two Sixties students who were now members of the new cabinet (these were former student union leader Jack Straw and one-time anti-apartheid activist Peter Hain).

Weeks later MI5 began to shred over 120,000 of the files they'd held on UK subjects – including one on John Ono Lennon. Rather than fight this outrageous action, the government actually seemed to encourage it – perhaps grateful that the youthful excesses of their senior and junior ministers would now never be made public. Those who'd been less successful in life than high-ranking government members – those who might have had their careers slowed or even destroyed by secret action – were the losers. They would not be able to claim compensation without proof. And that proof was rapidly being turned into pulp by the south bank of the Thames.

But the US copies of the MI5 Lennon files – or at least those that were sent to the FBI – *did* still exist. And after much prompting from Wiener and his civil liberties legal team, the FBI agreed to ask for British permission to finally release the last ten Lennon documents – those FBI files which had originated in, contained information from, or were copied to, Military Intelligence 5 and 6.

Yet, despite all their freedom of information pledges, Blair's regime hesitated for a few days, and then said "No". Lennon's 'All You Need Is Love' might have been good enough for the government's Millennium Dome party VIP singalong on New Year's Eve 1999 – and for the Queen's Golden Jubilee celebrations in 2002 – but the remaining FBI files on him were to remain secret, if Downing Street and Whitehall were to have anything at all to do with it.

But why have successive British governments gone to all this trouble, this decades-long trail of obstruction? Why did Blair's New Labour administration, which was often enough on the rack over PR spin and unfulfilled promises, effectively give up on open government? What are they – and the new Con-Dem government of David Cameron – really protecting? The fact that a few youthful indiscretions, much censored, might slip out? They cannot be worried about revealing the names of former radical, or showbiz, informers, since those specific names could be blanked out anyway. So what really concerns them? That the files might reveal that, under the successive Wilson, Heath and Thatcher regimes, that there was a level of surveillance in the UK that almost matched that of East Germany's Stasi? Or could it possibly be something even more sinister? Were MI5, and possibly MI6, passing on UK approval for foreign surveillance and harassment of a UK citizen, John Lennon? Surveillance by the FBI and CIA? It all sounds so over the top, so far-fetched – even an all-American assassination – and yet, John Lennon *is* dead, JFK, MLK and RFK *were* all assassinated, the official inquiries *were* unquestionably worthless.

More importantly, the bland mainstream view that no conspiracies ever happen is, quite simply, wrong. The Watergate conspiracy is a *fact*, as are the Contragate and Irangate conspiracies. They *did* happen – as is a matter of legal record – and their conspirators *were* caught and then disciplined, demoted or sacked and, in a few cases, jailed. And it is also a fact that the FBI *did* fight a 16-year court battle to try and prevent most of their 281 pages on Lennon ever being seen (and even now, despite America's Freedom of Information Act, 13 of the pages since released are effectively unreadable).

And since Lennon's death, MI5 and the Thatcher, Major, Blair-Brown and Cameron-Clegg administrations *have* all taken their turn to sit on the dustbin lid, *have* all taken their turn at keeping the rest of us in the dark. And it is, of course, the same in the US. The CIA's pages on Lennon, numbering in their dozens, remain unreleased. And, despite the flood of assassination files that the Kennedy Assassination Records Collection Act of 1992 forced from the CIA, they still have over *one million* unseen files on the JFK killing alone.

As a British citizen I now find it almost embarrassing that, Fenton Bresler aside, time and time again it has been *Americans* – principally Jon Wiener, Dan Marmalefsky and Mark Rosenbaum, whose actions have put most pressure on the FBI, and thus on MI5 and the UK government – to reveal the truth about the persecution of Britain's John Lennon. A truth still not yet fully told.

John Lennon was a British citizen by birth and he spent the first 31 years of his life based here. During his time here he employed dozens of people directly and thousands indirectly. He paid millions of pounds in taxes to Britain and helped generate millions more. He gave hundreds of thousands to charities, anti-war organisations and popular causes, most of them honourable. For his services to the British music industry he was awarded the MBE and though he returned the accompanying medal – in protest over the slaughter in Biafra and Vietnam – the Member of the British Empire medal is an honourary award which still stands. When he died he was officially still John Lennon MBE.

Summer 2009. Sales of Beatles recordings now exceed one billion. If cover versions, downloads, bootlegs and solo recordings by John Lennon and the others are included, then the figure rises to two billion – *two thousand million discs* – more recording copies than there are families on planet earth. Well over 112 million of these have been bought since Lennon's death.

A single one of the 60 cut-outs from the *Sergeant Pepper* cover was auctioned at Christies in London. The five-foot piece of cardboard realised over £86,000 ($130,000).

At any moment, at literally any time of the day or night, at least three Lennon-McCartney songs are being played on radio stations somewhere in the world.

What would once have been considered laughable in the pubs and art schools of Liverpool, is now just plain fact. The work recorded by John Lennon, with both the Beatles and Yoko Ono, will continue to be played and enjoyed and covered, as long as music is played. He, with their help, turned a fading musical fad into the biggest cultural force of the twentieth century – obligatory for every advert, movie, TV show, club, party and social gathering. The multi-generational soundtrack of an entire globe.

Where would John Lennon be now, in this post-Cold War world, this globalised, multicultural, designer world? A planet that now has mobile video phones, a world wide web and credit-card sized computers, as well as 800 million citizens still going hungry.

Musically it's easy to imagine Lennon warming to the

dance and technology explosions of the Eighties and early Nineties. He had, after all, helped break Motown, and thus Soul, in both Britain and in the US in the Sixties and he was always interested in studio technology, though he would perhaps have become concerned at the growing number of musicians being prematurely thrown on the scrap heap (and at the growing number of 'new' tracks that are simply sampled rip-offs of older songs).

Britpop and the various indie revivals would no doubt have raised a rye, appreciative smile – new wave of new wave of New Wave, anyone? – as would the music, and antics, of Oasis and other such groups.

It's pretty certain too he'd still be standing for peace, though he'd be suspicious of any 'peace' that merely meant that the killing would quietly go on out of sight, in the secret torture chambers of dictators. Similarly, he'd still be promoting racial and sexual equality, though he'd probably be too streetwise to wholly embrace the Political Correctness mentality and its own blend of reverse racism and endless hypocritical hierarchies.

Although he had said his wild days were 'over', Lennon might also have continued to put in the odd word for the decriminalisation of softer drugs such as cannabis. He lived, remember, in a world that hadn't yet created 'skunk' cannabis, a drug four times stronger than ordinary 'weed' or 'hash'; a new drug that medical researchers insist creates 600 per cent more mental health problems than its older, weaker predecessors.

John, and Yoko's, love of nature and organic food suggest he would now be in the forefront of those protesting against deforestation and the dangers of GM 'Frankenstein' food, as well as the ruthless globalisation of the world economy with which such phenomena are inextricably linked.

And yet even the most carefully weighed speculation,

whilst fascinating, is, in the end, wrong-headed. At least in all the ways that really count. Such speculation starts off from the wrong point like, say, Robert Harris' otherwise brilliant 'what-if' novel *Fatherland* – a book that had Beatles' songs being played across a Nazi-occupied Britain (as if Hitler's brutal culture police could possibly have nurtured Merseybeat in the same distant way that Atlee, Churchill and Eden inadvertently did).

You cannot just plonk John Lennon down in the twenty-first century. If he had been alive all along throughout the Eighties and Nineties – if he had *not* been killed – then things, no matter how small the change, would have been different. Things would be different now. It was Lennon, after all, who had sung about wanting to change the world, and it was not a line delivered from a position of total inexperience, it was something he had already done once before.

Lennon's fame and wealth, and *conscience*, could, and undoubtedly would, have been used again to support the causes close to his heart. His physical presence added tens of thousands to demonstrations and his words brought global media attention.

In the words of one of his few journalistic friends, ex-musician Roy Carr, "John could connect with the disenfranchised, the guy in the street, he could speak in terms that they understood – when he wanted to. And people *did* listen to him. When you've got the ears of that many people and you're not in government, or a government-sponsored opposition, then you're a threat to them, you're a real threat."

John could identify with the vulnerable because he was vulnerable himself. The triple blow of his parents' separation and the death of his mother and step-father left huge scars (and must account for much of his adolescent misbehaviour). Many lesser men have ended up in asylums, or prisons, after such a start in life. It is a testimony to Lennon that, despite this background and despite his inner demons that surfaced when he drank – he instead became the most important artist of his generation. An artist, moreover, who dared to talk about the political realities of his age. Today Roy Carr, like Fenton Bresler and many others, now believes that US intelligence had something to do with both Lennon's death and the subsequent cover-up.

This political 'threat' of which Roy Carr speaks is the real reason Lennon was placed under FBI surveillance in the first place – in Wiener's memorable phrase, the start of a sort of 'rock'n'roll Watergate. Because of John Lennon's opposition to the war in Vietnam he was a potential 'threat'. An enemy of the war-mongers.

There were, of course, millions of victims before the Cold War was 'won'. But few of them were musicians and fewer still were world famous – only one was John Lennon, ex-Beatle, poet, composer, peace activist.

It now seems obvious that his death was actually *not*, as many commentators have blithely concluded, the first fatal celebrity stalking. It was instead, almost certainly another 'successful' MK-ULTRA killing – 'delivered', at least in part, by an 'assassin' so deeply 'programmed', that even now, decades on, he still has no idea why he helped commit one of the most shocking crimes of the late twentieth century (an attitude that ensures his continuing imprisonment).

And in that sense Lennon's killing was the last of the Sixties' assassinations – the most important state executions of the twentieth century. For all their faults, the Kennedys, Martin Luther King and even, in the last months of his life, Malcolm X, had all stood for brotherhood, for the possibility of positive change, for the belief that love was stronger than hate and that, ultimately, people were more important than money.

It was something that John Lennon, for all his

indulgences, also believed in. It was something that the first post-Fifties decade had, for all its extremes, rapidly come to stand for. And so the target that dark December night was thus John Lennon himself, at the height of his comeback. For he was the man who symbolised, more than anyone else, The Beatles. The band who, more than any other, *were* the Sixties – those ten tumultuous years that the right-wing Tory MP Norman Tebbit once called "that cheap, over-rated decade"; the ten years that most other people remember as the last real decade of hope.

But the media battles about assassinations and the Sixties aren't something new. They began *in* the Sixties. During 1967 a CIA directive on criticism of the Warren Report was sent worldwide to all its Station Chiefs, a directive aimed at all its 'media assets'. This document was marked for destruction, but James DiEugenio managed to track down one surviving copy. It makes interesting reading:

1. Our Concern. From the day of President Kennedy's assassination, there has been speculation about responsibility for his murder, this was stemmed for a time by the Warren Commission report, [yet] there has been a new wave of books and articles criticising the Commission's findings, critics have speculated as to the existence of some kind of conspiracy.
2. This trend of opinion is a matter of concern to the US government, including our organisation, the aim of this dispatch is to provide material countering and discrediting the claims of the conspiracy theorists, so as to inhibit the circulation of such claims in other countries.
3. Action. We do not recommend discussions of the assassination be initiated where it is not already taking place. Where discussion is active [business] addresses are requested:
a. To discuss the publicity problem with liaison and friendly elite contacts (especially politicians and editors), pointing out that the Warren Commission made as thorough an investigation as humanly possible.

b. To employ propaganda assets to [negate] and refute the attacks of the critics. Book reviews and feature articles are particularly appropriate for this purpose. The unclassified attachments to this guidance should provide useful background material for passing to assets. Our play should point out, as applicable, that the critics are:
(I) wedded to theories adopted before the evidence was in,
(II) politically interested,
(III) financially interested,
(IV) hasty and inaccurate in their research, or
(V) infatuated with their own theories.

And so it goes on, for page after page. That CIA document doesn't formally admit anything, of course, but, as befits a file that was always supposed to stay secret, there is also a certain crude honesty to it; phrases like 'employing propaganda assets to refute attacks' and 'book reviews and feature articles are particularly appropriate for this purpose' leave no room for doubt – this is the perfect guide for those who wish to attack anti-CIA authors, for those who wish to deny what any basic research makes obvious to any researcher within days – that US intelligence was deeply involved in the JFK assassination and many of those that followed, including John Lennon's.

Again and again we see the same pattern; a popular hero is killed, a lone nut is blamed. On closer inspection the 'lone nut' turns out to be neither a nut nor a loner (Oswald and Chapman both travelled extensively, both learned Russian, both tried to get into the Soviet Union – and like James Earl Ray they both have mysterious gaps in their CVs: weekends, weeks or even entire months when their whereabouts is unknown, their contacts secret).

If the mad loner story publicly breaks down we are then told that it's all to do with the Mafia, an embarrassing admission you would have thought, for America's intelligence networks and legal system to confess to; that every US election between 1960 and 1976 has been decided by the gun, with the weapons being wielded by either madmen or the Mob, hardly something for the world's most powerful democracy to boast about. The fact that organised crime, or at least its killers, often *are* involved, on some level, only helps to muddy the waters.

If any media personnel have pursued the story they usually stop at the 'lone nut' killer. When the spirit of investigation is prompted by public demand – as when the *JFK* movie became a huge hit – most reporters stop at the 'Mafia alone' theory. Anyone who wants to look closer at the wealth of evidence that goes beyond this is instantly labelled a 'conspiracy freak' or 'conspiracy nut'. At the same time, writers, often 'agent-journalists', use books, documentaries and magazine articles to continue to push the 'madness or mob' theories. They, or their colleagues, then use spin against the assassins' dead victims. So JFK was, supposedly, a 'Mafia dupe' and even a 'cocaine addict',

The other myth about JFK still in circulation is that he was a Vietnam War hawk who thrust America into that unwinnable military struggle. This is almost the exact opposite of the truth, as Kennedy was undoubtedly trying to withdraw from the conflict at the time of his death in 1963. The facts about JFK's proposed Vietnam withdrawal, as outlined in Chapters 6 and 7, are so easily accessed, it's both strange and disturbing that Kennedy critics of left, right and centre continue to deny their existence.

The other major attack on JFK is the suggestion that he was so lonely and penniless that he became a Mafia puppet, begging mobsters for money and company (as if Kennedy, married and with access to his family's $400 million fortune, ever needed such cash). Meanwhile RFK was allegedly 'the cold-blooded killer of Marilyn Monroe' and MLK was a 'constant womaniser', while Lennon is the man 'who killed Stuart Sutcliffe' then killed May Pang between peddling heroin to the children of America.

Lies, all lies. Even the more moderate claims are usually wild exaggerations of rumours by those 'now free to talk' – for a price. These stories are often peddled by authors or publishers with an axe to grind – or a secret job to do. In the US, remember, the CIA had some 40 'agent-journalists' on their payroll not that long ago. I doubt if they've all gracefully taken early retirement and I doubt if their replacements have given up either. These journalist-operatives don't just change their own stories to fit the Agency's agenda, they often meddle with other people's articles.

One obvious example of this is when John Leonard reviewed two JFK assassination books for the *New York Times*. The piece was headlined 'Who Killed John F. Kennedy?' and it included two paragraphs in which Leonard listed just some of the many unanswered questions about the case, the questions the Warren Commission had avoided. Leonard also expressed his own scepticism over the official view of the killing.

Within hours though, as Lisa Pease noted in her 'Failure of The Fourth Estate' article in *Probe*, the headline was changed to 'The Shaw-Garrison Affair' and those two crucial paragraphs were removed. Although he spent time investigating these changes, Leonard was never able to find out who had made these alterations, or when, or why. He later said, "We've every right to be paranoid."

And in the UK press, when Fenton Bresler's *Who Killed John Lennon?* was initially published in 1988 – the first book to seriously discuss the links between Lennon's death and US intelligence – it was savagely attacked in the UK broadsheet newspapers by the reviewer known as Miles Copeland, although what his review didn't tell readers was that Copeland's father was actually one of the CIA's co-founders.

The motives for all this are obvious – and two-fold. Firstly, blame the messenger, and maybe even call him a liar, because then there is, apparently, no case to investigate. Secondly, ensure that physical assassination is followed by character assassination. Because such mud-slinging naturally lessens the demand for a full public investigation. *Why bother to see what really happened when the victims were, we're now telling you, all killers or hypocrites anyway?*

And the authorities are happy for that drive for truth to be undermined. In Britain the New Labour Party is a corrupt shadow of its former pre-Blair self, whilst in the US the Democrat Party is now an equally shiny empty shell, no more a threat to big business and state secrecy than the Republicans. Both parties are now run by, and for, millionaire lawyers.

Although New Labour and the Democrat leadership pay lip service to the dead heroes who inspired their rank and file members, neither party has ever seriously tried to investigate the demise of those heroes, even when in office. Like the rock culture to which both parties once had tenuous links, these organisations were supposed to be a crusade or nothing. For all their apparent power, the obvious implication is that they are now nothing. The McAlternative, as photographer David Binns has called them. An extension of the amateur dramatic societies of Congress and the Commons.

In other words, these parties continue to pretend to be anti-establishment in order to hide the fact that, to all intents and purposes, they really now *are* the establishment, and have been for years.

In early 2003, the UK's BBC TV invited British viewers to vote for the Greatest Briton of all time. Millions of votes were cast over a period of months. The poll was topped, of course, by the other Winston, the original one –

Britain's wartime leader Churchill – the man widely held to have delivered the nation from Hitler. But to the astonishment of conservative critics – who'd envisaged a list that would be completely dominated by prime ministers, generals, scientists and royalty – John Lennon reached as high as Number 3 before finally settling at Number 7. Not bad for a rock'n'roller who had not been in cynical Britain for over three decades; a 'nowhere man' who'd then been dead for some 23 years.

A blue plaque – for 'JOHN LENNON 1940-1980 MUSICIAN & SONGWRITER' – was unveiled that summer by Sir John Mills at the site of the old Apple boutique in London's Baker Street. The event was attended by various celebrities, including movie star Jean-Claude Van Damme, Liver Bird Nerys Hughes, singer Jess Conrad, dancer Lionel Blair, actress Anita Harris and John's old acting pal Victor Spinetti. The paparazzi were present too, as were hundreds of fans, many of them smiling through their tears.

"He knew he meant a lot to people," said May Pang the same month, "[but] I think he would have been astounded at how profoundly his death was felt throughout the world."

A one-hour BBC TV show was dedicated to Lennon. It was narrated by actor Alan Davies who had flown up to Liverpool's John Lennon International Airport. It was broadcast a couple of months before a remix of Yoko Ono's 'Walking On Thin Ice' reached Number 1 in the US dance charts, just as Lennon had said it would during the very last afternoon of his life.

It was some 18 years after his assassination that a John Lennon box set, *The Lennon Anthology*, was released. This EMI issue contained 94 tracks, many of them out-takes, spread across four CDs. There was a 64-page booklet too. In the latter Yoko described Lennon as a 'heavy dude', someone who was a 'king', not a mere pop prince. She also, poignantly, included the open letter to New York – and the world – which the pair of them had sent to the *New York Times* in May 1979, at the height of Lennon's hermit-like 'retirement'.

It was the note that, for all its mystical isolation, contained the first hints that Lennon was not just watching the wheels go round – the first signs of his explosive comeback; the comeback that was to be cut short; the comeback that was to prove to have such fatal consequences: "We understand that, we, the city, the country, the earth are facing very hard times, the future of the earth is up to all of us, everybody is asking us What, When and Why."

The partnership that propelled Lennon back into art – and into prolonged political activism – had begun with a single positive, the word 'Yes', which Yoko Ono had taped to the ceiling of London's Indica art gallery in 1966. The relationship ended – in the physical sense – some 14 years later with the same word, Lennon's last word before he was silenced. It was a faint, mumbled answer – almost unintelligible – to a cop's question, as he lay dying in the back of a NYPD police car, it was the same question that had ended 'Fame', the Bowie hit he'd co-written:

"What's your name? Are you John Lennon?"

"Yes."

So it was perhaps appropriate that John and Yoko's May 1979 letter, while discussing flowers and angels and silence, should also end on a straightforward, positive note:

"Remember, our silence is a silence of love and not of indifference. Remember, we are writing in the sky instead of on paper. Remember, we love you."

CHAPTER TWENTY

POSTSCRIPT

I'll outlive the bastards in more ways than one.

John Lennon

These pacifist revolutionaries are historically killed by the government, anybody who thinks that Mark Chapman was just some crazy guy who killed my dad for his own personal interests is insane, I think, or very naïve.

Sean Lennon

Rock is always being castigated for failing to change the world. But it changed individual lives for the better when it got its act together, braved opposition and aimed for something possible. If it doesn't do that now, it's not because it can't change anything. It's because it doesn't have the balls.

Gary Mulholland,
Popcorn: 50 Years of Rock'n'Roll Movies, 2009

A lot has happened in the years since I first wrote the notes for the above chapters, much of it concerning both John Lennon and the major assassinations of the Sixties and Seventies.

On a personal level several strange things happened. When my first book on a related subject, *John Lennon & The FBI Files*, was released in 2003, I was unable to send or receive emails from the USA for several weeks. Friends in New York complained that I was ignoring them. No technical explanation was ever forthcoming. Coincidence? Probably.

During this same period I had endless problems with noise on my telephone line. Coincidence? Probably. And then the literary agency I was with had their offices burgled. Of the dozens of writing agents there, only *my* agent had anything taken – his laptop. Coincidence? Possibly. Then a researcher on the book was mugged. Despite carrying cash, gold jewellery, designer clothing and several credit cards, only his phone and filofax were taken. Then there was another series of strange incidents with my telephone.

Now all of this could be happenstance. It *probably* is, but, to be honest, I have my doubts.

More significantly, there has since been a revelation about the small but important 9/11 Kennedy photo connection. In 1958, American-based photographer Jacques Lowe began to snap John F Kennedy, who was then a virtual unknown who could still sit with his wife in diners and cafes, drinking coffee unnoticed and unmolested.

Lowe had first started taking pictures of Bobby Kennedy during his anti-racket campaign in the Senate. He then followed JFK during his successful attempt to become President in 1960. From the 1961 inauguration, right through to that fateful day in Dallas in 1963, Lowe – by now a family friend – kept exposing roll after roll of negatives, making a living by occasionally selling pictures to newspapers and magazines.

In all, he shot over 40,000 images of JFK and his family, both on the stump, at media events and at home. Knowing the worth of his work, particularly after Kennedy's death, Lowe kept all the negatives in a fire-proof safe.

No company would insure the pictures but Lowe knew that the shots of rallies and speeches were of a value that went beyond money – they were historical pictures from another age: a time, he told his daughter Thomasina, "when people still believed in something".

It's likely too – after other photographers' random shots of Dallas showed Jack Ruby's shadowing both JFK and Oswald on 22 November 1963 – that Lowe was also aware that his photos might just contain images of people who had not wanted to be photographed. So, before he died, Lowe had the fire-proof safe placed inside a fire-proof vault within the World Trade Centre.

After the 9/11 tragedy his daughter tried for six months to retrieve her father's safe and its priceless load. In February 2002 the bank in question telephoned her to say the Lowe safe had indeed been found amidst the wreckage, but to Thomasina's 'surprise and horror' the safe was intact but *completely* empty. A neat square hole had been drilled where the lock once was – and not a single negative, singed or otherwise, was still inside. All the photographic images had been carefully removed.

It seems that even the horror of 9/11 can be exploited by elements within America's intelligence services – or those working with them. And so the JFK cover-up continues, over 45 years later.

The convenient disappearance of Lowe's photos was revealed in late 2003. In November of that year a diverse group of writers, lawyers and judges demanded that the CIA 'come clean' about their role in assassinations, especially the killing of President John F Kennedy. Included in the group were legal experts G Robert Blakey, the Chief Counsel of the House Select Committee on Assassinations, which investigated Kennedy's death in the Seventies and yet, under Blakey, did not seriously pursue the CIA, and John Tunheim, the federal judge who'd chaired the Assassination Records Review Board for the US government in the mid-1990s. It seems they had changed their minds about the CIA's role. The 'dupes' were finally, it appeared, no longer so happy to be 'duped'.

Also in the group was the late Norman Mailer and some commentators saw his participation in the demand as a belated attempt to make amends for his *Oswald's Tale* book, another tome that had unsuccessfully tried to perpetuate the myth that Lee Harvey Oswald and his 'magic bullets' were somehow responsible for JFK's death.

Later that year more archive film emerged, firstly on TV channels and then throughout the world wide web, showing JFK's secret servicemen running alongside the presidential limo at Love Field airport Dallas on that bright November day in 1963. This was what they were trained to do, to make it almost impossible for any would-be assassins to get a clear shot at the President. Within seconds, though – and before they've even left the airfield – we see the incredible sight of the secret servicemen being *ordered* to break protocol and leave the side of Kennedy's car. One of the SS men visibly protests at this blatant breach of security but he is over-ruled.

In 2004 speculation began to mount about the identity of the Dakota Building's anti-Castro doorman 'Jose', the man on duty the night John Lennon was killed. Strangely, his full name had not been revealed until 1987, almost seven years after the assassination – no official reason has ever been given as to why his identity was kept so secret for so long. His real full name is said to be Jose Joaquin Sanjenis Perdomo, and his alleged aliases are Joaquin Sanjenis and Sam Jenis. Various other books, and newspaper accounts, have established links between the Dakota doorman 'Jose' and a Jose who was an active anti-Castro Cuban. Cuban Information Archives have shown that a 'Jose Joaquin Sanjenis Perdomo' was active during the CIA's 1961 Bay of Pigs invasion, as an armed member of Brigade 2056.

Salvador Astucia, author of *The FBI's War On Rock*

Stars, now believes that Sturgis' friend Jose Perdomo *was* deeply involved with Lennon's death, with Mark David Chapman being another mere 'mind control patsy'. One of the first policemen on the scene that night – and, indeed, one of Chapman's arresting officers – was Peter Cullen whose first impression was that Chapman was, technically at least, innocent, and that the Dakota's handyman was the real 'shooter'.

Frank Sturgis – Watergate burgler and CIA operative – knew Jose Joaquin Sanjenis Perdomo personally, though Sturgis later claimed that the Perdomo he knew had died mysteriously in 1974. He offered no evidence to back up his claim of Perdomo's death, nor of how, why or where he died, and Sturgis himself is now dead.

If, as some commentators believe, the CIA abandoned Nixon around the time of Watergate – 'throwing him to the wolves' as punishment for his growing involvement with the Cold War thaw of detente – then the Sturgis connection makes perfect sense. Should someone discover Jose's real identity, the first person he would be linked with is Nixon's old Watergate 'plumber' Sturgis. For Lennon to be a Mafia target in 1980 was always pretty unlikely, but for him to be a target for a bitter and vengeful Nixon? Now that was closer to being believable. And, once again, we have another Plan B story that takes the focus off the CIA itself.

In January 2007 Sturgis' one-time colleague, former CIA agent, E Howard Hunt, passed away. Later that month Hunt's son issued a deathbed tape that his father had recorded. On the tape Hunt senior finally names a CIA agent as one of *several* assassins responsible for the assassination of John F Kennedy. The man named, Sturgis, was still working for the CIA in November 1963, and the other direct implication of Hunt's dying words were that Lee Harvey Oswald was comparatively innocent; the 'patsy' he'd always claimed to be.

In 2008 an audio tape of the Bobby Kennedy killing, a recording made accidentally by independent journalist Stanislaw Pruszynski, was subjected to the latest analytical techniques. It proved that at least 13 shots *were* fired at RFK, five *more* than Sirhan Sirhan could possibly have got from his eight chamber handgun. But the legal system of California has ignored this revelation, as it has ignored all the other RFK revelations since that fateful summer over 40 years ago.

Lennon's FBI Files were also prised opened a little further at this time but no great revelations were allowed out, aside from some references to possible CIA infiltration into Britain's far left during 1968-1973. And the rest of Lennon's CIA file remains unseen, as do the hundreds of blanked-out lines in his 'released' FBI Files.

The summer of 2009 saw a remarkable article appear in *The Times*, as respected journalist Dominic Wells investigated claims by James 'Tappy' Wright – Jimi Hendrix's one-time road manager – that Hendrix had not died of an accidental sleeping pill overdose in September 1970 but had, instead, been murdered. The man who ordered the killing was, according to Wright, Mike Jeffery a tough ex-Army man who was Hendrix's manager. Jeffery had, in fact, confessed all this to Wright, or so the latter claimed.

It seemed an unlikely tale, but the more Wells' looked into the story, the more supporting evidence – and witnesses – he found. People were indeed seriously frightened of Jeffery, who died in a plane crash in the 1990s, and descriptions such as 'dangerous' and 'killer' abounded. And the original sleeping pills overdose story, which had come from Hendrix's girlfriend Monika Dannemann, has long been discredited. The door to their flat was wide open for a start – suggesting a gang getaway rather than a quiet night in – and Hendrix was fully dressed (again unlikely if he was taking pills to sleep). The doctor who examined Hendrix after his death also found huge amounts of wine in the rock star's lungs yet only a strangely small measure of alcohol in his bloodstream – another strong indication of foul play. The doctor, John Bannister, told *Times* reporters, back in 1993, that Hendrix had been dead "for hours, rather than minutes" when the ambulance brought his body to the hospital – something that again contradicts Dannemann's claims (claims that have often changed times and details). She cannot be questioned about this anymore, though, having committed suicide three years after *The Times'* 1993 story appeared.

Tappy Wright's own claims are now in his *Rock Roadie* book – along with hundreds of pages of rock'n'roll excess – and the implication seems to be that Jeffery's motive for ordering the killing, aside from a little jealousy, was mainly financial. His managerial contract with Hendrix was indeed about to expire. As Hendrix was insured by Jeffery for millions, he would have made much more out of the counter culture hero's death, than he would have done watching his contract run out (a contract that Hendrix didn't want to renew).

But there is another possible connection – and hence another motive – that neither Wright nor Wells fully pursue. Jeffery was in the British Army's 'secret service'; a man who'd seen action and allegedly killed people in the Middle East, according to Wright and others. "Army secret service" may well have been Jeffery's way of saying MI6 (Military Intelligence Six – the name for Britain's overseas spy service). Either way, it is also a fact that Jeffery learnt to speak Russian during the Cold War. And that he had contacts with both the Mafia and the FBI, Perhaps his motive for killing Hendrix wasn't purely cash-based?

Increasingly, as more and more evidence emerges, it is beginning to look as if the West's security services in general – and America's FBI-CIA in particular – waged a vicious, and undeclared, war against the new culture during the Sixties and Seventies; a war that almost matched the cultural oppression of the KGB and Stasi; a war that also included all the major counter culture horrors of that era, from the political assassinations to the Manson killings to the tragic deaths of Jimi Hendrix, and John Lennon.

Various John Lennon books and films have been released over recent years. Some try and chronicle his post-Beatles relationship with Paul McCartney, (*Two of Us*), while others do a fair job of capturing his earlier years, such as 1993's *Backbeat* and the striking *Nowhere Boy*, 2009. Most of those productions that deal with Lennon's actual death, however – including the multi-million dollar films *Chapter 27* and *The Killing of John Lennon* – seem to ignore all the new evidence that has been revealed and depressingly stick with the established mainstream view: that Lennon was murdered by an 'attention-seeking fan' who was a fanatical 'autograph-hunter'; that this 'Lennon fan' was a 'lone nut', a 'celebrity stalker' who somehow acted alone, and in such a deadly way, for no apparent reason. The fact that Chapman avoided the publicity of a full trial. The fact is Chapman avoided the publicity of a full trial, had no autograph book, had no Lennon music collection. All these facts are ignored. Again.

We may never know the full story now but even the most cursory glance at the facts outlined in the above chapters must make deeply disturbing reading for anyone concerned about Western democracy and the individual's right to free speech. The media outcry over the CIA's exposed catalogue of torture and lies at Guatanamo Bay, perhaps, shows that the Agency's word is, finally, no longer taken at face value by at least some sections of the mainstream press.

But so what? Asks the cynic. What does all this matter? *Maybe Lennon, the Kennedys, King, maybe they did all mean something once. But that's decades ago, how can their lives, their deaths, possibly mean anything now?*

Yet the assassinations of John Lennon, Martin Luther King, RFK and JFK *are* still relevant, partly because the never-ending cover-ups – and their truth-stare apologists – show us exactly how the modern world, and its twin cancers of private and state intelligence, continues to cheat us all.

At the moment, the 'cover-ups' still officially stand, although fewer and fewer people believe them, despite the lack of investigative interest from both the media and the powers-that-be.

What did these 'non-investigations', by both the bulk of the Press and the authorities, lead to? The cover-up of JFK's assassination led to an uneasy silence that, in turn, led to the murders of both Robert Kennedy and Martin Luthor King. If you can get away with public murder once, why not try it again?

And what did this bloodshed achieve for those who had arranged it? Killing the Kennedys and MLK allowed the CIA to more easily lead the US deeper into a long-running, if undeclared, war in Vietnam. Although US arms manufacturers and oilmen made some money from this, that conflict ultimately resulted in 58,000 American deaths and over three million local casualties. It also ended in a humiliating defeat.

Killing John Lennon allowed the Reagan-Bush administration to more easily pursue a new nuclear arms race, as well as murderous policies in Central American and Afghanistan. The results were just as negative. Hundreds of thousands of innocents were killed in these proxy wars; the world secretly came close to nuclear conflict – in both 1983 and 1987; and the following years saw America's border states flooded with refugees and armed drug gangs.

By late 1991 the Soviet Union's peace-maker, Gorbechev, had been bankrupted and forced from power and the Cold War was not then followed by peace and reason – for it was not won peacefully or reasonably – but by a slowly rising tide of gangsterism and terrorism. And then war. Again.

If Americans ever want to genuinely reform their society, if they ever want a truly fair legal system, if they want to stop creating terror groups that then turn on them, if they ever want to hold their secret intelligence networks, both state and corporate, to account, then there is one first indispensable and only step – tell the truth about the assassinations. A full public enquiry, one that will let us see *all* the assassination files – including the one million plus still hidden in the CIA's vaults – and *every* part of those files, not just the chaff. It would be a massive *mea culpa*, one that would be as shocking as Watergate but would have far more meaning. For it would serve as a warning to anyone within US intelligence who was planning future outrages.

Britain should be pressing for these facts to be made public too; not just because British subject John Lennon was an assassination victim, not just because alleged assassin James Earl Ray was arrested here, but because such honesty might well improve America's relationship with the rest of the world – and, therefore, Britain's. The current holier-than-thou stance does nothing for anyone.

America's early rock'n'rollers, the ones who first inspired Lennon, thought their music was silly yet also earth-shatteringly important – *Roll Over Beethoven!* – partly because its raw joy and pulsing energy brought young people together. And how strange it is, despite all the brilliance of Dylan, the Byrds, the Beachboys, that the one man to finally, tragically, prove this importance beyond all possible doubt was not an American. He was an Englishman of Anglo-Irish descent, John Lennon.

Popular culture in general, and its rock'n'roll strand in particular, will almost certainly not regain the prominence it held in the years 1945 to 1991 and all the raw posturing, like the idiot rap boasts and the hollow shrieking of the X-Factor-Idol shows, just confirms this.

But there was once an age, in my own lifetime, when a non-politician like John Lennon – a mere dream weaver, an imperfect seeker after truth, a man who sang of both equality and love – could end up amongst presidents and kings, his image on every TV and cinema screen, his passing mourned by hundreds of millions, his name etched on to streets, parks and international airports, gestures that proved, as he'd said all along, that love, and those who dare talk of it, *are* very important and if love was intelligently applied to every avenue of life, it would indeed be all we need.

Lennon was born in comparative poverty in the back streets of Liverpool. He was killed 40 years later in New York City, where his commercial worth was estimated at 110 million pounds sterling. His value as a humanitarian, a philosopher and a visionary artist was – and *is* – worth so much more. He lived an amazing life and shaped the times he lived in.

As for myself – as someone who has been a police witness at murder trials, as someone who has written about culture, social issues and crime for over quarter of a century – I am now as convinced as any human being can be that elements of both the FBI *and* CIA were undoubtedly behind a 'cover-up' in December 1980.

They were also deeply involved in the actual killing

itself, the assassination at the heart of this cover-up, their vain attempt to 'kill' the spirit of the Sixties, to kill it with the violent death of John Winston Ono Lennon MBE.

YOKO'S STATEMENT

Lenono
Studio One
1 West 72nd Street
New York New York 10023

I TOLD SEAN WHAT HAD HAPPENED. I SHOWED HIM THE PICTURE OF HIS FATHER ON THE COVER OF THE PAPER AND EXPLAINED THE SITUATION. I TOOK SEAN TO THE SPOT WHERE JOHN LAY AFTER HE WAS SHOT. SEAN WANTED TO KNOW WHY THE PERSON SHOT JOHN IF HE LIKED JOHN. I EXPLAINED THAT HE WAS PROBABLY A CONFUSED PERSON. SEAN SAID WE SHOULD FIND OUT IF HE WAS CONFUSED OR IF HE REALLY MEANT TO KILL JOHN. I SAID THAT WAS UP TO THE COURT. HE ASKED WHAT COURT – A TENNIS COURT OR A BASKETBALL COURT? THAT'S HOW HE USED TO TALK WITH HIS FATHER. THEY WERE BUDDIES. JOHN WOULD HAVE BEEN PROUD OF SEAN IF HE HAD HEARD THIS. SEAN CRIED LATER. HE ALSO SAID, "NOW DADDY IS PART OF GOD. I GUESS WHEN YOU DIE YOU BECOME MUCH MORE BIGGER BECAUSE YOU'RE PART OF EVERYTHING."

I DON'T HAVE MUCH MORE TO ADD TO SEAN'S STATEMENT. THE SILENT VIGIL WILL TAKE PLACE DECEMBER 14TH AT 2 P.M. FOR TEN MINUTES.

OUR THOUGHTS WILL BE WITH YOU.

Love
Yoko & Sean
Dec. 10 '80
N.Y.C.

THE LAST WILL & TESTAMENT OF JOHN WINSTON ONO LENNON

1, JOHN WINSTON ONO LENNON, a resident of the County of New York, State of New York, which I declare to be my domicile do hereby make, publish and declare this to be my Last Will and Testament, hereby revoking all other Wills, Codicils and Testamentary dispositions by me at any time heretofore made.

FIRST: The expenses of my funeral and the administration of my estate, and all inheritance, estate or succession taxes, including interest and penalties, payable by reason of my death shall be paid out of and charged generally against the principal of my residuary estate without apportionment or proration. My executor shall not seek contribution or reimbursement for any such payments.

SECOND: Should my wife survive me, I give, devise and bequeath to her absolutely, an amount equal to that portion of my residuary estate, the numerator and denominator of which shall be determined as follows:

1. The numerator shall be an amount equal to one-half (1/2) of my adjusted gross estate less the value of all other property included in my gross estate for Federal Estate Tax purposes and which pass or shall have passed to my wife either under any other provision of this Will or in any manner outside of this Will in such manner as to qualify for and be allowed as a marital deduction. The words "pass", "have passed", "marital deduction" and "adjusted gross estate" shall have the same meaning as said words have under those provisions of the United States Internal Revenue Code applicable to my estate.

2. The denominator shall be an amount representing the value of my residuary estate.

THIRD: I give, devise and bequeath all the rest, residue and remainder of my estate, wheresoever situate, to the Trustees under a Trust Agreement dated November 12, 1979, which I signed with my wife YOKO ONO, and ELI GARBER as Trustees, to be added to the trust property and held and distributed in accordance with the terms of that agreement and any amendments made pursuant to its terms before my death.

FOURTH: In the event that my wife and I die under such circumstances that there is not sufficient evidence to determine which of us has predeceased the other, I hereby declare it to be my will that it shall be deemed that I shall have predeceased her and that this, my Will, and any and all of its provisions shall be construed based upon that assumption.

FIFTH: I hereby nominate, constitute and appoint my beloved wife YOKO ONO, to act as the Executor of this my Last Will and Testament. In the event that my beloved wife YOKO ONO shall predecease me or chooses not to act for any reason, I nominate and appoint ELI GARBER, DAVID WARMFLASH and CHARLES PETTIT, in the order named, to act in her place and stead.

SIXTH: I shall nominate, constitute and appoint my wife YOKO ONO, as the Gurdian (sic) of the person and property of any children of the marriage who may survive me. In the event that she predeceases me, or for any reason she chooses not to act in that capacity, I nominate constitute and appoint SAM GREEN to act in her place and stead.

SEVENTH: No person named herein to serve in any fiduciary capacity shall be required to file or post any bond for the faithful performance of his or her duties, in that capacity in this or in any other jurisdiction, any law to the contrary not withstanding.

EIGHTH: If any legatee or beneficiary under this will or the trust agreement between myself as Grantor and YOKO ONO LENNON and ELI GARBER as Trustees, dated November 12, 1979 shall interpose objections to the probate of this Will, or institute or prosecute or be in any way interested or instrumental in the institution or prosecution of any action or proceeding for the purpose of setting aside or invalidating this Will, then and in each such case, I direct that such legatee or beneficiary shall receive nothing whatsoever under this Will or the aforementioned Trust.

IN WITNESS THEREOF, I have subscribed and sealed and do publish and declare these presents as and for my Last Will and Testament, this 12th day of November, 1979.
(signed) John Lennon."

JFK: KILLED AGAIN

The following assassination story was to have appeared in Private Eye *magazine in December 2003, following a BBC broadcast of a documentary* Beyond Conspiracy *that had half-convinced some intelligent people I knew, such as Tony Wilson, that the 'lone nut' theory might still be valid, History was, I felt, being re-written – and falsely – and so I attempted to step in. Unfortunately, the ill health of my only* Eye *contact, Paul Foot, prevented the piece appearing that month. Soon after he became seriously ill and died and the story was forgotten. It is reprinted here, as it is a concise summing up of the JFK assassination – and also because it reveals some of the ways the mass media use to neuter the past.*

The dumbing down of the BBC took another mighty leap forward during the recent Kennedy assassination anniversary. Leading the way was Gavin Esler's 90-minute TV epic *JFK: Beyond Conspiracy*, a pseudo-documentary that attempted – via a succession of half-truths, omissions and less than credible witnesses – to resurrect the bizarre 'lone nut with magic bullet' theory. The latter theory is much favoured by CIA apologists, since it exonerates 'the company's' role in both President Kennedy's death and the consequent cover-up.

There are, of course, plenty of problems for those who try to blame the entire JFK assassination – the shooting of Kennedy, Governor Connolly, Officer Tibbit and the wounding of passer-by James Tague – on Lee Harvey Oswald alone (Oswald allegedly firing just three bullets from *behind*, at the moving targets, his base being the Texas School Book Depository over 260 feet, and several floors, away).

For a start, there is the awkward testimony of a dozen Dallas doctors and nurses – including those who first treated Kennedy at Parkland Hospital – all of them clearly stating that at least one of JFK's wounds was inflicted with a *frontal* shot. Their statements are corroborated by some 28 witnesses – including police officers and ex soldiers – who saw gun-smoke, or heard gun-shots, coming from in *front* of Kennedy, from the now infamous grassy knoll.

Evidence of collusion abounds too – in 1993 photos were finally made public showing Oswald in a Civic Air Patrol group alongside CIA pilot, and anti-Castro fanatic, David Ferrie, the latter being a long time JFK assassination suspect. Just three months before the JFK killing a variety of witnesses, in the small Southern towns of Clinton and Jackson, also saw Oswald and Ferrie together with Clay Shaw, the man who New Orleans' DA Jim Garrison later charged with JFK's assassination. Shaw's trial was the basis for the 1992 Oliver Stone film *JFK*.

Another problem for Esler was the cheap $12 assassination weapon allegedly used by Oswald, a 20-year-old Mannlicher-Carcano antique that was in such dangerously poor condition that FBI riflemen later refused to test-fire it until it had undergone a complete barrel re-bore. The Mannlicher-Carcano was anyway known as the 'humanitarian' gun during World War II, because it seemingly never hurt anyone, and other rifle experts have called it both 'poorly designed' and 'inaccurate'. It is, quite simply, the last weapon any serious marksman would ever choose – and yet with this dodgy relic, Oswald was supposed to have performed Olympian acts of marksmanship against a moving target over 260 feet away.

Esler & Co got round all these huge problems by simply ignoring them. Instead, alongside some bizarre computer graphics, he and director Mark Obenhaus, served up a selection of witnesses, many of them long discredited, in order to damn Oswald as the fanatical commie 'lone nut' (who just happened to have incredible shooting skills that his career in the marines had somehow failed to reveal).

First up was one-time *Dallas Morning News* hack Hugh Aynesworth who later led the press attacks on Garrison (this was when Garrison linked Oswald, Ferrie and Shaw during Shaw's 1969 trial). Aynesworth was presented on screen as an independent journo – there was no mention whatsoever of his contacts with the FBI, or of the October 1963 CIA memo that noted that Aynesworth was 'offering his services' to the Agency.

And it was Aynesworth, according to local friends like Holmes Alexander, who constantly urged the FBI and Warren Commission to portray Oswald as a crazy 'leftist' killer. Aynesworth also arranged the sale of Oswald's 'diary', making a small fortune by peddling it to three different publications. Hardly a model of disinterested neutrality.

Also joining in the 'fun' was Wall Street lawyer, and 'lone nut' fanatic, Gerald Posner, author of *Case Closed*, the book that some critics dubbed 'Mind Closed'. It is also the tome about which respected historian Professor David Wrone said, "[it] stands as one of the stellar instances of irresponsible publishing on the subject." As expected, Posner touted his usual 'lone nut' line.

Oswald's killer, Jack Ruby, was then described as having no Mafia connections, though it was never explained how the nickel-and-dime Chicago street hustler suddenly became the wealthy manager of The Carousel, a large strip club almost a thousand miles away in Dallas. Ruby's time working for Richard Nixon and his 'UnAmerican Activites' team was not mentioned either, although Ruby leaving his dog in his car and wiring a few dollars to a stripper were somehow given as serious reasons why he could not possibly have been part of any wider conspiracy.

"The people who knew Ruby didn't believe he was part of a conspiracy," Esler blithely claimed, yet the vast majority of the facts point in the opposite direction. Carousel Club employees Karen Bennett Carlin, Janet 'Jada' Conforto, William D Crow Junior, Ester Ann Mash and Wally Weston have *all* previously given statements saying that Ruby knew Oswald *before* the assassination and Carlin even said she believed Ruby, Oswald and other individuals were key elements in a plot to assassinate Kennedy. Ms Carlin herself was shot dead in Houston, Texas, in August 1964, several months after daring to make her plot statement – something else that *Beyond Conspiracy* bravely neglected to mention.

We were also told that the Kennedy administration had agreed to have Cuban leader Castro assassinated – yet this dream project of the CIA's never had JFK's approval and it is a matter of record that he spoke out strongly *against* political assassination several times, including to Florida Senator George Smathers and *New York Times* reporter Tad Szulc.

Esler rounded things off with an attack on the late Jim Garrison and his 1969 prosecution of Clay Shaw. Garrison was portrayed as a corrupt, obsessed fool who rested his entire case on the testimony of the one man prepared to implicate Shaw, Perry Russo (Russo said he'd seen Oswald, Ferrie and Shaw together, plotting to kill JFK before the assassination).

Esler did admit that Ferrie had died during this period but he didn't reveal that Ferrie's death was a suspicious suicide, which occurred before he could take the stand at the Shaw trial, a 'self-inflicted' death which happened just weeks after Ferrie had told friends that he would 'never' commit suicide. And Esler's 'entire case on one man' jibe at Garrison isn't quite true either. Garrison also had several witnesses from the towns of Clinton and Jackson and he would have had dozens more witnesses from elsewhere in the US had not other States totally refused to extradite any of them.

In fact, though, rather than avoid contradictions, *Beyond Conspiracy* rushed to embrace them, often in the same reel, sometimes in the same minute. Various 'experts' told us how Oswald was proud of killing Kennedy, 'proud of it and constantly smiling'. Seconds later rare real footage revealed a nervous and unsmiling Oswald emphatically denying the murder of JFK.

So after an expensive hour and a half – cost to the licence-payer of at least £200,000 – what are we left with? The CIA and US intelligence are somehow exonerated; the ridiculous 'commie assassin' and 'magic bullet' theories get another airing; some has-beens, including various unsavouries, get yet another public platform; and Gavin Esler and his crew get to have a nice working holiday in sunny Texas. What an intelligent, responsible way for the BBC to mark one of the most important events of the twentieth century!

BIBLIOGRAPHY

The Assassinations James DiEugenio, Lisa Pease & Judge Joe Brown (Feral House 2003)

An Act of State: The Execution of Martin Luther King William F Pepper (Verso 2003)

Encyclopedia of The JFK Assassination Michael Benson (Checkmark 2002)

Let Me Take You Down Jack Jones (Virgin 2001)

Lennon In America Geoffrey Giuliano (Robson Books 2001)

Choosing War: The Lost Chance For Peace & The Escalation of War In Vietnam Frederick Logevall (2001)

Lennon: The Definitive Autobiography Ray Coleman (Pan 2000)

Nowhere Man: The Final days of John Lennon Robert Rosen (Soft Skull 2000)

Gimme Some Truth: The John Lennon FBI Files Jon Wiener (California 1999)

For The President's Eyes Only: Secret Intelligence & The American Presidency From Washington To Bush Christopher Andrew (HarperCollins 1996)

Revolution In The Head: The Beatles' Records And The Sixties Ian MacDonald (Fourth Estate 1994)

Nancy Reagan: The Unauthorized Biography Kitty Kelley (Bantam Press 1991)

Who Killed John Lennon? Fenton Bresler (St Martin's Press 1989)

Guts & Glory: The Rise & Fall of Oliver North Ben Bradlee Jnr (Grafton 1988)

One Brief Shining Moment William Manchester (Michael Joseph 1983)

Loving John May Pang & Henry Edwards (Warner Books 1983)

The Lennon Tapes (BBC 1981)

The Killing of RFK Donald Freed (Dell 1975)

Coup d'Etat In America; The CIA & The Assassination of John F Kennedy A.J. Weberman & Michael Canfield (1975)

Executive Action Donald Freed & Mark Lane (Dell 1973)

RFK Must Die! Robert Blair Kaiser (Dutton 1970)

DISCOGRAPHY

JOHN LENNON SOLO UK HIT SINGLES

Give Peace A Chance (1969)

Cold Turkey (1969)

Instant Karma (1970)*

Power To The People (1971)*

Happy Xmas (War Is Over) (1972)*

Mind Games (1973)

Whatever Gets You Through The Night (1974)*

Number 9 Dream (1975)

Stand By Me (1975)

Imagine (1975)

(Just Like) Starting Over (1980)

Woman (1981)

Watching The Wheels (1981)

Love (1982)

Nobody Told Me (1984)

Borrowed Time (1984)

Jealous Guy (1985)

* with the Plastic Ono band and others

SOLO UK HIT ALBUMS

John Lennon & The Plastic Ono Band (1971)*

Imagine (1971)*

Sometime In New York City (1972)*

Mind Games (1973)

Walls And Bridges (1974)

Rock'n'Roll (1975)

Shaved Fish (1975)

Double Fantasy (1980)**

The John Lennon Collection (1981)

Milk And Honey (1984)**

Live In New York City (1986)

Imagine – Music From The Motion Picture (1988)***

* with the Plastic Ono band and others

** with Yoko Ono

*** with some tracks by The Beatles

JOHN LENNON'S BEATLES SONGS

The following Beatles' singles were mostly, or wholly, written by John Lennon:

Please Please Me

Ask Me Why

Thank You Girl

I'll Get You

I Want To Hold Your Hand

You Can't Do That

A Hard Day's Night

She's A Woman

Ticket To Ride

Help!

Day Tripper

Rain

Strawberry Fields Forever

All You Need Is Love

I Am The Walrus

Lady Madonna

Revolution

Don't Let Me Down

Ballad Of John And Yoko

Come Together

You Know My Name (Look Up The Number)

The following Beatles' album tracks were mostly, or wholly, written by John Lennon:

Misery

There's A Place

It Won't Be Long

Little Child

Not A Second Time

If I Fell

Any Time At All

I'll Cry Instead

When I Get Home

You Can't Do That

No Reply

I'm A Loser

Baby's In Black

Eight Days A Week

The Night Before

You're Gonna Lose That Girl

It's Only Love

Tell Me What You See

Norwegian Wood

Nowhere Man

The Word

I'm Looking Through You

In My Life

Run For Your Life

I'm Only Sleeping

She Said, She Said

And Your Bird Can Sing

Doctor Robert

Tomorrow Never Knows

Lucy In The Sky With Diamonds

Fixing A Hole

Benefit Of Mr Kite!

A Day In The Life

Dear Prudence

Glass Onion

Wild Honey Pie

Bungalow Bill

Happiness Is A Warm Gun

I'm So Tired

Why Don't We Do It In The Road

Julia

Everybody's Got Something To Hide Except For Me And My Monkey

Sexy Sadie

Revolution 9

Cry Baby Cry

All Together Now

Hey Bulldog

I Want You (She's So Heavy)

Mean Mr Mustard

Polythene Pam

Carry That Weight

Two Of Us

Dig A Pony

Across The Universe

Dig It

The One After 909

Previous publications by Phil Strongman:

As Author:
Pretty Vacant (Orion 2007)
Metal Box: Stories of John Lydon & PiL (Helter Skelter 2007)
John Lennon & The FBI Files (Sanctuary 2003)
Cocaine (Abacus 1997 reprinted 1997, 1998, 1999, 2000)

As Editor:
Friday On My Mind by Don Hughes (Armadillo 2010)
My Amazing Adventures With the Sex Pistols by Dave Goodman
(The Bluecoat Press 2007)

As Contributor:
White Lines Edited by Hyde & Zanetti (Thunder's Mouth Press 2002)
A Century of Jazz Editor Roy Carr (Boxtree 2000)
Classic Albums (Harper Collins 1999)
Rockers John Stuart (Plexus 1987)
Up They Rise Jamie Reid & Jon Savage (Faber & Faber 1987)

JOHN LENNON & THE FBI FILES
'Book of the Month' *Hi-Fi Choice*

PRETTY VACANT
'Powerfully narrated, phenomenally well-informed.' *The Times*

METAL BOX: STORIES OF JOHN LYDON & PiL
'One of the best music books for a very long time.' *Irish Post*

COCAINE
'Worthy of Hunter S. Thompson … hallucinatory!' *Uncut*